The American Dole

Recent Titles in
Contributions in American History

The American Dole

Unemployment Relief and the Welfare State in the Great Depression

JEFF SINGLETON

Contributions in American History, Number 189

GREENWOOD PRESS
Westport, Connecticut · London

Library of Congress Cataloging-in-Publication Data

Singleton, Jeff, 1947–
The American dole : unemployment relief and the welfare state in the Great Depression /
   Jeff Singleton.
       p.   cm.—(Contributions in American history, ISSN 0084–9219 ; no. 189)
       Includes bibliographical references and index.
       ISBN 0–313–31400–4 (alk. paper)
       1. Public welfare—United States—History—20th century. 2. Insurance,
   Unemployment—United States—History—20th century.   3. Social security—United
   States—History—20th century.   4. Depressions—1929—United States.   I. Title.
   II. Series.
   HV91.S555   2000
   362.5′82′09043—dc21   99–462054

British Library Cataloguing in Publication Data is available.

Library of Congress Catalog Card Number: 99–462054
ISBN: 0–313–31400–4
ISSN: 0084–9219

First published in 2000

Greenwood Press, 88 Post Road West, Westport, CT 06881
An imprint of Greenwood Publishing Group, Inc.
www.greenwood.com

Printed in the United States of America

The paper used in this book complies with the
Permanent Paper Standard issued by the National
Information Standards Organization (Z39.48–1984).

10 9 8 7 6 5 4 3 2 1

Contents

Preface

Thus study began, as many do, with a surprising finding gleaned from a primary source. Reviewing data collected by the U.S. Children's Bureau on relief spending in the early depression, I noticed that most relief during the Hoover years was financed by public funds, not voluntary contributions. Like most historians of American social policy, I presumed that welfare prior to the New Deal was financed by private funds in the spirit of "voluntarism." Upon further review of the Children's Bureau series I noticed another striking fact: there was no significant increase in relief spending in the early months of the New Deal when, according to legend, Harry Hopkins, the new relief "czar," saved local relief with big new federal grants. There were, it seemed, a number of myths surrounding the origins and implementation of the first federal welfare program.

Mythology and welfare policy seem to fit comfortably together. Today, for example, we hear that the federal dole has virtually ended and that Aid to Families with Dependent Children (now called Temporary Assistance to Needy Families) has been turned back to the states. Yet federal welfare spending is actually significantly higher than it would have been had the recent reforms not passed, and the 1996 law actually imposes some rather formidable federal *mandates* (time limits and work requirements). Then there are the more popular myths about the moral character of welfare recipients and the cost of supporting them. In fact, public assistance is a relatively inexpensive way of assisting the poor, most of whom would rather work than be on the "dole." The New Deal found this out when it attempted to replace relief with public employment; states such as Wisconsin, which are attempting to carry out the provisions of the 1996 law in good faith, are relearning the lesson.

This study is, in part, designed to challenge some of the myths surrounding the relief system of the early depression years: the myth of the traditional "voluntarism" of the Hoover years; the myth of the New Deal welfare "entitlement"; the myth that the Social Security Act enshrined a "two-tiered" welfare state in American social policy. In the process I hope to make a small contribution to the ever-expanding literature on the origins of the American welfare state. This research, I believe, has generally failed to take depression-era unemployment relief sufficiently into account. I also hope to challenge the way we look at the economic and institutional crisis of the early depression years and, in particular, to place more emphasis on the impact of the modernizing policy legacies of the 1920s.

But I do not wish to carry this project too far. To be an academic naysayer in an era of radical policy changes is to be marginalized. A little mythology can, at times, be a good thing. Conservatives now claim the end of welfare as perhaps their greatest policy victory of the 1990s. But this should also mean that they can no longer use the dole as a political club to bludgeon liberals. They may also find that in order to carry out their promise to replace welfare with work, they will need to support expanded day care subsidies, universal health coverage, increases in the minimum wage and continued expansion of the earned income tax credit.

Radical changes in welfare policy have a way of producing unintended consequences. This is another lesson of the era of the "American dole."

I would like to thank the many archivists, librarians, janitors, cooks and coffee-makers who make our research facilities a joy to work in. They certainly help increase the excitement and minimize the pain of the big project. Several readers made their way through versions of this book, including Arnold Offner, Bob Bruce, Saul Engelbourg, Joseph Boskin, Mark Gelfand (who read the most recent version) and my sister, Sara Singleton (a former recipient of the dole and now a highly successful rational choice theorist). Major thanks must go to the History Department at Boston College, which has paid me well for part-time teaching and has given me an office to work in.

Of course, particular thanks are due to my family—my mother and my father, who taught me to read, write and think—and to Doris Singleton, who put up with me while I worked in the National Archives. Most importantly, I must pay tribute to my wife, Dori, who gave me the time and space to finish this project, and to my son, Daniel, who broke through the gloom of unemployment in the 1930s by using me as a climbing structure.

The American Dole

Chapter 1

Unemployment Relief and the Welfare State

From 1930 to the end of 1935 general relief administered by local public and private agencies was the primary source of aid to the unemployed. Relief during these years was very much like what we now call "welfare"—a grant by a local agency to a needy family to supplement an inadequate income. The key difference is that welfare today is targeted to single mothers and children. General relief in the 1930s required only an income test to determine eligibility, and most of the caseload consisted of male workers and their families or single men.[1] There were, to be sure, other important differences: depression-era relief tended to be given "in kind" (food baskets, grocery orders, used clothing) rather than in cash; local relief administration was highly unstable, with frequent organizational shifts resulting from funding crises or abrupt changes in federal policy; the system was the focal point of a great deal of protest and grassroots organizing, among both recipients and social workers; the social work profession itself was less mature and still resembled a social reform movement. Still, the 1930s "dole," like contemporary welfare, was essentially an inadequate, bureaucratic, highly variable, income-tested program targeted to the poor that retained many of the characteristics of traditional "poor law" relief. It was generally despised by recipients, who considered it degrading, was attacked by conservatives, who viewed it as a source of moral decay, and was a political albatross for liberals, who couldn't seem to get rid of it.[2]

The explosive growth of general relief in the early depression years was a crucial episode in the history of American social policy. Not only did the system assist millions of unemployed workers and impoverished farmers in the depths of the Great Depression, but it federalized public assistance to the poor. Neither the Works Progress Administration (WPA) nor the Social Security Act can be adequately explained outside the context of the approximately 5 million recipients receiving federal relief monthly in late 1934. In the end, the unemployment relief crisis of the early 1930s nationalized public welfare, placing it at the very center of the nascent American "welfare state." It is therefore somewhat surprising that so little attention has been paid to relief policies implemented during these years. Although there are a number of valuable state and local studies of unemployment relief, the origins and implementation of the first full-blown federal welfare program have attracted relatively little scrutiny.[3] This phenomenon is particularly striking in the context of the explosion of literature attempting to explain the origins of the American "welfare state" and its unique emphasis on means-tested relief. There has been a great deal of debate over the reform movements of the Progressive era, the role of gender in formulating social policy, and the legislative history of the Social Security Act. But much of this literature has tended to minimize what was, arguably, the first federal welfare program.[4]

The rather casual treatment of depression-era welfare policy appears to reflect several assumptions. First, there has been an understandable tendency to view the expansion and federalization of relief as a more or less automatic response to needs generated by mass unemployment. By the spring of 1933 the unemployment rate approached 30 percent, and the depression had passed its fourth winter. This was such an extreme economic dislocation that, in retrospect, it seems only natural that it should disrupt traditional relief arrangements, forcing federal intervention. Second, accounts of depression-era relief have been profoundly shaped by the apparent contrasts between the policies and rhetoric of Herbert Hoover and those of Franklin D. Roosevelt. Because Hoover opposed federal relief, using rhetoric reminiscent of nineteenth-century welfare ideologies, it has been assumed that relatively little was done to assist the unemployed prior to the New Deal. Because Roosevelt spoke of federal responsibility to assist the "forgotten man," it is assumed that a vast new federal welfare program was initiated at the beginning of the New Deal under relief "czar" Harry Hopkins. Thus, the political realignment of the 1930s has provided an easy framework for explaining the emergence of federal welfare.[5] Finally, the role of unemployment relief has been obscured by the emphasis placed on the Social Security Act of 1935. Because the act appears to institutionalize the distinction between popular social insurance policies (old age pensions and workmen's compensation) and more controversial "welfare" programs (most notably, Aid to Dependent Children), it has been natural to look to the origins and implementation of the law to explain our "two-tiered" welfare system.[6]

Yet there are good reasons to question all these assumptions. While the federalization of relief was certainly the result of mass unemployment, the view that sees means-tested welfare as an inevitable response to "need" ignores a considerable body of evidence that suggests that the expansion of the welfare state was a complex response to a variety of changes in the modern social order. These include the collapse of traditional systems of social support; the evolution of a "free labor" market; economic growth, which generates new demands and the governmental revenues to satisfy them; the impact of mass protest, unionization and the rise of socialist political parties; and the professionalization of social work, the expansion of state "administrative capacity" and the rise of interest groups attached to the public bureaucracies. These developments strongly influenced the response of the existing welfare system to the depression and helped produce a great debate over the appropriate level of government action to satisfy the "need."[7] Furthermore, means-tested public welfare was certainly not the only possible legacy of mass unemployment. The United States might have implemented a more generous public employment policy, as many liberals desired, or might have avoided a federal public welfare program entirely. In short, while unemployment was undoubtedly the primary cause of the expansion of relief, the public welfare system that emerged from the depression-era relief crisis reflected a range of influences that need to be scrutinized more closely.

If modernized public welfare was not an inevitable consequence of unemployment, neither was it necessarily a product of the transition from Herbert Hoover to Franklin D. Roosevelt. The perspective that interprets public policies in the early depression years as primarily reflecting the contrasting ideologies of the two presidents has been seriously undermined by a large and influential body of literature that stresses the continuities between the two administrations. There remains, to be sure, considerable disagreement over claims that Hoover was a "Progressive" whose policies presaged later New Deal reforms. Yet it now seems clear that Hoover was not a classic anti-statist conservative and that his response to the depression, whatever its limitations, should not be characterized as simply "traditional."[8] At the same time, there is now a consensus that the program of Roosevelt's famous first 100 days was not marked by the fiscal liberalism and economic populism that would come to characterize the later New Deal.[9] Rather, it was an experimental period in which a range of somewhat contradictory philosophies influenced policy. As we shall see, there was a good deal more continuity in relief policies actually implemented at the end of the Hoover administration and at the beginning of the New Deal than is generally supposed. Both Hoover and Roosevelt consistently opposed the idea of a permanent federal "dole," but both were unable to avoid it.

Finally, a rather simple observation casts doubt on the tendency to hold the Social Security Act responsible for the emphasis on means-tested welfare in American social policy. When the Committee on Economic Security, which wrote the Act, first met in the summer of 1934, there was already a full-blown federal relief program with a caseload approaching 5 million (ironically, this was approximately the size of the national caseload at the time of the welfare reforms of 1996).[10] The Social Security Act transformed the program into one that targeted single-parent families rather than unemployed workers and sharpened the contrast with social insurance by establishing more generous policies for the elderly and unemployed. But in most other respects the "second tier" of the American welfare state had already been established by the time the 1935 law was implemented. The goal of Social Security, in conjunction with the WPA, was to eliminate federal relief, not institutionalize it.

One result of the lack of attention given to the role of welfare policies in the early depression years is that popular accounts of unemployment relief continue to be highly impressionistic, reflecting the lingering influence of the old Hoover versus Roosevelt paradigm. We are all familiar with these images, which often resemble a "before and after" advertisement for the New Deal. Workers, hands in pockets, wait in long lines for bread and soup during the Hoover years. These same workers, their sleeves rolled up, are busy at work on useful projects devised by New Deal officials. Herbert Hoover assures the nation that "no one is starving" while local relief agencies go bankrupt; New Deal relief czar Harry Hopkins, working feverishly in an office cluttered with unopened file boxes, distributes federal aid to save local relief in the spring of 1933. One would never know, from these accounts, that there were over 5 million workers and farmers on federally financed public welfare when Roosevelt was inaugurated and that a key goal of New Deal relief policy was to get rid of this national "dole."

THE POLICY

One way to evaluate traditional assumptions about unemployment relief policy is to look more closely at available data on relief spending, caseloads and standards of aid. The limited research in these sources is striking because the early depression years coincided with the first attempts to collect national relief statistics on a systematic basis. This effort was initiated by the Russell Sage Foundation, which began an "urban relief series" in 1929. The study was expanded in response to the big increase in relief spending in 1930 and taken over by the U.S. Children's Bureau the following year. In late 1932 the Bureau began receiving data from federal relief agencies, first the Relief Division of the Reconstruction Finance Corporation and then the Division of Research and Statistics of

Table 1
Quarterly Relief Spending (120 Urban Areas), 1930–1935

Year	Spending (Millions)	% Public Spending	Year	Spending (Millions)	% Public Spending
1930			1933		
1	11.1	68	1	105.1	89
2	9.9	67	2	107.5	94
3	9.2	68	3	96.0	95
4	20.0	65	4	99.1	95
1931			1934		
1	38.7	55	1	86.5	95
2	31.4	66	2	154.7	98
3	25.9	74	3	165.0	98
4	42.0	64	4	190.5	98
1932			1935		
1	69.5	65	1	222.1	99
2	61.2	80	2	208.4	99
3	58.3	83	3	186.8	99
4	76.7	88	4	133.3	96

Source: Emma Winslow, *Trends in Different Types of Public and Private Relief in Urban Areas, 1929–1935* (Children's Bureau Publication No. 237) (Washington, DC: Government Printing Office, 1937), 69–71 (see Appendix).

the Federal Emergency Relief Administration (FERA).[11] As a result, we have relatively good data on monthly relief expenditures in 120 "urban areas" from 1930 through 1935 and annual estimates of caseloads and benefit levels. The following descriptive data analysis is thus based on a large sample of urban relief agencies. It is supplemented by data on national expenditures collected by the FERA between 1933 and 1935. The FERA sample includes all agencies, urban and rural, receiving federal funds and includes estimates of the relative shares of federal, state and local spending.[12]

Table 1, constructed from the Children's Bureau's urban relief series, shows spending by public and private agencies quarterly from 1930 through 1935.[13] The data tends to highlight the seasonal trend of relief, with spending increases during the winter months (first and fourth quarters), followed by cutbacks during the spring and summer. Although the spending series shows the relative significance of public and private relief, it does not show the increasing importance of state and federal expenditures. During the first two years of the depression, relief was financed by local public appropriations, donations to private agencies and large, citywide relief drives modeled on the Liberty Loan campaigns of World War I. Beginning in the fall of 1931, local funds were supplemented by the first state appropriations for general relief.[14] The federal government entered the relief picture in July of 1932, distributing loans to the states through the Reconstruction Finance Corporation (RFC). This federal welfare program (the loans were never repaid) was financed by a $300 million congressional appropriation. The New Deal's relief agency, the FERA, began allocating grants to states at the end of May 1933. Thereafter, most funds for unemployment relief came from federal appropriations (there were five in all under the New Deal), although state and local financing continued to play an important role.[15] It should be noted that the appearance of a relief cut during the winter of 1933–1934 is misleading. At the time, several million recipients were taken off the relief rolls and placed on projects financed by the Civil Works Administration (CWA). This led to a reduction in spending by agencies reporting to the Children's Bureau but not a cut in federal aid to the unemployed. Had the cost of CWA been included in the data, there would have been a massive increase in relief spending during these months.[16]

The Children's Bureau series suggests we need go beyond impressionistic accounts and take a closer look at policies actually implemented during the early years of the Great Depression. First, despite the inadequacies of locally financed relief, there was a massive expansion of public welfare and private charity prior to the New Deal. While this finding would certainly not surprise most historians of early-depression social policy, the dimensions of the increase and the economic context need to be evaluated more carefully. During the first year of the depression relief spending increased from approximately $11 million (first quarter, 1930) to over $38 million (first quarter, 1931). It should be noted that this increase occurred when the level of unemployment was probably not significantly higher than previous downturns in the business cycle.[17] As unemployment reached unprecedented levels, and tax revenues fell in late 1931, the burden of relief began to generate a major local fiscal crisis. Still, voluntarist relief drives and new public appropriations financed a big increase in relief spending, which reached nearly $70 million by the first quarter of 1932. Spending rose nearly 50 percent during the winter of 1932–1933, the period of the greatest unemployment in all the years of the Great Depression, exceeding $100 million during the quarter preceding the creation of the FERA.

Second, "voluntarism"—that is, private financing of relief through mass fundraising appeals—would not appear to be an appropriate way to characterize policy during this period. Public funds financed over 60 percent of all relief as early as the first quarter of 1930.[18] Even during the winter of 1931–1932, when private spending increased dramatically

as a result of the national relief drive sponsored by the Hoover administration, public funds financed well over half of all relief in the 120
urban areas. During the second quarter of 1932, there was a precipitous
decline in private financing, as the emergency relief committees created
the previous fall were bailed out by public appropriations. By the beginning of 1933, private funds played a very small role in financing the
national relief system.

One of the most striking aspects of the Children's Bureau data is that
it fails to show a significant increase in relief expenditures during the
early months of the New Deal. The first FERA grants were distributed
in May and June of 1933. Traditional accounts of early New Deal welfare
policy would lead one would expect a big increase in relief expenditures
during the second quarter of 1933, when the Federal Emergency Relief
Administration was created. In fact, there was a very small rise followed
by a decline during the summer months. While this pattern is consistent
with the seasonal trend of relief shown throughout the series, it contra-
dicts the mythology that has the FERA's Harry Hopkins doling out large
sums to save local relief in the spring of 1933. Spending for relief did
increase significantly under the New Deal, but this occurred during the
spring of 1934. The Children's Bureau series shows a big jump in expenditures in the second quarter of the year, coinciding with the demobilization of the New Deal's first large public employment experiment, the
CWA. Spending continued to increase over the next year so that by the
first quarter of 1935, it was more than double the level that had prevailed
in 1933. It remained at this level until the fall, when the WPA was created, and federal relief grants to the states were discontinued (WPA expenditures are not included in the relief series). Thus, the early months
of the New Deal relief policy show continuity with the Hoover period,
but there appears to be an important shift in 1934, coinciding, as we will
see, with the Roosevelt administration's first public employment experiments.

These generalizations about relief under the New Deal are supported
by FERA data for the nation as a whole. Table 2 shows expenditures for
all public agencies—urban and rural—receiving federal funds from 1933
through 1935.[19] While the sample and aggregate spending are considerably larger than those of the Children's Bureau, the trend of relief is
essentially the same. Once again, the data fails to show a significant rise
in relief expenditures during the early months of the FERA, shows a
decline during the summer of 1933 and shows a big increase when the
CWA was dismantled in the spring of 1934. The FERA data is useful for
another reason: the agency, unlike the Children's Bureau, recorded the
relative shares of federal, state and local relief outlays. We can therefore
test one possible explanation for the failure of the data to record the
large grants purportedly made by Hopkins in May of 1933: federal grants

Table 2
Quarterly Public Relief Expenditures (National), 1933–1935 ($ Millions)

Year	Amount	Federal	Federal %
1933			
1	209	126	60
2	210	135	64
3	181	119	66
4	194	114	59
1934			
1	184	87	47
2	369	271	74
3	425	318	75
4	512	390	76
1935			
1	569	427	77
2	549	416	76
3	425	325	76
4	286	181	63

Source: Federal Works Agency, *Final Statistical Report of the Federal Emergency Relief Administration* (Washington, DC: Government Printing Office, 1942), 88.

may have simply replaced depleted state and local funds so that aggregate spending would not have increased. However, the FERA's estimate of the percentage of relief financed by federal funds fails to support such an explanation. The federal share of total relief expenditures increased only slightly during the early months of the New Deal. A more significant rise in federal spending occurred in early 1934, once again after the CWA's demise.

A particularly noteworthy aspect of the national spending data is the high percentage of relief financed by federal funds before the FERA was established. During the first quarter of 1933, which included the last two months of the Hoover administration, federal aid constituted approximately 60 percent of all relief nationally. These funds were appropriated by Congress in mid-1932 and distributed by the RFC. Because the Hoover administration resisted federal relief, and the RFC initially adopted conservative loan policies, this important relief program has been almost entirely ignored in most accounts of welfare policy in the 1930s.[20] The fact that the federal government financed most relief on the eve of Roosevelt's inauguration would no doubt surprise most historians. It certainly came as a shock to Harry Hopkins, who told a group of social workers soon after he became FERA director, "I was the most surprised

Table 3

Average Monthly Spending, Caseloads and Allowances in 120 Urban Areas, 1930–1935

Year	Spending ($ Millions)	Caseload	Relief/Case
1930	4,180,933	199,187	20.99
1931	11,501,901	541,521	21.24
1932	22,147,996	1,056,175	20.97
1933	33,962,351	1,581,115	21.48
1934	49,885,272	1,824,626	27.34
1935	62,551,970	2,043,514	30.61

Source: Emma Winslow, *Trends in Different Types of Public and Private Relief in Urban Areas. 1929–1935* (Children's Bureau Publication No. 237) (Washington, DC: Government Printing Office, 1937), 29–30.

man in the world when I got to Washington and found the federal government was paying eighty percent [*sic*] of all unemployment relief in the United States."[21]

Aggregate spending is, of course, a rudimentary measure of welfare policy. Spending totals do not tell us how many unemployed workers were on relief or whether relief payments were adequate. Increases in spending might reflect relief higher caseloads or increased benefits to those receiving aid. If unemployment and caseload increases outpaced appropriated funds, significant cuts in standards of relief might have occurred. Social workers lobbying for a federal relief program often argued that this was the case during the Hoover years. The relationship between spending, caseloads and relief standards is also an important issue when evaluating policy under the New Deal. As we shall see, FERA officials initially hoped to reduce caseloads and thereby free funds to increase payments to those remaining on the relief rolls. But increased benefits also meant that more workers qualified under the income test and, when coupled with work relief and the payment of benefits in cash, tended to reduce the stigma of applying for aid. Thus, the effort to raise relief standards may have also encouraged caseload increases.[22]

Table 3 presents annual estimates of average monthly caseloads and benefit levels in the 120 urban areas derived from the Children's Bureau series.[23] The data suggests that nearly all the spending growth during the early years of the depression was fueled by the massive numbers of unemployed applying for general relief. For example, the caseload in the urban sample increased from an estimated 199,187 in 1930, to 1,056,175 in 1932, or approximately 400 percent. The spending estimate shows a virtually identical increase. As a result of the close fit between spending and caseloads, average monthly benefits appear to have remained stable during these years. The Children's Bureau's estimate of the relief standards shows a monthly allowance of $20.99 in 1930 and $20.97 in 1932. During the New Deal period, however, the relationship between caseloads, benefit levels and spending changed. Caseloads continued to increase but at a measurably slower rate than spending. The relief caseload increased by approximately one-third from 1933 to 1935, but spending nearly doubled. As a result, relief allowances increased by almost 50 percent, from approximately $21 per month in 1933 to over $30 in 1935. We should note that the increase in relief standards came in 1934, consistent with the big spending increases after the CWA.

The data on benefit levels raises the issue of the adequacy of general relief, a much-debated topic during the early depression years. Were relief allowances adequate to "prevent starvation"? Did they fall below pre-depression norms as a result of the relief crisis? One way to evaluate this question is to compare the standards of relief with prevailing wages of industrial workers. According to the *Statistical Abstract of the United States*, weekly earnings of unskilled workers in a large sample of manufacturing enterprises averaged approximately $28.55 in 1929. By 1933 weekly earnings had declined to under $18.[24] The Children's Bureau estimated that average *monthly* relief per case in the latter year was $21.48. Thus, relief payments during the Hoover years appear to have been less than one-quarter of the average wages for unskilled workers in manufacturing just prior to the depression. New Deal policy, despite a significant increase in standards of aid, barely made a dent in lost wages. Another way to measure adequacy is to compare general relief rates to minimum standards advocated by social workers and implemented by private agencies and the relatively generous "Mothers' Aid" programs. A careful estimate of the cost of a "Minimum Grocery Order" produced by a "home economist" at the Federated Jewish Charities in 1930 was $10.42 per week. At a congressional hearing in early 1933, Walter West of the American Association of Social Workers cited Russell Sage Foundation data showing private agencies in the industrial Northeast provided benefits slightly over $50 per month in 1930. He also noted that the Children's Bureau series reported that Mothers' Aid allowances averaged approximately $44 per month during the same period. Thus, it would appear that relief standards during the Hoover years were slightly under one-half of those paid under the more generous charity organizations and public programs. Reporting on a study of relief in forty-four cities in 1932, Harry Lurie of the American Association of Social Workers estimated that if "essential relief were to be given at a minimum budgetary standard, including food, clothing, rent, light, heat, and medical care, it would become necessary at least to double the total relief expenditures of these cities."[25]

Table 4

Estimated Relief Caseload and Unemployment (Average/Month), 1930–1935

Year	Caseload	Unemployment	% Unemployed on Relief
1930	199,187	1,905,984	10
1931	541,521	3,890,760	14
1932	1,056,175	5,926,888	18
1933	1,581,115	6,117,413	26
1934	1,824,626	4,927,804	37
1935	2,043,514	4,665,674	44

Source: National Industrial Conference Board, *Conference Board Economic Record* (March 20, 1940), 81–82, 86; U.S. Department of Commerce, Bureau of the Census, *Fifteenth Census of the United States: Unemployment, Vol. 1* (Washington, DC: Government Printing Office, 1930), 24–45.

On the other hand, if we move beyond comparisons with the more generous and professionally administered social agencies, the data does not appear to show that the relief crisis produced a decline in average relief payments, which remained stable throughout the Hoover years. In fact, benefits received by general relief recipients may have increased slightly in real terms. According to the Department of Commerce, the cost of goods and services purchased by "wage earners and lower salaried workers" declined 23.1 percent between December 1929 and December 1932.[26] Thus, an average payment of approximately twenty-one dollars would mean, for example, a more adequate grocery order in 1932 as compared with 1930. Furthermore, standards of aid increased by nearly 50 percent under the New Deal. In short, while relief in the early depression years was clearly inadequate, the depression-era crisis did not produce a decline in standards of aid but instead revealed the inadequacies of existing general relief policies. This, in turn, generated pressures that produced more adequate relief. Indeed, the tendency for welfare officials like West and Lurie to compare general relief allowances with those of private charity organizations and Mothers' Pension programs was part of this process.[27]

Another key measure of the adequacy of relief is the percentage of unemployed receiving aid. Presumably, the higher the percentage of unemployed workers on relief, the more adequately the relief system was meeting needs generated by mass unemployment. Indeed, the whole question of relief policy must be considered in the context of changes in the level of unemployment. Table 4 presents an estimate of average annual unemployment in the 120 urban areas using the April 1930 census as a benchmark and projecting forward with labor force and employment estimates made by the National Industrial Conference Board in the 1930s.[28] An estimate of the percentage of unemployed workers receiving relief was derived by dividing the caseloads reported in Table 3 by the number of unemployed. It should be noted that these estimates probably understate the percentage of unemployed who actually received aid from local agencies during the course of a year. First, the average relief "case," or family, reporting to the Bureau frequently contained more than one "employable" adult.[29] Second, yearly caseload averages do not reflect the fact that significant numbers of the unemployed moved in and out of the relief system during the course of a year: an average monthly case-load of 1.1 million in 1932, for example, would certainly mean that more than 1.1 million workers came in contact with the relief system at some point in the twelve-month period.[30]

The estimates shown in Table 4 suggest that while an increasing number of unemployed workers received relief during the Hoover years, the percentages remained relatively small.[31] During 1931 only one in seven unemployed workers is estimated to have received aid from relief agencies monthly; by the next year, the average had increased to barely 20 percent. These low percentages are noteworthy in light of the fact that mass applications for aid had resulted in the collapse of local relief and the first federal welfare program. Despite the big increases in relief spending, which transformed the national relief system, the percentage of needy workers on public assistance did not increase substantially. Under the New Deal, on the other hand, the relationship between unemployment and relief changed rather dramatically. The number of unemployed in the 120 urban areas declined from an estimated average of slightly over 6 million in 1933 to approximately 4.7 million in 1935, a 23 percent decline. Yet relief caseloads rose from an estimated 1.6 million to approximately 2 million. As a result, the estimated percentage of unemployed on relief rose to 44 percent by 1935. Given the fact that this was most certainly an underestimate, it would appear probable that by the last year of the New Deal's relief program, more than half of all unemployed workers received relief at some point. Once again, the data suggests an important shift in relief policy during the New Deal period, but the gains appear in 1934, rather than in the early months of the FERA.

Data on caseloads, spending and benefit levels, of course, tells us little about crucial aspects of relief policy—the political conflicts over federal policy, the relationship between social work and relief and, above all, the impact of "the dole" on unemployed workers. But it does provide a useful starting point for our story and helps us to evaluate some traditional assumptions about relief. For example, one simply cannot account for the growth and federalization of public welfare by focusing on the political transition from Hoover to Roosevelt. Public financing played a crucial role in the relief picture during the Hoover years, and by the winter of 1932–1933 there was a full-blown federal welfare program. There was a good deal of continuity, according to our policy measures, in the policies of the later Hoover period and those of the early months of the New Deal. There was an important policy shift under the FERA, but this appears to have occurred in early 1934. Second, while mass unemployment was certainly the major cause of the expansion and federalization of relief, it cannot explain crucial aspects of national welfare policy during this period. This is particularly true under the New Deal, when unemployment declined, but relief spending and caseloads continued to rise. Finally, the data confirms the argument that the role of the Social Security Act has been somewhat exaggerated in accounts of the institutionalization of means-tested welfare. As early as January of 1933, there was a large federal "dole," which was the focus of many of the same criticisms that have beset contemporary "welfare."

THE WELFARE STATE

If the American "dole" was not simply a predictable consequence of economic conditions or the political realignment of the early 1930s, how are we to explain the prominence of means-tested welfare in American social policy? An effort to answer this must situate the relief system just described in the context of recent research on the growth of "welfare states" in Europe and the United States. Here, one encounters a daunting body of work emanating from two distinct sources—historians attempting to understand the nature of twentieth-century reform and social scientists seeking to elaborate and test broader theories of the "state." The historians have traditionally been concerned with the reform movements and the rise of the social work profession. Debates have centered on the motives of social reformers and the implementation of specific policies. More recently, there has been an effort to link this institutional approach with social histories of the poor and with feminist research on gender and the state.[32] Social scientists have undertaken the more ambitious project of explaining why all advanced capitalist countries develop welfare states and what accounts for the considerable variations between them. Indeed, the two issues are often conflated, with cross-national comparisons used to test different "theories of the state."[33] Although there is not an easy fit between the historical and social science approaches, which involve different methodologies and professional concerns, two questions are paramount for the purpose of this study. First, what factors account for the expansion of social welfare spending and institutional capacity in the United States and all advanced capitalist countries? Second, how are we to account for the unique character of the American welfare state, with its low levels of public expenditures, decentralized administration and reliance on means-tested "welfare"?

The starting point for all efforts to evaluate these questions is modernization theory, or "developmentalism," as it is often called when applied to welfare policy. This approach argues that rapid economic development, accelerated by the Industrial Revolution, broke down traditional social structures that addressed the problem of poverty. Industrialization also produced new "needs": the business cycle generated periodic mass unemployment, and lower mortality rates produced a larger dependent elderly population. Finally, economic growth produced increases in wealth, creating an economic surplus that could be taxed for new social programs. Thus, the national systems of unemployment insurance, old age pensions, universal health care and family allowances reflect broad structural changes that have occurred in all advanced capitalist countries.[34]

Although modernization theory has come in for a good deal of criticism in recent years, it remains, in my view, the best synthetic explanation for the central paradox of the modern state: all nominally "free market" national capitalist systems have also developed large, publicly financed social welfare bureaucracies. Its insights are particularly noteworthy in the context of contemporary political debates over the future of social policy in the West, which are often premised on the notion of a fundamental conflict between capitalism and the bureaucratic state. Modernization emphasizes that the market-based economic systems generate needs and demands that cannot be satisfied without a heavy dose of intervention by the state and creates the resources to respond to those demands. Furthermore, the state, according to this view, does not simply respond to the needs generated by capitalism. Rather, the centralization of state power and the expansion of bureaucracy ("administrative capacity," as the new policy historians call it) reflect similar tendencies in the private sector. Historically, there is a very close relationship between the development of "corporate capitalism" and the growth of the state—a division of labor rather than a fundamental conflict.[35]

Yet modernization theory raises two fundamental (and closely related) questions. First, what are the precise mechanisms by which the social changes it describes produce specific welfare programs? Second, what explains the rather striking variations in social welfare policies between "advanced" capitalist countries, variations that do not seem well correlated with measures of economic development, as the modernization approach would seem to predict?[36] These questions are particularly crucial when considering American social welfare policy. The United States does not appear to exhibit the combination of pressures that have produced the European welfare states—powerful socialist political parties challenging the capitalist order, entrenched centralized bureaucracies ready

to plan and implement reform and a nationalist ideology that emphasizes social solidarity. The United States, a relatively "advanced" country
according to the common measures of social and economic development,
has lagged behind European states in the creation of social insurance
and is far less generous in its policies.[37] Thus, it took the shock of the
Great Depression to bring this country into line with developments else-
where.

Efforts to elaborate the mechanisms that produce welfare-state growth
and explain cross-national variations have produced a variety of "theories of the welfare state."[38] Some have argued that the welfare policies
reflect changing "values," with modern societies rejecting individualistic
ideologies in favor of collective responsibility for social welfare. This
perspective seems to fit comfortably with the large body of historical
literature that focuses on the efforts of humanitarian reformers and liberal public officials to implement more generous social policies. The relatively primitive American welfare state, according to this perspective,
reflects a more individualistic or anti-statist value system embedded in
the political culture.[39] Another set of explanations emphasizes the role
of social class and class conflict in shaping welfare policies. Some see the
modern welfare state as a response to "pressure from below" in the form
of mass socialist political parties or, in the case of the United States,
"poor people's movements" that disrupt existing institutional arrangements for "regulating the poor." Others see various liberal capitalists
themselves as initiating reforms to preempt socialist demands or rationalize the labor market.[40] Class-based interpretations tend to stress the
relative weakness of socialist or labor parties and the influence of "corporate liberal" capitalists in explaining the unique features of the American welfare state. A third, increasingly influential approach locates the
sources of growth and difference in welfare policy in the state itself and
in the political structures linked to it. Social welfare systems—indeed,
all public policies, according to this view—strongly reflect the presence
or absence of entrenched bureaucracies (often referred to as "administrative capacity") that initiate or shape programs. They also reflect the
strength of linkages between political parties, interest groups and the
state bureaucracies. Policy variations can best be explained by different
state structures and political systems, rather than broader social or ideological determinants.[41] "Institutionalists" like Theda Skocpol, Stephen
Skowronek and Margaret Weir explain the unique features of the American state as a product of decentralization and the role of political parties
in social policy.

One can certainly find evidence of all these influences in the conflicts
attendant on the expansion of relief in the early 1930s. The Great Depression was a period when dominant values about the relationship between state and society were challenged. The relief system was no doubt

influenced by the widespread rejection of what Robert McElvaine has termed "acquisitive individualism" and by the tendency, stressed in Lizbeth Cohen's widely acclaimed study of the Chicago union movement, to look to the state for support once provided by local voluntary organizations.[42] Relief policy was also influenced by the intense social conflicts of the period, as evidenced by the wide variety of grassroots organizations among the unemployed and the so-called rank-and-file movement within the social work profession. Yet it would be difficult to explain the "dole" as a product of American values, which the policy would appear to directly contradict, or as a response to protest, a good deal of which was directed against means-tested relief.

Rather, as institutional historians have suggested, the relief system was profoundly shaped by certain unique characteristics of the American state inherited from the nineteenth century—a "federalist" system, which relied heavily on state and local government to implement policies; a party system which marginalized social-democratic politics and intensified the relative power of "reactionary" elites; and powerful middle class reform coalitions which lobbied for professionalized bureaucracies to address social problems.[43] In the absence of European-style bureaucracies and socialist political parties, reformers were most successful in efforts to expand and modernize the local system of poor law relief and private charity inherited from the nineteenth century. For example, during the Progressive era, "maternalist" reformers, women's organizations and public officials created state-level Mothers' Pension programs to assist poor single women and serve as vehicles for administrative reform.[44] Public welfare and private charity expanded during the 1920s, developments closely linked to the professionalization of social work and efforts by "welfare capitalists" to find American alternatives to a European-style "dole" (see Chapter 2). When the Great Depression struck, these policy legacies resulted in the rapid expansion and federalization of means-tested relief. The New Deal created a political opening for European-style social insurance programs and public employment. But the continued commitment to a decentralized administrative state and the power of the conservative coalition in Congress "placed severe limits on the policies that could prevail." As a result, social insurance was less generous than in Europe; public employment was limited; and bureaucratic, state-administered "public welfare" remained at the center of American social policy.

Yet it would be an enormous error to place undue emphasis on the role of institutional actors in creating the American "dole." First, the economic crisis, as Frances Fox Piven and Richard A. Cloward have emphasized, severely disrupted existing institutional arrangements, nearly destroying the private family relief organizations that had played such a key role in social policy during the 1920s and bankrupting local public

welfare agencies. At the same time, the political realignment caused by
the Great Depression greatly increased support for more liberal social
insurance and public employment policies that might have replaced
means-tested relief. Thus, while institutional and political legacies profoundly shaped welfare policies that emerged from this era, this was also
a period of institutional disruption, political reordering and a great deal
of policy experimentation. Furthermore, while the social reformers and
public officials who loom so large in most institutional histories certainly
played key roles in shaping national welfare policy, the expansion and
federalization of relief were not primarily the product of a great welfare
reform movement. Indeed, key federal officials in both the Hoover and
Roosevelt administrations sought to avoid a federal relief program. Hoover's relief policy was designed to avoid federal public welfare, with
mass private relief drives modeled on the Liberty Loan fund drives of
World War I; the New Deal's Harry Hopkins, the most influential relief
official of the period, sought to replace the national "dole" with public
employment. State relief officials sought to institutionalize public welfare
but generally saw it as a second cousin to social insurance. The broader
movement of reformers and professionals in the social work community
aggressively defended relief, but they often sharply divided on key policy questions, and their influence on national policy was problematic.

What was so striking about unemployment relief in the 1930s (and
"welfare" since then) was the degree to which all parties in policy debate—protest organizations of the unemployed, politicians, the public,
federal relief administrators, social reformers—disliked means-tested relief as the solution to mass unemployment. Yet there it was, at the very
center of American social policy, where it would remain in various forms
until the end of the century.[45] Part of the explanation for this painful
irony is that there is a closer relationship between state and society, at
least as far as public welfare policy is concerned, than most institutional
accounts assume. The expansion of relief was the product of many small
decisions by workers and farmers who rejected the stigma of applying
for the dole and swelled the relief caseloads. Often these decisions were
simply a response to desperate need caused by unemployment, drought
or the collapse of regional economies. Yet they also occurred in response
to important policy shifts initiated by public officials—the publicity associated with a mass relief drive; the announcement of a new work relief
program; the transition from "in kind" to cash relief. In short, the expansion and federalization of relief during the early depression years
involved complex and unpredictable interactions between the emerging
public bureaucracies, the mass of unemployed workers and the political
party system undergoing realignment. What emerged was a public welfare system that satisfied no one, that conformed to no reform blueprint

and that was thus vulnerable to periodic political attacks and failed efforts at "reform."[46]

NOTES

1. Gladys L. Palmer and Katherine D. Wood, *Urban Workers on Relief*, Part 1 (WPA Research Monograph IV) (Washington, DC: Government Printing Office, 1936), 9–12, 24–25. This is not to suggest that the depression had no impact on families headed by single women or on the mothers' pension programs inherited from the Progressive era. Spending for the latter may have increased by as much as 40 percent between 1929 and 1933. Furthermore, as the federal government came to finance most relief, the general relief caseload increasingly absorbed these families. See Emma Winslow, *Trends in Different Types of Public and Private Relief in Urban Areas, 1929–1935* (Children's Bureau Publication 237) (Washington, DC: Government Printing Office, 1937), 38, 69–70; Linda Gordon, *Pitied but Not Entitled: Single Mothers and the History of Welfare* (New York: Free Press, 1994), 184–186. The statement that families on general relief were "headed" by males is certainly problematic. Feminist historians have recently marshaled a good deal of evidence that shows that the economic crisis and relief disrupted traditional gender roles within families. See, for example, Lois Scharf, *To Work and to Wed: Female Employment, Feminism and the Great Depression* (Westport, CT: Greenwood Press, 1980); Ruth Milkman, "Women's Work and the Economic Crisis: Some Lessons from the Great Depression," in Nancy F. Cott and Elizabeth Pleck, eds., *A Heritage of Her Own: Toward a New Social History of American Women* (New York: Simon and Schuster, 1979), 507–541; Lizbeth Cohen, *Making a New Deal* (Cambridge: Cambridge University Press, 1990), 246–248; Elaine Tyler May, *Homeward Bound* (New York: Basic Books, 1988), 49–51.

2. James T. Patterson, *The New Deal and the States* (Westport, CT: Greenwood Press, 1981), 74; Michael Katz, *Improving Poor People* (Princeton, NJ: Princeton University Press, 1995), 20; Frances Fox Piven and Richard A. Cloward, *Regulating the Poor: The Functions of Public Welfare* (New York: Random House, 1971), 80. For an analysis that stresses the historical continuities in welfare policy see Michael Katz, *In the Shadow of the Poorhouse* (New York: Basic Books, 1986), ix. Linda Gordon, on the other hand, argues in *Pitied but Not Entitled* that "in two generations the meaning of welfare has reversed itself," suggesting that changes in public assistance policies created the negative connotations associated with the word. I argue that attitudes toward means-tested relief have remained constant and generally quite negative. Welfare was once a positive term because it was not closely associated with relief. See Chapter 2.

3. The most detailed account of relief policy during the Great Depression remains Josephine Brown's classic *Public Relief, 1929–1939* (New York: Henry Holt and Co., 1940). The best recent studies are William R. Brock's *Welfare, Democracy and the New Deal* (Cambridge: Cambridge University Press, 1986) and Edwin Amenta, *Bold Relief* (Princeton, NJ: Princeton University Press, 1998). Brock treats relief policy primarily as an episode in state–federal relations, following the tradition of Patterson's seminal *The New Deal and the States*. Patterson's monograph stimulated a number of valuable state and local studies that cover

relief policy. Among the most influential of these are Bonnie Fox Schwartz, "Unemployment Relief in Philadelphia: A Study of the Depression's Impact on Voluntarism," in Bernard Sternsher, ed., *Hitting Home: The Great Depression in Town and Country* (Chicago: Quadrangle Books, 1970); Barbara Blumberg, *The New Deal and the Unemployed: The View from New York City* (Lewisburg, PA: Bucknell University Press, 1977); Bruce Blumell, *The Development of Public Assistance in the State of Washington during the Great Depression* (New York: Garland, 1984); David Maurer, "Public Relief Programs and Politics in Ohio" (Ph.D. diss., Ohio State University, 1962); John F. Bauman, "The City, the Depression and Relief: The Philadelphia Experience, 1929–1939" (Ph.D. diss., Rutgers University, 1969). Good accounts of federal policy can be found in biographies of Harry Hopkins, most notably Searle F. Charles, *Minister of Relief: Harry Hopkins and the New Deal* (Syracuse, NY: Syracuse University Press, 1963) and George McJimsey, *Harry Hopkins, Ally of the Poor, Defender of Democracy* (Cambridge, MA: Harvard University Press, 1989). Also indispensable is Piven and Cloward, *Regulating the Poor*, Part 1 and *Poor People's Movements* (New York: Random House, 1977), ch. 2.

4. "Welfare" here is defined narrowly as direct relief, or transfer payments to individuals. I am suggesting that there is a direct line of descent from the federal relief program of the early 1930s to the present federal welfare policy. One can certainly find earlier examples of federal welfare programs, more broadly defined. These would include relief given to former slaves under the Reconstruction-era Freedman's Bureau, the pension program for Civil War veterans, and social service programs established just after World War I (the infant and maternal health program funded under the Sheppard-Towner Act being the best known of these). See Edward Berkowitz and Kim McQuaid, *Creating the Welfare State*, 2nd ed. (New York: Praeger, 1988), 4–7, 73–83; Theda Skocpol, *Social Policy in the United States* (Princeton, NJ: Princeton University Press, 1995), ch. 2.

5. Charles H. Trout, "Welfare in the New Deal Era," *Current History* 65 (July–December 1973): 11; Robert S. McElvaine, *The Great Depression* (New York: Times Books, 1993), 80, 151–152; Anthony Badger, *The New Deal* (New York: Hill and Wang, 1989), 49, 191. On the Hoover–Roosevelt contrast see Albert U. Romasco, "Hoover–Roosevelt and the Great Depression: A Historiographic Inquiry into a Perennial Comparison," in John Braeman, Robert H. Bremner and David Brody, eds., *The New Deal: The National Level* (Columbus: Ohio State University Press, 1973), 3–26; and Frank Friedel, "Hoover and FDR: Reminiscent Reflections," in Lee Nash, ed., *Understanding Herbert Hoover: Ten Perspectives* (Stanford, CA: Hoover Institution Press, 1987).

6. See, for example, Christopher Howard, "Sowing the Seeds of 'Welfare': The Transformation of Mothers' Pensions, 1900–1940," *Journal of Policy History* 4 (1992): 188–227; Gordon, *Pitied but Not Entitled*, ch. 9; Jerry Cates, *Insuring Inequality: Administrative Leadership in Social Security, 1935–1954* (Ann Arbor: University of Michigan Press, 1983).

7. As Linton Swift told a congressional committee in late 1931, the answer depended in part "upon the social attitude of the individual himself—his conception of the responsibility of the community toward the unemployed as human beings." U.S. Congress, Senate Committee on Manufactures, *Unemployment Relief*, Hearings . . . on Secs. 174 and 162, 72nd Cong., 1st sess., December 1931–January 1932, 91. For important discussions of the role of gender in the debate over

"needs" see Nancy Fraser, "Struggle over Needs: Outline of a Socialist-Feminist Theory of Late-Capitalist Political Culture," in Linda Gordon, ed., *Women, the State and Welfare* (Madison: University of Wisconsin Press, 1990), 199–200; Gordon, *Pitied but Not Entitled*, 160–165.

8. Ellis Hawley, *The Great War and the Search for a Modern Order*, 2nd ed. (New York: St. Martin's Press, 1992), 188 and Hawley, "Neo-Institutional History and the Understanding of Herbert Hoover," in Lee Nash, ed., *Understanding Herbert Hoover: Ten Perspectives* (Stanford, CA: Stanford University Press, 1987). For Hoover's response to the depression see, in particular, the essays in J. Joseph Huthmacher and Warren Susman, eds., *Herbert Hoover and the Crisis of American Capitalism* (Cambridge, MA: Schenkman, 1973). For a critique of the "Hoover revisionism" see Arthur Schlesinger, Jr., "Hoover Makes a Comeback," *The New York Review of Books* (May 8, 1979): 10–16.

9. On the relationship between the early New Deal and modern liberalism see Alan Brinkley, *The End of Reform* (New York: Alfred Knopf, 1995), 4–8.

10. Federal Works Agency, *Final Statistical Report of the Federal Emergency Relief Administration* (Washington, DC: Government Printing Office, 1942), 23.

11. Winslow, *Trends in Urban Areas*, 2–6. Extensive documentation regarding the history of the series may be found in Children's Bureau Files (National Archives Record Group 102 [hereafter Children's Bureau], Box 102, File 12–8-1 and Box 412, File 12–7-4 (0).

12. Federal Works Agency, *Final Statistical Report*, iii–v, Appendix A.

13. Table derived from Winslow, *Trends in Urban Areas*, 69–71. The data includes spending for public and private general relief but excludes categorical relief (mothers' aid, Old Age Assistance, Aid to the Blind). See Appendix.

14. Rowland Haynes, *State Legislation for Unemployment Relief* (Washington, DC: Government Printing Office, 1932).

15. Federal Works Agency, *Final Statistical Report*, 88, 99–102.

16. Winslow, *Trends in Urban Areas*, 12; Ralph Hurlin, Memo on CWA and Relief Statistics, Children's Bureau, Box 538, File 12–7-4 (0).

17. Lebergott estimates average unemployment at 8.9 percent in 1930 and 16.3 percent in 1931. He estimates unemployment levels of 11.7 percent during 1921, 8.5 percent in 1915 and 8.0 percent in 1908. Stanley Lebergott, *Manpower in Economic Growth* (New York: McGraw-Hill, 1964), 512. Thus, I argue that during the winter of 1930–1931, unemployment was comparable to that of previous depressions in this century. By the summer of 1931, the levels exceeded previous downturns in the business cycle. This point is stressed because there has been a tendency, when emphasizing the inadequacies of local relief during the Hoover years, to evaluate early relief efforts and controversies as if they were responses to the extreme levels of unemployment that prevailed later in the depression. See, for example, Cohen, *Making a New Deal*, 218–223; Badger, *The New Deal*, 49; McElvaine, *The Great Depression*, 75, 78–80. An influential exception is Schwartz, "Unemployment Relief in Philadelphia."

18. If categorical relief were included in the data, the percentage of public spending would be even higher. For example, public expenditures for all forms of relief, including mothers' aid, old age assistance and aid to the blind, constituted 77 percent of all relief in 1930. Winslow, *Trends in Urban Areas*, 69.

19. Table 2 is derived from data in Federal Works Agency, *Final Statistical Report*, 88.

20. See Chapter 4, note 8. Notable exceptions have been Brock, *Welfare, Democracy and the New Deal*, ch. 4 and Udo Sautter, *Three Cheers for the Unemployed* (New York: Cambridge University Press, 1991), 311.

21. Harry Hopkins, "The Developing National Program of Relief," *Proceedings of the National Conference on Social Work* (Chicago: University of Chicago Press, 1933), 67.

22. For the early FERA attitude toward relief standards see discussion in Chapter 4 and Executive Committee of the Board of Directors of Louisiana Emergency Relief Commission, "Report of Meeting with Hopkins," June 14, 1933, FERA Files, Box 111, File: Louisiana, May–December 1933. On the problem of higher standards producing higher caseloads see Aubrey Williams to Harry Hopkins, July 24, 1933, FERA-Old Subject File, Box 3, File: Alabama Field Reports 1934.

23. The Children's Bureau published only annual estimates for spending and caseloads, and the sample of agencies reporting was smaller than the spending sample. Table 3 is derived from the data in Winslow, *Trends in Urban Areas*, 29–30, but I have adjusted the data to make it consistent with the spending estimates in Table 1. See Appendix for description of estimating procedures.

24. U.S. Department of Commerce, *Statistical Abstract of the United States*, no. 58 (Washington, DC: Government Printing Office, 1936), 329. The sample covered 1.5 million workers in twenty-five industries.

25. S. Etta Sadow, "Testing the Practicability and Palatability of the Minimum Food Order," *The Family* 11, no. 7 (November 1930): 235; U.S. Congress, Senate, Committee on Manufactures, *Federal Aid for Unemployment Relief*, Hearings . . . on Sec. 5125, 72nd Cong., 2nd sess., January 3–17 1933, 70–71 (Lurie Testimony), 359–360 (West Testimony).

26. U.S. Department of Commerce, *Statistical Abstract of the United States*, no. 58, 304. For a contemporary analysis that supports the view that general relief standards may well have increased in real terms see Anne Geddes, "Relief in a Rising Market," *Survey* 69, no. 10 (October 1933): 346.

27. In addition to the comments by West and Lurie, see Helen Tyson Testimony in Senate Committee on Manufactures, *Federal Aid for Unemployment Relief* (1933), 416; Jacob Billikopf Testimony, U.S. Congress, Senate Committee on Manufactures, *Unemployment Relief*, Hearings on Sec. 174 and 262, 72nd Cong., 1st sess, December 1931–January 1932, 115.

28. This procedure has produced annual unemployment rates for the urban sample that are comparable to the national estimates of Stanley Lebergott, the most frequently cited unemployment data for the 1930s. See Appendix for estimating procedures and comparisons with Lebergott.

29. An FERA analysis of 83,641 relief cases in sixteen cities in 1934 revealed that 40 percent of families had one "gainful worker," 44 percent had two and 13 percent had three or more. "Number of Gainful Workers in Relief Families," June 12, 1934, FERA-Old Subject File, Box 11, File: Field Study—June 1934. See also the analysis by Joanna Colcord and Russell Kurtz in *Survey* 70, no. 4 (April 1934): 134. Colcord and Kurtz cited an FERA study of the Cincinnati relief caseload that showed that the average "case" contained 1.5 employable persons.

30. A survey of 91,662 California relief cases conducted by the FERA in June 1934 showed that 24 percent of the cases were either opened or closed during the month. The turnover may have been particularly high in the immediate aftermath of the CWA. FERA, Box 25, File: California—Field Reports.

31. At hearings of the Senate Committee on Manufactures in December 1931, William Hodson estimated that there were approximately 800,000 persons out of work in New York City, of whom 100,000 were receiving relief (12.5%). In December of 1932 the relief committee of the American Association of Social Workers (AASW), using a questionnaire sent to members, attempted to estimate the percentage of unemployed on relief. Estimates from the forty-three cities that answered ranged from 18 to 58 percent. The average was 32 percent. The estimates for Table 3 produced percentages of 14 percent per month in 1931, 18 percent in 1932 and 26 percent in 1933. Hodson Testimony: Senate Committee on Manufactures, *Unemployment Relief*, 1931–1932, 12–13; AASW Study: Senate Committee on Manufactures, *Federal Aid for Unemployment Relief*, January 3–17, 1933, 67.

32. For critical analysis of traditional social welfare history see Raymond Mohl, "Mainstream Social Welfare History and Its Problems," *Reviews in American History* 7 (December 1979): 469–476; Clarke Chambers, "Toward a Redefinition of Welfare History," *Journal of American History* 73 (September 1986): 407–433. Studies that attempt to bridge the gap between social welfare history and the "new social history" include James T. Patterson, *America's Struggle against Poverty*, 3rd ed. (Cambridge, MA: Harvard University Press, 1994) and Katz, *In the Shadow of the Poorhouse*. A newer policy history places the expansion of the welfare state in the context of broader institutional developments in the public and private spheres, with less emphasis on the history of reform and the social work profession. See essays by Ellis Hawley, Donald Critchlow, Edward Berkowitz and Morton Keller in Critchlow and Hawley, eds., *Federal Social Policy: The Historical Dimension* (University Park: University of Pennsylvania Press, 1989). Feminist approaches to social welfare history include Mimi Abramovitz, *Regulating the Lives of Women*, 3rd ed. (Boston: South End Press, 1992), Gordon, *Pitied but Not Entitled* and Robyn Muncy, *Creating a Female Dominion in American Reform, 1890–1935* (New York: Oxford University Press, 1991). A seminal essay of feminist scholarship on the welfare state is Gordon's "The New Feminist Scholarship on the Welfare State," in *Women, the State and Welfare*.

33. This summary and the analysis that follows draw heavily on the review of the social science literature in Theda Skocpol, *Protecting Soldiers and Mothers* (Cambridge, MA: Harvard University Press, 1992), 11–40. Also helpful are Jill Quadagno, "Theories of the Welfare State," *Annual Reviews in Sociology* 13 (1987): 109–128; Frances Fox Piven and Richard A. Cloward, "Explaining the Politics of the Welfare State or Marching Back toward Pluralism?," in R. Friedland and A.F. Robertson, eds., *Beyond the Marketplace: Rethinking Economy and Society* (New York: Aldine de Gruyter, 1990), 245–269; Jerald Hage, Robert Hanneman and Edward T. Gargan, *State Responsiveness and State Activism* (London: Hyman 1989), chs. 1, 4; Daniel S. Levine, *Poverty and Society* (New Brunswick, NJ: Rutgers University Press, 1988), 6–11; Francis C. Castles, "The Impact of Parties on Public Expenditures," in Francis C. Castles, ed., *The Impact of Parties: Politics and Policies in Democratic Capitalist States* (Beverly Hills, CA: Sage Publications, 1982), 22–34.

34. For the classic statement of developmentalism, which explains the welfare state as a product of the "logic of industrialization," see Harold Wilensky and Charles Lebeaux, *Industrial Society and Social Welfare* (New York: Free Press, 1965). In 1975, however, Wilensky moved away from a simple industrialization framework, arguing that "economic growth and its demographic and bureaucratic outcomes are the root cause of the general emergence of the welfare state" and suggesting that variations between advanced capitalist countries can be explained by "specific differences in political, social and economic organization." See Wilensky, *The Welfare State and Equality* (Berkeley: University of California Press, 1975), xiii–xiv, 68. For a version of modernization theory that focuses on institutional and political developments in Europe see Peter Flora and Jens Alber, "Modernization, Democratization and the Development of Welfare States in Western Europe," in Peter Flora and Arnold J. Heidenheimer, eds., *The Development of Welfare States in Europe and America* (New Brunswick, NJ: Transaction Press, 1981), 38–48. Hage, Hanneman and Gargan in *State Responsiveness and State Activism*, 11–15, draw rather sharp distinctions between Wilensky's "economic model" and modernization approaches that focus on social and insitutional factors (urbanization, transportation and communication). For modernization approaches that stress the role of ideas and values in explaining the variation between advanced capitalist states see Kirsten A. Grønbjerg, *Mass Society and the Extension of Welfare* (Chicago: University of Chicago Press, 1977), 9–12, 153–154; W. Andrew Achenbaum, *Shades of Gray* (Boston: Little, Brown, 1983), 6–24.

35. John Kenneth Galbraith, "Blame History Not the Liberals," *New York Times*, September 19, 1995, A21; John Kenneth Galbraith, *The New Industrial State*, 2nd ed. (Boston: Houghton Mifflin, 1971), 289–290; Berkowitz and McQuaid, *Creating the Welfare State*, xii–xiii. For an influential Marxist analysis that sees state policy mirroring the structure of the modern capitalist economy see James O'Connor, *The Fiscal Crisis of the State* (New York: St. Martin's Press, 1973).

36. Skocpol, *Protecting Soldiers and Mothers*, 13; Hage, Hanneman and Gargan, *State Responsiveness and State Activism*, 107, 127–128; Flora and Alber, "Modernization, Democratization and the Development of Welfare States in Western Europe," 65.

37. Skocpol, *Protecting Soldiers and Mothers*, 13–14; Ellis Hawley, "Social Policy and the Liberal State in Twentieth Century America," in Hawley and Critchlow, *Federal Social Policy*, 119. The resistance to the modern, centralized state in the United States is a central theme in Barry Karl's influential *The Uneasy State: The United States from 1915 to 1945* (Chicago: University of Chicago Press, 1983). See also Alan Brinkley, "Writing the History of Contemporary America: Dilemmas and Challenges," *Daedalus* 113 (1984): 134–137.

38. Historians of social welfare policy have been skeptical of social science efforts to elaborate theories of the state. See Walter I. Trattner, *From Poor Law to Welfare State*, 6th ed. (New York: Free Press, 1999), xxxii–xxxiii; Katz, *Improving Poor People*, 8–9.

39. Social science studies that stress the impact of values on social policy include Gaston Rimlinger, *Welfare Policy and Industrialization in Europe, America and Russia* (New York: Wiley 1971); Daniel Levine, *Poverty and Society: The Growth of the American Welfare State in International Comparison* (New Brunswick, NJ: Rutgers University Press, 1988); Grønbjerg, *Mass Society and the Extension of Welfare*

and Grønbjerg, David Street, and Gerald D. Suttles, *Poverty and Social Change* (Chicago: University of Chicago Press, 1978), 3–6; Achenbaum, *Shades of Gray*, 17–24. The emphasis on national values fits comfortably with traditional American social welfare history, which focuses on the role of social work reformers implementing policies that reflect modern, Progressive values. See, for example, James Leiby, *A History of Social Welfare and Social Work in the United States* (New York: Columbia University Press, 1978).

40. There are important differences between these two formulations, particularly with regard to the importance of social conflict and the attitude of the "capitalists" toward the welfare state. Those who stress the "social-democratic model" and the impact of protest tend to see capitalists opposing expansion of the state. See, for example, John D. Stephens, *The Transition from Capitalism to Socialism* (London: Macmillan, 1979); Walter Korpi, *The Democratic Class Struggle* (London: Routledge and Kegan Paul, 1983); Michael Shalev, "The Social Democratic Model and Beyond," *Comparative Social Research* 6 (1983): 315–351; John Myles, *Old Age in the Welfare State* (Boston: Little, Brown, 1984), ch. 4. The classic study of the impact of protest on American welfare policy remains Piven and Cloward, *Regulating the Poor*. Interpretations that stress the role of "corporate liberal" capitalists in formulating social policy, on the other hand, often downplay the impact of working-class pressure, particularly in the American case. An influential example of this approach is Berkowitz and McQuaid, *Creating the Welfare State*. See also Jill Quadagno, *The Transformation of Old Age Security* (Chicago: University of Chicago Press, 1988). The classic statements of the theory of "corporate liberalism" include James Weinstein, *The Corporate Ideal in the Liberal State* (Boston: Beacon Press, 1968) and G. William Domhoff, *The Higher Circles* (New York: Random House, 1970). For an attempt to combine corporate liberalism and protest models see J. Craig Jenkins and Barbara A. Brents, "Social Protest, Hegemonic Competition and Social Reform: A Political Struggle Interpretation of the Origins of the American Welfare State," *American Sociological Review* 54 (1989): 891–909 and a critique by Edwin Amenta and Sunita Parikh, "Capitalists Did Not Want the Social Security Act: A Critique of the Capitalist Dominance Thesis," *American Sociological Review* 56 (1991): 124–129.

41. Skocpol, *Protecting Soldiers and Mothers*; Skocpol, *Social Policy in the United States* (Princeton, NJ: Princeton University Press, 1995), ch. 1; Stephen Skowroneck, *Building the New Administrative State: The Expansion of National Administrative Capacities, 1877–1920* (Cambridge: Cambridge University Press, 1982); Margaret Weir, *Politics and Jobs: The Boundaries of Employment Policy in the United States* (Princeton, NJ: Princeton University Press, 1992); Amenta, *Bold Relief*; James G. March and Johan P. Olsen, "The New Institutionalism: Organizational Factors in Political Life," *American Political Science Review* 78 (1984), 734–739. The "new institutionalism" is mirrored in the work of organizational historians such as Ellis Hawley, Louis Galambos and Brian Balogh. See especially Hawley, *The Great War and the Search for Modern Order*; Hawler, "Neo-Institutional History and the Understanding of Herbert Hoover," 69–73; Louis Galambos, "Technology, Political Economy and Professionalization: Central Themes of the Organizational Synthesis," *Business History Review* 57 (Winter 1983): 471–493; Brian Balogh, "Reorganizing the Organizational Synthesis," *Studies in American Political Development* 5 (1991): 119–172.

42. McElvaine, *The Great Depression*, ch. 9; Cohen, *Making a New Deal*, 283–289, 333–349.

43. Skocpol, *Social Policy in the United States*, 23–25.

44. Ibid., 26–28; Skocpol, *Protecting Soldiers and Mothers*, Part 3.

45. For a discussion of this phenomenon in recent discussions of welfare reform see Katz, *Improving Poor People*, 20–21.

46. The inability to reform an unpopular welfare policy has been frequently noted. Michael Katz has argued that "stale ideas about poor people" have made reform efforts failed exercises in social control. Stephen Teles, on the other hand, has stressed that the sharp, ideological debates among policy elites have made it difficult to implement the public consensus of the need to reform welfare. Katz, *Improving Poor People*, 21 and Stephen Teles, *Whose Welfare? AFDC and Elite Politics* (Lawrence: University of Kansas Press, 1996). A central argument of this study is that the inability to reform relief has been produced by a fundamental contradiction embedded in the political culture: Americans have consistently opposed means-tested relief but have also resisted financing the reforms necessary to eliminate it. On the fiscal constraints inhibiting welfare reform see Laurence E. Lynn, Jr., and David deF. Whitman, *The President as Policymaker: Jimmy Carter and Welfare Reform* (Philadelphia: Temple University Press, 1981), 232–240.

Chapter 2

The "Rising Tide of Relief"

In 1937 the WPA's Division of Social Research published a monograph entitled *Trends in Relief Expenditures, 1910–1935*. The study, authored by Anne E. Geddes, a member of the work program's research division, placed the expansion of relief during the Great Depression within in the context of long-term trends in welfare spending. Geddes reviewed a range of studies on public and private relief expenditures during the two decades that preceded the depression. The data, although "scattered and fragmentary," consistently showed significant increases in spending for relief during this period. In a sample of sixteen large cities, for example, public expenditures for all forms of relief increased from an aggregate of $1.6 million in 1911 to nearly $19 million in 1929. Correcting for population increases, Geddes found per capita expenditures rising from $.10 to $.90 per inhabitant. Another study focused on a large sample of public and private agencies in the most populous cities in the nation. It found that public relief spending increased by 216 percent between 1916 and 1925; private relief showed a more modest, but impressive, rise of 143 percent during the same period.[1] The studies showed that relief spending had increased both during the latter part of the Progressive era, the period of reform prior to World War I, and during the 1920s, when there was relatively less public concern about the problem of poverty. Geddes concluded that the relief crisis of the early 1930s was not simply an anomaly caused by the economic crisis but represented "a sharp acceleration of a tendency manifest during the preceding two decades."[2]

Geddes' conclusion suggests that even before the Great Depression, means-tested relief was becoming the safety net for low-wage workers.[3] This finding, although not stressed in most histories of social welfare and social work, is consistent with a good deal of research in the field. Walter Trattner's classic general history, *From Poor Law to Welfare State*, pointed to a "Renaissance of Public Welfare" during the Progressive era and its aftermath.[4] Recent studies attempting to explain the unique structure of the American welfare state, with its heavy emphasis on income-tested relief, have stressed the role of the Progressive-era Mothers' Pension programs as "sowing the seeds" of contemporary welfare policy.[5] Studies focusing on professionalization and modernization of the American administrative state have come to similar conclusions. William R. Brock has described a significant effort to reform state and local public welfare administration during the 1920s, a decade that has long been appreciated as the time when the social work profession emerged in its modern form.[6] In general, the 1920s is no longer viewed as a static decade, dominated by business elites implacably hostile to reform, but a "new era" marked, in Ellis Hawley's words, by "an enhanced vision of enlightened private orders enlisted in the national service and working with public agencies to advance the common good."[7]

Yet we get a very different, almost contradictory picture when we turn to accounts of the early years of the Great Depression. Massive unemployment is portrayed as a storm washing over a system of private charity and poor law relief that had changed little since the late nineteenth century. The initial responses of urban welfare systems to the depression are often described as "traditional" and "inadequate." The expansion of public relief during the Hoover years, culminating in the first federal welfare program, is seen as a radical break with tradition, the end of "voluntarism" in social welfare policy. The policy changes that occurred during the early decades of the century and their impact on early depression relief efforts are almost entirely ignored.[8]

The question of the relationship between the Great Depression and the American welfare state is not simply a historiographic problem. The traditional narratives suggest that the federalized welfare system that emerged from this period was forced on an unsuspecting and unprepared political culture by a catastrophe.[9] This approach would appear to buttress, perhaps unintentionally, the popular view that the modern American welfare state is simply a product of the depression and New Deal. For conservatives, the depression destroyed an effective voluntarist system dominated by private charities, creating dangerous tax-funded "entitlements." Contemporary liberals, on the other hand, see the privatist welfare system of the 1920s as "inadequate"; believe the depression revealed those inadequacies; and laud the New Deal for its guarantee of a basic floor under income. But what if the system of the 1920s was not, in fact, voluntarist but was evolving, albeit slowly, toward a modern system of public welfare? What if the modern features of this emerging welfare state influenced and even exacerbated the crisis of the early depression years? This might change not only our approach to social policy in the early depression but also our view of the origins of our contemporary welfare dilemma. The study of social policy prior to 1930 also challenges us to rethink commonly held notions about the relationship between the modern state and society, particularly between the public and private spheres. Rather than as opposing forces, locked in a zero-sum battle, they evidenced similar tendencies toward centralization, bureaucratization and a sense of public entitlement.[10] As we shall see, the expansion of relief prior to 1930 was the product of institutional and social forces that ignored the perceived divide between the public and the private.

The increase in relief-giving between 1910 and 1930 has been noted in passing by a number of historians but is not well understood.[11] Part of the problem is that the forces that are usually seen as producing changes in social policy—reform movements, grassroots social protest organizations and interest groups attached to the emerging public bureaucracies—do not seem to explain the growth of public and private relief.[12] With the notable exception of new state programs to aid widows ("mothers' pensions"), the expansion of relief does not appear to be a product of legislative activity. As we will see, most of the key developments in social welfare policy from 1910 to 1930—the professionalization of social work, the development of casework, the enormous increase in private fundraising associated with the Community Chests, the public welfare movement—were not designed to create an expanded relief system. Even the Mothers' Aid programs, clearly new public relief measures, were often justified as efforts to pull single women out of the existing "poor law" relief system and provide them with a "pension," not a traditional "dole." How, then, are we to account for the expansion of relief?

One way to approach this question is to look at the experience of a single agency, Boston's public welfare department (The Overseers of the Public Welfare), which administered most relief in a large city during the early decades of the century. While Boston was certainly not a typical city in its relief policies—per capita expenditures were among the highest in the nation, and its reliance on public administration was exceptional—the welfare department's annual reports provide a relatively consistent data series that can help us pinpoint the timing and sources of expenditure growth. Table 5 shows total and per capita expenditures for relief and the estimated caseload of the department for five-year periods from 1900 to 1930 (I include the data for 1929 to show expenditure and caseload growth in the 1920s before the 1930 depression). The data shows that the city's relief expenditures and caseload were stable during the first decade of the century (the early years of the Progressive era did not produce a liberalization of welfare policy) but rose significantly dur-

Table 5
Boston Overseers of the Poor/Public Welfare: Caseload, Expenditures and
Mothers' Aid Cases, 1900–1930

Year	Total Cases	Mothers' Aid	Spending	Relief/Case
1900	2,707		$78,996	$29.17
1905	2,202		$79,575	$36.13
1910	1,995		$83,738	$41.97
1915	5,515	1,338	$601,125	$109.06
1920	3,605	1,476	$879,072	$243.85
1925	5,334	1,167	$1,562,145	$292.86
1929	7,463	975	$2,480,382	$332.35
1930	11,478	1,007	$3,667,561	$319.53

Note: The Mothers' Aid program began in September 1913. Expenditures and relief per
    case are in current dollars (not adjusted for inflation).
Source: "Annual Report of the Boston Overseers of the Poor [Public Welfare]," Documents
    of the City of Boston (1900–1930).

ing the next twenty years. Between 1910 and 1920 spending increased
from $83,738 to $879,072, and the caseload rose from 1,195 to 3,605. Caseloads continued to grow in the 1920s, more than doubling to nearly 7,500
recipients in 1929, while expenditures nearly tripled to $2,480,232.[13]
These trends are consistent with Geddes' findings for public and private
agencies during this period.[14]

Analysis of the welfare department's annual reports makes it possible
to evaluate the sources of spending and caseload growth. Most of the
expansion prior to 1920 can be explained by implementation of the state's
Mothers' Pension law beginning in 1913. Like most states during the
World War I era, Massachusetts established a mandate requiring that
localities aid single women with children "in their homes." The impact
on the caseload of the Boston welfare department was dramatic: the
number of cases jumped from 2,978 recipients to 4,507 between 1912 and
1913 and reached 5,515 in 1915 (although many of the new cases were
single women, the recession of 1914 had a significant, short-term impact
on the department's caseload).[15] Because mothers' pension cases received
significantly higher monthly payments than traditional general relief recipients, the impact on total expenditures during the period was even
greater. Yet although the Mothers' Aid program appears to have initiated
the increase in relief-giving, it does not account for the increases during
the 1920s. During this period, the mothers aid caseload actually declined
(from 1,476 cases in 1920, to 1,167 in 1925, to 975 cases in 1929), whereas

the overall caseload nearly doubled and expenditures rose at an even greater rate.[16] Data collected by the department on the "sources of dependency" (including "old age," "disability," "alcoholism" and "disease") shows increases in all categories of the poor. Particularly noteworthy was the tendency to absorb increasing numbers of unemployment relief cases: the number of those listing "unemployment" as a reason for receiving aid rose sharply during the recession of 1921–1922 (from 331 to 1,260) and failed to return to previous levels with the end of the cyclical downturn. By 1929 the unemployment relief caseload had doubled from the level of 1920.[17]

The Boston data suggests that the Mothers' Aid program initiated the expansion of relief reported in the Geddes study but does not account for its growth during the 1920s. This suggests a complex relationship between mothers' pensions and general (noncategorical) relief in the predepression era. The new program for female-headed families may well have liberalized the policies toward all classes of the poor. Ironically, at the very time the mothers' aid caseload had stabilized, its impact on the treatment of other classes of recipients was being felt. These generalizations are confirmed by contemporary observers. According to a 1924 report on the Overseers by the Boston Finance Commission, an independent fiscal watchdog agency closely linked to the city's business elite, the Mothers' Aid law changed attitudes of both recipients and administrators. Traditionally, the stigma of public charity meant that "only those in desperate circumstances applied for it." But since the passage of the Mothers' Pension law, "there has grown up a noticeable change in attitude of the people toward receiving aid from the poor department." At the same time, the new program influenced conceptions of adequacy within the department:

The law requires the furnishing of adequate aid to dependent mothers and their children. This has tended to increase the aid also to those who do not come within the mothers' aid act. The distinction in many cases is so slight between those aided under the mothers' aid act and those aided under the poor laws that it is impossible for the same board administering both funds not to accord similar treatment.[18]

Prior to the law, "the overseers gave $2 or $3 a week, often in groceries regardless of the size of the family or its need." The influence of mothers' aid "with its insistence on adequacy of relief has been shown in the more liberal assistance now being given to the other families and individuals aided by the city."[19] Robert Kelso, a nationally known public welfare official and prolific writer on the subject, believed that mothers' pensions had inaugurated profound changes in the administration of poor relief. In Massachusetts the process had begun when, under the auspices of the

Mothers' Aid program, the state Department of Public Welfare "entered the field and began a cooperative reconstruction of local outdoor poor relief." Kelso also noted that more liberal policies toward mothers' aid cases influenced the treatment of recipients aided under the traditional poor laws, since the latter were "relieved from the same offices by the same agents living in the same neighborhoods."[20]

Historians have occasionally noted the impact of mothers' aid on public welfare and private charity, but the relationships have received relatively little attention or analysis. Rather, most accounts of implementation of the Mothers' Aid programs have emphasized the ways policies failed to live up to the expectations of the reformers who lobbied for them. Benefits did not provide adequate family incomes, forcing women and their children into the low-wage labor market; long waiting lists developed for the limited number of slots; private charity workers, who had initially opposed the programs, were called upon to staff the bureaucracies that implemented them; they imposed income tests and morals standards that stigmatized recipients, making mothers' pensions resemble traditional charity. A number of historical accounts have suggested that these developments paved the way for the low status of "welfare" in contemporary social policy (Mothers' Aid programs are the forerunners of today's federal program for single parents).[21] Another reason for the failure to appreciate the impact of mothers' pensions on pre-depression welfare policy is that in most localities, Mothers' Aid programs were administered outside the regular relief-giving bureaucracies. The Boston case, where the same agency administered both mothers' pensions and "general relief," was not the norm. In most localities, the Juvenile Courts, volunteer boards or new public agencies administered the program. In these cases, agencies tended to draw on the services of private charity organizations for administrative personnel.[22] These administrative arrangements reflected, in part, the effort by advocates of the program to distinguish mothers' aid from traditional "poor law relief."[23]

Yet while Mothers' Aid programs may not have lived up to the expectations of reformers and were often administered outside the traditional relief machinery, they appear to have encouraged the expansion of all forms of relief prior to the depression. In part, this is because they provided additional funds for a class of recipients that had always made up a large segment of the relief rolls. Joanne Goodwin has found that just prior to the implementation of the Illinois Mothers' Aid program, approximately 50 percent of all recipients on the rolls of the Cook County (Chicago) poor board were female-headed families. Similarly, the Boston Overseers reported in 1906 that its caseload contained, "a large numbers of the families . . . of [widowed or deserted] women with very young children."[24] One goal of the Mothers' Aid programs was to pull this class of recipients out of the poor relief machinery, but this effort did not always succeed. A key reason was inadequate appropriations for state-mandated programs, which required supplemental aid from public agencies and private charities. A Children's Bureau study found that numerous localities supplemented inadequate benefits with funds from other sources. In Allegheny County (Pittsburgh), for example, the four private family agencies gave supplemental aid to families on the mothers' aid rolls and to those on the waiting list; the local public agency assisted seven families receiving mothers' aid and thirty on the waiting list. In Wayne County (Detroit), Michigan, the Mothers' Aid program was administered by the Juvenile Court under the supervision of a former private charity official. But the Detroit public welfare department "had a liberal policy in regard to supplementing mothers' aid when the maximum grant was inadequate."[25]

These examples suggest that Mothers' Aid programs not only encouraged expansion of public and private relief but may well have broken down the distinction between the two. Historians of mothers' pensions have emphasized that social workers from private charities were called upon to staff the new programs, which they had initially opposed as dangerous expansions of "outdoor relief." In the process, it has been argued, they imposed morals tests and intrusive investigations on recipients that reflected traditional attitudes about the behavior of the poor.[26] But it is also important to recognize that the attitudes of charity officials and social workers were not static. Implementing Mothers' Aid programs may well have influenced prevailing attitudes about adequacy, dependency and the role of public welfare. "We can smile at the warning, issued years ago by those of us who were the opponents of Mothers' Assistance Fund legislation that such laws would create a new crop of dependent families," wrote Helen Tyson in a paper presented to the 1926 National Conference on Social Work:

The law has not created them; it has simply discovered them. With all our mis-givings about this new type of family work there is one that, in Pennsylvania, we have never had—the fear that unsuitable families are receiving relief or that there has been any slackening of effort on the part of the families themselves to graduate from the assisted group. Our great concern at present lies with those on our waiting lists whom we are not helping at all, and with those whom . . . we are not helping sufficiently.[27]

Tyson's comments (and those of Boston's Finance Commission previously quoted) suggest that central to this process was changing the attitudes toward the question of the adequacy of relief within the social work community. Implementation of Mothers' Aid programs coincided with the proliferation of "standard budgets" produced by various aca-

demic experts and disseminated by national welfare agencies, including
the U.S. Children's Bureau. Probably the most influential of these was a
budget produced by the Chicago Council of Social Agencies in 1920.
(Other standard budgets included one produced by the New York National Council and the so-called Jaffa Budget, developed at the University
of California.)[28] These were essentially lists of items to be included in the
basic relief grant—a "standard food order" designed to maintain a family of a given size in "health and decency." They were primarily designed
as guidelines for agencies and social workers determining individual
grants, but, invariably, they became yardsticks for measuring the adequacy of local relief. It soon became obvious that Mothers' Aid programs
rarely measured up to the standards of reformers whose goal was to
encourage single women to leave the labor force.

Accounts of implementation abound with stories of women being
forced into low-wage labor to supplement inadequate grants. (A Children's Bureau study even provides examples of women being forced to
indenture children to other families.)[29] But it is often not emphasized
that the social workers who administered mothers' aid were highly critical of these trends and lobbied hard to increase relief standards. Emma
Lundberg, while emphasizing the inadequacy of mothers' aid grants,
contrasted the approach of social workers to the problem with the
"deadly complacent" attitude assumed toward traditional relief:

Discontent with the standards of mothers' aid is prevalent enough, but it is often
shared by the persons charged with the administration of the aid. It is not the
hopeless dissatisfaction that led to the abolition of public relief in certain cities
and in some other localities which expects nothing and therefore gets what is
expected.[30]

Although Lundberg stressed the impact of mothers' aid on public "outdoor relief," it appears that social workers were developing a yardstick
that influenced relief practices in private agencies as well.[31] Edward
Lynde described the changing policies of a private family agency, clearly
influenced by the mothers' aid approach to relief-giving, in Philadelphia
between 1916 and 1926:

Another comparison in Philadelphia shows the difference in treatment of the
families of men who drink heavily, the wife in each instance being in need of an
operation. In 1916, such a family with five children was given a total of $7 in
relief and the record closed with the comment that the woman refused to undergo an operation and that court action was advised for the man. In 1926 a
similar family with six children was given $663 in relief, *in order that the mother
might remain at home from work* [emphasis added]. The husband's wages alone,
even when he worked regularly, had been insufficient to maintain their large
family. At first reluctant to undergo an operation because of her husband's op-

position, she finally consented. Very intensive and very costly psychiatric case work resulted in the man's giving up liquor and working more regularly than for years back. It also affected almost a miraculous improvement in the relationship among all members of the family.[32]

Lynde's reference to "intensive psychiatric casework" suggests that the changes in relief practices initiated by the Mothers' Aid programs were magnified by other trends in social welfare provision. Casework, for example, was at the heart of the professionalization of social work in the 1920s. This much-discussed development followed a predictable pattern—the creation of national organizations like the American Association of Social Workers and the Family Welfare Association to promote standards for individuals and agencies; the establishment of training institutions, particularly schools of social work attached to major universities; and the elaboration of a quasi-scientific methodology to justify claims to expertise.[33] Casework was this methodology. The goal, as has been frequently noted, was to assist "dysfunctional" individuals and families adjust to modern social life. The caseworker was required to draw on theories of human behavior, including therapeutic approaches associated with Freudian psychology, as well as knowledge of local social conditions and the range of available community services, to create a program designed to "rehabilitate" clients. The casework movement has been frequently criticized for ignoring the social roots of poverty, discouraging activism and encouraging "social control" of the poor by middle-class professionals. With so much emphasis on reforming individual behavior, rather than the political economy, social workers became, in Michael Katz's words, "second class therapists."[34]

The relationship between the new, professional social worker and relief was complex and ambiguous. For example, caseworkers sought to de-emphasize the relief-giving aspects of their profession in favor of "constructive" skills that made families "self-sufficient." A key goal of the new social agencies, it was argued, was to eliminate the automatic giving of relief. On the other hand, the provision of adequate relief was a central task of the professional social worker. One *Survey* column neatly captured this ambiguity: "There has been a shifting of emphasis from mere relief to the constructive and preventative aspects of [family casework] . . . [yet] relief work itself is more intensive and fundamental to the well-being of families whom it does touch." Another columnist listing twelve "Personal Aims and Methods in Social Case Work "expressed a similar attitude. The caseworker was advised how to deflect the demands of a "grasping" client "that demanded help from a fund left for those in need." On the other hand, social workers were urged to "preserve the self-respect" of clients by providing adequate aid and avoiding intrusive and judgmental investigations.[35] These contradictory

attitudes were resolved by the theory that social work would limit the
number of those receiving aid but provide adequate assistance to the
"truly needy" clients who required extensive casework.[36] This was a neat
theory that proved extremely difficult to implement in practice. An increase in the standards of adequacy automatically increased the number
of low-wage workers who were judged truly needy. Rejecting clients
whose incomes fell below minimum standards simply because they did
not appear to have other "pathologies" could subject the welfare agency
to a good deal of public criticism.[37]

In fact, relief-giving was far more important to the new professionals
than they were perhaps willing to admit. The provision of adequate relief
was one of the central policies that distinguished modern social workers
from those who administered traditional "poor law relief," the primary
negative reference for the emerging profession.[38] The giving of inadequate "doles" was constantly cited by those who criticized local poor
law agencies that had not implemented modern standards of professionalization. The calculation of family budgets was part of the "expertise"
involved in the casework method. This could be a complex process,
which involved translating food prices into a "standard budget"; recal-
culating for price increases; and attempting to adjust these amounts for
the needs of cases of different sizes and levels of income. Then the social
worker needed to help the client obtain the maximum health benefit from
the food order. "It is not sufficient to turn the family who cannot manage
over to the home economics department and expect magic to be per-
formed there," reported one social worker in *The Family*. "The adoption
and use of the Minimum Food Order is dependent upon education in
its use."[39] "Family budgeting required skill for its execution," Blanche
Coll writes in her recent monograph on the implemenation of the Social
Security Act, "the skill of home economists to develop and keep current
a realistic minimum standard of living applicable to a given area and,
most of all, the skill of social workers to apply the general to the particular, to personalize, to individualize from the mass."[40]

Thus, while it is certainly true that professional social work incorporated traditional attitudes about relief and the dangers of "dependency,"
the overall impact of professionalization was to liberalize relief policies.[41]
Increasingly, relief came to be seen as a valuable tool in social work and,
with a proper dose of casework, not harmful to the client. Some social
workers were even rejecting the idea that relief was "pauperizing." Grace
L. Marcus, a casework consultant to the Charity Organization Society of
New York, published several articles and a short monograph in the late
1920s on casework and relief. In the *Family*, an influential journal of family casework, Marcus argued that relief was the "modus operandi" of
the caseworker in establishing and maintaining a relationship with the
client: "Relief gives the caseworker a reason for being on the casework

scene." Having established a relationship with the client, paternalistic attitudes by the caseworker or servility by the client could undermine the central goal of the casework method: encouraging the client to become self-sufficient. She went on to suggest that relief "is often made the scapegoat for the development of dependencies that existed in the make-up of the clients long before relief became a factor in their lives . . . [there is a] nervousness about relief which has interfered with casework in various ways."[42] The director of a Catholic relief agency, speaking at the 1930 National Conference on Catholic Charities on "The Influence of Relief Giving on Personality and its Development," put it more bluntly: "In conclusion, let me say that relief is a tool in casework [which] in and by itself pauperizes no one."[43]

In evaluating the attitudes of social workers and the practice of local agencies, public and private, it is also important to keep in mind that while the casework method encouraged an emphasis on individual, rather than social, roots of poverty, professionalism did not entirely eclipse the commitment to reform that characterized the early years of the profession. As Clarke Chambers argued in his influential monograph *Seedtime of Reform*, many social workers in the 1920s advocated a program that served to link the reformist movements of the Progressive era with the social agenda of the New Deal years.[44]

Particularly noteworthy, in terms of the relief problem, was a new emphasis on unemployment and its impact on the families of low-wage workers. Growing interest in the issue of unemployment appears to have been sparked by a number of developments. The economic recession of 1921 produced a landmark federal "Conference on Unemployment," chaired by Secretary of Commerce Herbert Hoover. The conference although noticeably short on policy initiatives, represented, in Udo Sautter's words, a "remarkable departure" for the federal government.[45] The conference coincided with academic interest in the impact of "technological unemployment" (labor force reductions caused by the introduction of new machinery) and the possibility of stabilizing the business cycle through government spending policies, particularly public works. Finally, the late 1920s witnessed a concerted effort by "urban liberal" politicians, most notably, New York's Senator Robert Wagner, to rally Democrats around a new reform agenda focusing on unemployment.[46] Social workers were active in several local "employment stabilization" committees that experimented with job creation, public works and re-employment programs. In 1928 the National Federation of Settlements established a committee on unemployment and initiated a study of seasonal and technological unemployment. The following year, the *Survey* produced a special issue entitled "Unemployment and the Ways Out— Our Stake in Steady Jobs," which proclaimed, with typical Progressive faith in planning and expertise, that joblessness had become "a needless and controllable byproduct of industrial progress."[47]

Although reformers certainly did not see relief as the solution to unemployment, social workers concerned about the problem tended to focus on its impact on local relief-giving agencies.[48] In doing so, they may well have encouraged more liberal policies (and more applications for aid). The experience of the St. Louis Provident Association, a private family welfare agency, is a good example of this process at work. During the winter of 1926–1927, the agency made a study of the increasing number of unemployment relief cases applying for aid and began an intensive casework program designed to link workers with potential employers. The success of the program, however, led to increased contact between unemployed workers and the relief agency: "As a result of this attention to the unemployment problem in the casework program, requests for jobs increased to the point where the district was in danger of becoming an employment bureau." The initial response to this trend was more intensive investigation of potential recipients, but by the next year the agency was adopting more relaxed policies for unemployed applicants. Office interviews with the "unemployed man" were substituted for home visits, and "investigations were limited chiefly to economic and industrial sources." By the winter of 1928–1929, the number of unemployed cases has increased to the point where new "intake visitors" were added to help with the mounting caseload. The next winter a new intake department was created to "sift out the more difficult casework problems from the mass of unemployment problems with which we were swamped."[49]

St. Louis was not an isolated case. In Philadelphia there were an unusually large number of applicants to the local private family welfare agency during the winter of 1923. Although welfare officials believed seasonal unemployment was the primary cause, "the summer [of 1924] brought as many applications as did the winter, and at the end of the first nine months forty-two percent more families had come to the Society than in the same months in 1923." A special fund was raised for relief, but it was exhausted by September, and the family society had to stop intake for nearly five months. The rise in the relief caseload appears to have coincided with growing concern about unemployment and low-wage workers: in 1923 the agency initiated a study of unemployment and its impact on relief.[50] Chicago provides another example. In 1927 the private United Charities was "flooded with appeals" for aid from unemployed men. Social workers were perplexed by the phenomenon, since payroll indexes showed relatively high levels of employment. Yet it is also clear that leaders in the private field were increasingly concerned about the impact of unemployment on family welfare, and this may have influenced the attitudes of agencies toward potential applicants. In 1928 the Chicago Council of Social Agencies created a special committee on unemployment, circulating a questionnaire to members on the problem and its impact on casework.[51]

Concern about unemployment and its impact on the caseloads of private agencies appears to have influenced attitudes concerning the relationship between public and private relief. Casework, particularly as practiced by private charity organizations, was predicated on a well-rounded program of education, recreation and training and a great deal of consultation with individual clients. The program was quite labor-intensive, requiring that model social agencies have large staffs and finance a broad range of social services. Yet during the 1920s private family societies were under increasing pressure from unemployed workers who did not appear to need elaborate casework intervention. Social workers with mounting caseloads had less time for individualized counseling, and increasing relief expenditures drew funds from social services required to make casework effective. Agencies could respond to the dilemma by reducing the amount of casework for unemployed workers, as in the case of St. Louis, but this also had the tendency to encourage applications since relaxed investigative procedures tended to reduce the stigma of relief. This impact of these developments was to cause some social workers to argue that mass relief-giving was not a proper function of private charity but rather should be handled by public agencies. The notion of a division of responsibility between public and private agencies coincided with a weakening of the intense ideological opposition to public "outdoor relief," which had characterized the charity movement of the nineteenth century. According to Michael Katz, "as social workers became more self-consciously professional, they argued that the source of funds mattered less than their management and they redefined outdoor relief as a problem of administration rather than a matter of principle."[52]

The more favorable attitudes toward public relief were encouraged by efforts to impose "modern" principles of administrative organization on the provision of public social services. Traditional opposition to relief, particularly public relief, was partly based on the belief that public agencies were controlled by local political machines, dispensing aid in a haphazard and unprofessional manner. In this context, the "public welfare" movement, the effort to centralize and rationalize the vast array of social services that state and local governments had inherited from the nineteenth century, was one of the most important developments in social policy during the 1920s. At the local level, the effort was spearheaded by municipal reformers who sought to create new public welfare boards, consolidating the array of services targeted to low-income groups. State-level reform focused on reorganizing the various agencies that ran large institutions (prisons, asylums and public hospitals) and integrating newer programs such as public health and the Mothers' Aid programs into a rational administrative structure.[53] The goal was to apply the new ethic of efficiency, centralization and professionalism to social services. Both the goals and the rationale for the movement were extremely ambitious. Howard Odum, in an introduction to a special edition of the *Annals of the American Academy of Political and Social Science* on the subject, called public welfare "the outstanding contribution of the half century toward progress in American democracy" and possibly "the last and perfecting stage in an effective democracy." Robert Kelso, a welfare administrator whose career was marked by continuous movement between the public and private sectors, listed the specific functions a local public agency might perform—"police powers in matters of public health; the care and reformation of lawbreakers; relief of the poor; care and education of the blind and crippled; care and custody of the insane, the epileptic and the feeble minded . . . oversight of city and town planning; supervision of private social agencies; the licensing of various welfare enterprises such as boarding homes for infants, lying-in hospitals, dispensaries, dance halls and theaters."[54]

As Kelso's list implies, relief was only one function—and not the most important one—of the model public welfare agency. Furthermore, administrative reform meant applying casework methods that, in theory, de-emphasized the role of relief. Chicago's new Bureau of Public Welfare (Cook County), according Wilfred Reynolds, was created, in part, to "replace the old system of giving doles of material rations . . . by a system of family rehabilitation through adequate casework methods in which the supplying of material necessities is only one of many items of service included in a complete plan for the family."[55] In his widely read treatise *The Science of Public Welfare*, Kelso claimed that the hiring of a "trained social worker" by one Pennsylvania county had reduced the relief caseload by half.[56] But the overall impact of administrative reform was probably to produce more liberal attitudes toward relief. A central goal of the public welfare movement was the elimination of traditional "poor law relief." This was generally defined as the giving of "doles" in a haphazard manner by politically connected officials with no training in "modern" casework methods. Although reformers hoped to eliminate, in Kelso's words, "the malingerers" who did not deserve aid, they also sought to increase relief standards for those judged in need. "Mechanical doles," Kelso argued, "seldom afford adequate relief." The problem, as we have noted, is that this process inevitably increased the number of potential recipients eligible for aid under the means test. In practice, the policies of reducing caseloads but increasing standards for those judged "truly needy" tended to work at cross-purposes.

The public welfare movement may have also encouraged a subtle, but important, change in the image of local agencies that influenced day-today relief practices: relief now appeared to be part of a broader, more inclusive social agenda, rather than simply part of an effort to regulate the behavior of the poor. One can image a good deal less stigma attached to an application to the Boston Overseers of the Public Welfare than to its predecessor, the Overseers of the Poor. When the city changed the name of its almshouse to the "Long Island Hospital," the *Boston Herald* noted that the old name was "not in keeping with modern charitable practice, casting a stigma on the recipient of municipal aid. The city council about three years ago changed the name of the Overseers of the Poor to the Overseers of the Public Welfare for the same reason." Kelso himself feared that administrative modernization may have proceeded more slowly than the expansion of relief it had induced. In a 1923 article on "Recent Advances in the Administration of Poor Relief" he warned that the main impact of reform may have been to "increase the totals of out relief without parallel advance in the skill with which it is applied."[57]

Measured against the goals of reformers like Odum and Kelso, public welfare development appears to have been quite limited during the 1920s.[58] Administrative reform and modernization were far more advanced in the private sector, as the professionalization of social work coincided with a dramatic increase in organizational activity at both the local and national level. Charity organizations, which focused on relief-giving and the visiting of the poor by volunteers, were replaced by "family societies" that provided casework, dispensed relief, and coordinated a range of social services. Religious, ethnic, and nonsectarian organizations were joined into citywide "Welfare Councils" or "Councils of Social Agencies." National organizations of agencies, social workers and administrators—the American Association of Social Workers, the Family Welfare Association, the American Red Cross, the Association of Community Chests and Councils—proliferated.[59] These were led by "professional" (mostly male) administrators who attempted to project a "businesslike" image, shedding the perceived amateurism and sentimentality of the older charity movement.[60]

The centralization of private relief involved many of the same subtle changes in public image that influenced relief-giving in the public sphere. As societies for "improving the condition of the poor" became "family societies," the stigma of applying for relief was reduced. This was ironic, since the name changes were designed, in part, to emphasize the broad, nonrelief functions of the new agencies, particularly their casework orientation. Yet observers persistently complained that clients and the social workers who referred them continued to view private agencies primarily as dispensers of relief. Linton Swift, the director of the American Association for Organizing Family Social Work (Family Welfare Association), believed that centralization, and the way it was financed had played a key role in creating this perception. Writing in the journal *The*

Family in March of 1929, Swift sought to explain the " 'rising tide' of relief expenditures" that was "causing great concern to family social agencies and community chests." He went on to stress the impact of mass relief appeals, sophisticated forms of publicity and the dramatic increase in the number of contributors. These had transformed the public image of local agencies: "we have lost our former character as an independent private and experimental agency, and have drifted toward the status of a semi-official public agency, responsible to the entire community for the administration of a large central relief fund."[61]

Swift's analysis, emphasizing the rather fragile distinction between the public and the private in social policy, suggests that the concept of "voluntarism," a term often used to characterize pre–New Deal relief policy, needs to be reevaluated. This becomes clearer when we look more closely at the impact of the Community Chests, the quintessential voluntarist fundraising organizations, which played such an important role in the early years of the Great Depression. The first Chests were created by business elites just prior to World War I to consolidate the numerous and often conflicting appeals of local charities for donations. The Chests and similar organizations in non-Chest cities proliferated in urban areas during the 1920s, and the goals of the movement became considerably more ambitious. Influenced by (and in many cases a direct organizational outgrowth of) the "Liberty Loan" bond drives, which raised massive sums for the war effort, they employed new techniques of mass publicity, experts in the emerging field of "public relations" and new technologies of communication to greatly expand the financial base of private charity.[62] In the process, the Chests served an important ideological function: they promoted the notion that the United States had discovered a unique "American way" to assist the poor and unemployed, avoiding tax-funded subsidies and public bureaucracies. Modern techniques of mass communication and corporate organization could be marshaled to promote traditional, privatist goals.[63]

Moving beyond the ideological rationales, however, one finds a complex relationship between the Chests and the expansion of public welfare. Although Chest campaigns were designed as an antidote to tax-supported relief, their development was clearly part and parcel of the broader movement for professionalization, centralization and bureaucratization that was occurring in both the public and private spheres.[64] One private welfare official, returning to Cincinnati in 1924 after a decade's absence, described the impact of the Community Chest in terms of "the growth of humanitarian activity . . . from the neighborly aid of the early days in behalf of the sick and the starving to the massing of forces in modern times for promoting the common good in every phase of life." Such heady formulations tended to reduce sharp distinctions between public and private institutions, as this official stressed that the "cooperation of public and private agencies has long been a striking characteristic of social work in Cincinnati."[65] Not only did the centralization of relief financing and charity organization mirror developments in the public sphere, but, as we have seen, the "experts" and administrators employed by the Chests moved back and forth between public and private agencies. As a result, antipathy to public relief, which appeared as part of the rationale for the Chests, was not shared by the officials who administered the campaigns and the expanding social agencies they funded.

The key problem with Community Chests as antidotes to public "doles" was that they advertised the existence of large relief funds and encouraged the public to think of relief as both a community responsibility and a right. Emotional appeals that focused on the neediest citizens were the central tactic of the Chest campaigns. Recognizing the dangers in this approach, the *Survey* persistently encouraged the Chests to reorient publicity by stressing the "positive" aspects of casework and social services. The editors complained that "it looked for a time as if the little girl on crutches who always traveled with the label 'Suppose Nobody Cared?' was going to be the trademark for the Community Fund," noting with approval a new poster that featured a newsboy with a "friendly dog." By the late 1920s publicity more frequently emphasized the positive, nonrelief aspects of family societies, with "crippled children" replaced by "smiling clients."[66] Yet emotional appeals continued to be the most effective mechanism for raising funds, particularly during the annual drives for winter relief. In New York, a non-Chest city, funds were raised for private agencies through Christmas appeals for the "one hundred neediest." The *Survey* complained that the campaigns raised "thousands for relief . . . but how much for education?"[67]

The problem was not simply a distorted public image of the methods of modern social work. Emotional appeals, while raising unprecedented sums for private relief, could undermine the very agencies they were financing. A study of relief and private casework in New York City found a great deal of confusion about the goals of private family societies "indirectly encouraged by fundraising publicity." The problem was exacerbated by the broadening of the financial base from which private welfare organizations gained funds. Workers who had given small donations through so-called industrial solicitations ("voluntary" deductions from their pay for charity) would no doubt be encouraged to think of the "community fund" as precisely that: a resource that they might tap in times of need. Both clients and the social workers from referring agencies believed that the local family welfare organization was "under an obligation to furnish financial assistance since it obtains from the sympathetic public to help those whose problems appear to arise from financial need."[68] One speaker at the 1930 National Conference of Catholic

Charities put it this way: "It has been my observation that whirlwind campaigns with attendant blare of trumpets announcing hundreds of thousands of dollars each day, mass meetings and high-powered sales talks and general newspaper publicity tend to make many persons feel that it is their duty, not only to contribute to the fund, but to refer numerous clients to the office as well, and many clients are better informed than the case-worker on the exact amount of money raised."[69]

In this way, Chest publicity generated demands that, ironically, could be satisfied only by public appropriations. Thus, we see a few cities, just prior to the Great Depression, allocating small sums to private agencies in conjunction with Chest campaigns. In San Francisco the city government contributed approximately $20,000 to the Associated Charities during the winter months, in part to help relieve the private agencies of the relief burden so they could continue to allocate funds to casework and services. Similarly, in Los Angeles, the Community Chest received public appropriations from the City Council and the Board of Supervisors. In Birmingham, Alabama, where the Chests had assumed control of the financing of relief in 1925, Chest officials appealed (without success) to the city and county governments to help finance the rising relief caseloads in 1928 and 1929.[70]

Linton Swift believed that such trends would undermine the rationale for the Community Chests themselves. In the spring of 1930, on the eve of the first of the great "voluntarist" campaigns of the early depression years, Swift warned that high-profile fundraising campaigns were fostering a "community relief psychology which has already gone beyond our control . . . spilling over into pressure for the development of new types of public agencies and into community demands for new types of governmental relief such as old age pensions." Swift was particularly concerned with "industrial solicitations, which almost inevitably develop aspects of coercion [and] bring a great flood of demands later from thousands who treat their contributions as insurance against their own future needs."[71] The analysis, made at the 1930 National Conference on Social Work and reprinted in the *Survey*, was prophetic.

The central argument, here, is that efforts to reform and modernize public poor-law relief and private charity encouraged the expansion of relief in the 1920s and profoundly influenced the response of the American welfare system to the onset of the Great Depression. I am not suggesting that traditional relief had been eradicated by 1929. Indeed, as has often been noted, there is ample evidence that traditional methods of relief-giving and attitudes persisted well into the depression. The "modernization" process, as I have described it, was certainly confined to large urban areas, and even there it was incomplete.[72] But it was precisely in these large cities that the relief crisis of the early 1930s, which generated the pressures for the first large-scale federal relief appropriation, was the most intense, and the intensity of the crisis cannot be explained simply by pointing to unemployment. It was also produced by the fact that the "modern" system of public and private welfare organization was generating new demands for relief that could not long be satisfied by local financing mechanisms.

Nor am I suggesting that a national system of means-tested relief was the central goal of professionalizers and reformers of the era. In fact, reforms were often justified as efforts to eliminate traditional relief, reduce its role in the social work program or make it more efficient. For example, a great deal of energy was expended trying to distinguish between mothers' pensions and public relief. Mothers' Aid, according to a Children's Bureau study, was "much more than a relief measure in that the test of its worth and efficiency is not wholly and primarily the alleviation of material distress but also the well being of the children under supervision, as expressed in terms of adequate mother care, health, both physical and mental, school progress and preparation for effective womanhood and manhood."[73] Similarly, social workers in private family agencies appear to have been in a state of denial about the importance of their relief functions. One researcher who studied the "rise in relief-giving" found a great deal of defensiveness about the issue: "With very few exceptions [my] questionnaires were returned with emphatic statements to the effect that this or that organization was not a 'relief agency.'"[74]

Not only was the expansion of relief an unintended consequence of the modernization of the welfare system, but it was accompanied by rhetoric that suggested that this was a dangerous development. Frank J. Bruno, a private charity official from Minnesota, complained in the *Survey* that social workers had "grown complacent" concerning "the demoralizing effect of much of our relief giving." Bruno went on to argue that "the socialization of medicine, mothers' pensions, industrial compensation, the rising standard of living, the short-sighted nature of much social work publicity, have all driven us to the granting of still larger amounts of relief." Grace Marcus' 1929 study of relief and casework was framed by noting "the increasing sense of responsibility family societies feel for accounting to their boards and the directors of the community chests for the difficulty they are encountering in keeping their relief expenditures within the bounds set by their budgets." In her detailed examination of relief and casework, Marcus stressed "the existence of a many-sided conflict in the caseworker's attitude toward relief," arguing that "the core of the difficulty lies in the caseworker's fear of the dangers of relief."[75] Even Linton Swift, who as director of the Family Welfare Association in 1931 would become an outspoken supporter of public relief during the unemployment crisis of the early depression, warned that mass relief drives were creating a "community relief psychology" that would, in the end, produce a "great governmental relief system of the type which has wrecked states in the past."[76]

Swift's jeremiad represented the prevailing view concerning the real dangers of a national, tax-supported relief system, an attitude created in large measure by American perceptions of the financial difficulties confronted by the new European social insurance systems, particularly the British system of unemployment compensation. In its original form the British policy, inaugurated in 1911, could easily be distinguished from traditional relief. Financed entirely by contributions from employers and employees and containing a fifteen-week limit on benefits, the program was fiscally sound and linked to employment. After World War I, however, the British government, responding to the rapid demobilization of the military and mass unemployment, extended coverage to new classes of workers and extended the time limit. In the process, it began to contribute to the system from general revenues, financed, in part, by borrowing. Thus, according to the *New York Times*, "the dole made its appearance." By 1927 roughly two-thirds of the unemployed workers covered by the system were drawing "uncovenanted" benefits—that is, benefits financed by the general budget rather than contributions. Efforts to return to a strict contributory system were stymied by opposition from labor and the weakness of the British economy in the late 1920s.[77] These developments provided, according to the historian Daniel Nelson, a "wealth of ammunition" to American opponents of social insurance. By the early 1930s reformers advocating unemployment compensation in the United States "were almost unanimous in their condemnation of the British dole and in their demands that any American system emphasize the possibilities that lay in management initiative."[78]

What is particularly noteworthy here is that this particular "Atlantic Crossing" produced a public rhetoric that warned of the imminent danger of a national relief system financed by general tax revenues.[79] This was precisely what the term "dole" came to signify in the American political culture. The persistent American use of the term created defensiveness among British politicians on the Left and the Right. They argued that the system continued to be based on contributions and could be brought back into balance when the national economy revived. The *New York Times*, hardly an advocate for social insurance in the United States, defended British policy, calling the dole "that misleading name for unemployment insurance."[80] Americans, as one British industrialist told the U.S. Chamber of Commerce, widely misconstrued the British program as a "state of charity." Yet American perceptions were encouraged by the frequent demands for reform on the part of British leaders themselves. Albert Beveridge, the architect of the original program, argued that the policy had become "a general system of outdoor relief of the able-bodied, administered by a national tax" and that only the "ghost of insurance" remained. A 1931 study sponsored by an American industrial relations counseling firm picked up this theme and argued that the "basis of the scheme is now so altered that it has become a relief rather than an insurance measure." Similarly, the National Industrial Conference Board argued that in Britain, "mere charity relief has been superimposed on insurance, and the insurance system degenerates into a dole."[81]

These attitudes were easily transferred to American social welfare policy in the form of opposition to public relief. When a columnist in the *Survey Graphic* warned American readers of the dangers of "dole-itis," he was not simply referring to social insurance but to direct relief payments made from a centralized fund. "The dole has almost become a bogey of American popular literature," wrote the social insurance advocate I.M. Rubinow in the *Social Service Review*:

The fear of the dole system is, of course, based on the British experience. It is amazing how familiar the average American newspaper reader considers himself with economic and social conditions of the British Isles of the past, present and future, and particularly with the nature and extent and effects of the dole system. If the Rotarian or Kiwanian wants to record his objections to public relief for fear of an increase in the tax rate, he does not have to argue the point. All he has to do is wave his hand eloquently eastward and exclaim, "Look what the dole system has done to Great Britain."[82]

By the early 1930s, according to the historian Robert Cowley, the word "dole" had come to be "charged with the the the same amorphous malignity and colored with the sickly foreign taint as the word Red in 1919."[83] In this way, traditional hostility to public relief mingled with attacks on European-style social insurance to popularize the concept of a "dole" as a tax-supported system of aid to the unemployed that encouraged "malingering," increased the public debt and undermined the national character.[84]

Thus, side by side with the expansion of relief there developed a public rhetoric intensely hostile to this development yet seemingly unaware that it was occurring. Indeed, there was, a strong belief that the United States was well on the way to developing alternatives to the "dole."[85] While there was a good deal of truth in this idea—one certainly sees an American approach to social welfare during these years that sharply diverges from the European pattern—reforms designed to promote an "American way" appear to have encouraged precisely the trend they were created to obviate: a national system of means-tested welfare financed by public funds. By centralizing public and private welfare activities, increasing the resources available through new, mass fundraising techniques and implementing new standards in conjunction with the

Mothers' Aid programs and the professionalization of social work, they created new agencies to which low-wage workers could apply and tended to reduce the stigma of applying for aid. The result was a public relief system that perhaps more closely resembled a "dole" than the British system of unemployment compensation. This fact became painfully evident during the early years of the depression, as relief became the only alternative for millions of unemployed workers. The irony was not lost on Jacob Billikopf, a leader of Philadelphia's private emergency relief organization. Speaking to the National Conference on Social Work in the spring of 1931, Billikopf noted:

> If the spirit of irony . . . were hovering over this land, he would find a source of sardonic amusement in the spectacle of a country which for a decade has protested that it did not want unemployment insurance because it was a dole, and which so protests, slowly realizing that under its boasted American methods all that it can offer to those most in need is the real dole of public or private charity.[86]

As Billikopf spoke, the issue of federal aid for unemployment relief was moving to the center of the political agenda.

NOTES

1. Anne E. Geddes, *Trends in Relief Expenditures, 1910–1935* (WPA Research Monograph No. 10) (Washington, DC: Government Printing Office, 1937), 6–15.

2. Ibid., xiii.

3. The studies reviewed by Geddes were, in fact, the product of increasing concern about the "mounting bill for relief." These studies and the discussion of relief they encouraged in the journals of social work are key sources for this chapter. See John B. Dawson, "The Significance of the Rise in Relief-Giving during the Past Five Years: Its Relationship to Increased Costs and the Adequacy of Relief," *Proceedings of the National Conference on Social Work* [hereafter NCSW] (Chicago: University of Chicago Press, 1922), 228–236; Ralph Hurlin, "The Mounting Bill for Relief" and Raymond Clapp, "Relief in Nineteen Northern Cities," both in *Survey* 58, no. 4 (November 15, 1926): 207–211; "When Relief Soared," *Survey* 62, no. 6 (June 15, 1929): 352. For more developed analyses of the causes of the increase in relief see Edward E. Lynde, "The Significance of Changing Methods in Relief Giving," *The Family* 8, no. 5 (July 1927): 135–136; Linton Swift, "The Relief Problem in Family Social Work," *The Family* 10, no. 1 (March 1929): 3.

4. Walter I. Trattner, *From Poor Law to Welfare State*, 6th ed. (New York: Free Press, 1979), ch. 10; Michael Katz, *In the Shadow of the Poorhouse* (New York: Basic Books, 1986), 208. For a more negative assessment of developments in the 1920s see James T. Patterson's *America's Struggle against Poverty* (Cambridge, MA: Harvard University Press, 1994), 27–30.

5. Barbara J. Nelson, "The Origins of the Two-Channel Welfare State: Work-

men's Compensation and Mothers' Aid," in Linda Gordon, ed., *Women, the State and Welfare* (Madison: University of Wisconsin Press, 1990), 123–151; Christopher Howard, "Sowing the Seeds of 'Welfare': The Transformation of Mothers' Pensions, 1900–1940," *Journal of Policy History* 4, no. 2 (1992): 188–227; Theda Skocpol, *Protecting Soldiers and Mothers* (Cambridge, MA: Harvard University Press, 1992); Linda Gordon, *Pitied but Not Entitled* (New York: Free Press, 1994). Gordon, it should be noted, has placed less emphasis on the Mothers' Pension programs per se than on the "gendered" reform tradition that they embodied (see 157–181).

6. William R. Brock, *Welfare, Democracy and the New Deal* (New York: Cambridge University Press, 1986), chs. 1, 2 (see especially his analysis on 41–45); Roy Lubove, *The Professional Altruist: The Emergence of Social Work as a Career* (New York: Atheneum, 1983); Clarke Chambers, *Seedtime of Reform: American Social Service and Social Action, 1918–1933* (Minneapolis: University of Minnesota Press, 1963); James Leiby, *A History of Social Welfare and Social Work in the United States* (New York: Columbia University Press, 1978).

7. Ellis Hawley, *The Great War and the Search for a Modern Order*, 2nd ed. (New York: St. Martin's Press, 1992), v. For a textbook narrative that embodies this view of the 1920s see James Henretta et al., *America's History*, 3rd ed. vol. 2 (New York: Worth Publishers, 1997), 739.

8. Even William R. Brock, who describes in great detail the modernizing reforms of the 1920s, stresses the "archaic" aspects of the welfare system when he moves on to the depression. See *Welfare, Democracy and the New Deal*, 71. See also Patterson, *America's Struggle against Poverty*, 56–57; Katz, *In the Shadow of the Poorhouse*, 213; Lizbeth Cohen, *Making a New Deal* (Cambridge: Cambridge University Press, 1990), 218–224; Anthony Badger, *The New Deal* (New York: Hill and Wang, 1989), 34–35; William H. Mullins, *The Depression and the Urban West Coast, 1929–1933* (Bloomington: Indiana University Press, 1991), ch. 3; Bonnie R. Fox, "Unemployment Relief in Philadelphia: A Study of the Depression's Impact on Voluntarism," in Bernard Sternsher, ed., *Hitting Home: The Great Depression in Town and Country* (Chicago: Quadrangle Books, 1970). Fox's important essay has strongly influenced my thinking about early depression welfare policy. She describes a highly innovative effort by Philadelphia's business elites and social welfare leaders to organize a relief program financed primarily by private funds. Yet I argue that the program she describes was not really traditional (nor entirely "voluntarist") but rather reflected the developments in social organization described in this chapter.

9. Robert Higgs, *Crisis and Leviathan* (New York: Oxford University Press, 1987). Although Higgs notes that the welfare state expands incrementally in response to long-term social trends (61), his narrative places almost exclusive emphasis on a series of crises (depressions and wars) in explaining the growth of "Big Government."

10. Michael Katz, *Improving Poor People* (Princeton, NJ: Princeton University Press, 1995), 56–57; Edward Berkowitz and Kim McQuaid, *Creating the Welfare State* (New York: Praeger, 1980) xii–xiii.

11. See, for example, Katz, *Improving Poor People*, 50; Patterson, *America's Struggle against Poverty*, 27–28.

12. Skocpol, *Protecting Soldiers and Mothers*, 54–57; Edwin Amenta, *Bold Relief:*

Institutional Politics and the Origins of American Social Policy (Princeton, NJ: Princeton University Press, 1998), 27–37.

13. "Annual Report of the Boston Overseers of the Poor [Public Welfare]," Documents of the City of Boston (1900–1930).

14. Joanne Goodwin describes a somewhat different pattern in Chicago. She found the number of families aided by the county poor board, measured as a percentage of the population, declined from 1910 to 1920 but increased in the 1920s. Goodwin also found a significant per capita increase in relief expenditures in the 1920s, but argues that this did not keep pace with inflation. However, her data does not appear to include Mothers' Aid cases, which were given relief under the auspices of the Juvenile Court. In any case, Goodwin found that by the late 1920s, "public relief in Cook County surpassed private relief." See Goodwin, "Gender, Politics and Welfare Reform, Chicago 1900–1930" (Ph.D. diss., University of Michigan, 1992), 87, 119–122 and *Gender and the Politics of Welfare Reform* (Chicago: University of Chicago Press, 1997), 69, 80–84.

15. "Annual Reports of the Boston Overseers of the Poor [Public Welfare]," Documents of the City of Boston, 1912–1920.

16. Ibid, 1920–30.

17. Ibid.

18. Brian Gratton. *Urban Elders: Family, Work, and Welfare among Boston's Aged, 1890–1950* (Philadelphia: Temple University Press, 1986), 161–162; Boston Finance Commission (BFC), *Reports and Communications* (Boston: BFC, 1924), 11.

19. Ibid, 160, 178.

20. Robert Kelso, "Recent Advances in the Administration of Poor Relief," *The Journal of Social Forces* 1, no. 2 (January 1923), 91–92; Kelso, *The Science of Public Welfare* (New York: Henry Holt and Co., 1928), 174–175.

21. Howard, "Sowing the Seeds of 'Welfare,'" 201–205; Skocpol, *Protecting Soldiers and Mothers*, 472–479; Gordon, *Pitied but Not Entitled*, 49–50.

22. Mary F. Bogue, *The Administration of Mothers' Aid in Ten Localities* (U.S. Department of Labor, Children's Bureau, Publication no. 184 (Washington: Government Printing Office, 1928), 2–3, 5–6; Emma O. Lundberg, "Progress of Mothers' Aid Administration," *Social Service Review* 2 (September 1928), 436.

23. Separate administrative arrangements could produce conflict at the local level. Joanne Goodwin has shown that there was initially a great deal of friction in Chicago between the Cook county poor board, linked to the city's political machines, and the Juvenile Court, which administered mothers pensions and was allied with middle-class reformers, women's clubs and settlement houses. Goodwin, *Gender and the Politics of Welfare Reform*, 119–124. See also Roy Lubove, *The Struggle for Social Security* (Cambridge, MA: Harvard University Press, 1968), 101–106; Mimi Abromowitz, *Regulating the Lives of Women*, 3rd ed. (Boston: South End Press, 1992), 203.

24. Goodwin, *Gender and the Politics of Welfare Reform*, 69; "Annual Report of the Boston Overseers of the Poor [Public Welfare]," Documents of the City of Boston, 1905, 18; Abromowitz, *Regulating the Lives of Women*, 148, 156–157.

25. Bogue, *The Administration of Mothers' Aid in Ten Localities*, 8 (Pittsburgh), 172, 175 (Detroit); I.M. Rubinow, "Should Mothers Pensions Be Supported?" *Survey* 52, no. 10 (May 15, 1924), 234–235. For a brief discussion of the role of private agencies in supplementing mothers' pensions in New York City see George

McJimsey, *Harry Hopkins: Ally of the Poor and Defender of Democracy* (Cambridge, MA: Harvard University Press, 1987), 22–23.

26. Howard, "Sowing the Seeds of Welfare," 200; Nelson, "The Origins of the Two-Channel Welfare State," 139–140; Lubove, *The Struggle for Social Security*, 111; Gordon, *Pitied but Not Entitled*, 64.

27. Helen Glenn Tyson, "Measuring the Results in Securing the Essentials of Family Life: Some Suggestions Based on a Review of Mothers Assistance in Pennsylvania," NCSW, 1926, 299; I.M. Rubinow, "Can Private Philanthropy Do It?," *Social Service Review* 3, no. 3 (September 1929), 379.

28. Sydnor H. Walker, "Privately Supported Social Work," 1182; Bogue, *The Administration of Mothers' Aid in Ten Localities*, 8. Joanne Goodwin has stressed the impact of family budgets in her study of mothers' pensions in Chicago. Goodwin, *Gender and the Politics of Welfare Reform*, 172–175.

29. The most frequently-cited evidence is from a 1926 study of 2,404 Mothers' Aid cases in Pennsylvania. An aggregate of 56% of the income of these families was raised by their own efforts. The Mothers' Aid grant accounted for only 39.4% of the income, with the remainder being provided by private charities. "What Is Desirable Income," *Survey* 57, no. 10 (February 15, 1927). See also Tyson, "Measuring Our Results . . . ," 297–299; Emil Frankel, "Sources of Income, Standards of Mothers' Work and of Children's Education in Families Aided by the Mothers Assistance Fund," NCSW, 1927, 255–257.

30. Lundberg, "Progress of Mothers Aid Administration," 454–455; Goodwin, *Gender and the Politics of Welfare Reform*, 173.

31. Walker, "Privately Supported Social Work," 1182–1184; Leila Houghteling, "The Budget of the Unskilled Laborer," *Social Service Review* 1, no. 1 (March 1927), 1–3; Kelso, *The Science of Public Welfare*, 207.

32. Lynde, "The Significance of Changing Methods in Relief Giving,"140.

33. Katz, *In The Shadow of the Poorhouse*, 163–171; Lubove, *The Professional Altruist*, ch. 5; Leiby, *A History of Social Welfare and Social Work*, 181–185. For an excellent discussion of the recent literature on professionalization see Brian Balogh, "Reorganizing the Organizational Synthesis," *Studies in American Political Development* 5 (Spring 1991): 131–140.

34. Katz, *In the Shadow of the Poorhouse*, 166; Lubove, *The Professional Altruist*, 119.

35. Anne Lockard Chesley, "Personal Aims and Methods in Social Case Work," *Survey* 55, no. 2 (October 15, 1925), 89–90.

36. Lynde, "The Significance of Changing Methods in Relief Giving," 138; Walker, "Privately Supported Social Work," 1184. Both Lynde and Walker defended private social agencies, which were experiencing big increases in relief expenditures, by emphasizing that the proportion of clients receiving relief had declined.

37. Lynde, "The Significance of Changing Methods in Relief Giving," 141. Lynde advised that agencies reject families with men capable of employment and potential recipients of Mothers' Aid "with all the public approbrium and loss of support which such limitation of intake may sometimes entail."

38. Kelso, "Recent Advances in the Administration of Poor Relief," 91–92.

39. S. Etta Sadow, "Testing the Practicability and Palatability of the Minimum Grocery Order," *The Family* 11, no. 7 (November 1930): 236; "Budgets in Case-

work," *Survey* 43 (January 10, 1920): 398; [Maurice Taylor,] "Family Workers and Food," *Survey* 45, no. 4 (November 15, 1925): 205. Taylor complained about the formulaic process of calculating food budgets and urged agencies to implement in-service training on "the science of food values and bodily needs."

40. Blanche Coll, *Safety Net: Welfare and Social Security, 1929–1979* (New Brunswick, NJ: Rutgers University Press, 1995), 86; Gordon Hamilton, NCSW, 1931, 184–185.

41. Brock, *Welfare, Democracy and the New Deal*, 42–43.

42. Grace L. Marcus, "Social Attitudes as They Are Affected by Dependency and Relief-Giving," *The Family* 9, no. 5 (July 1928): 139. See also Marcus, *Some Aspects of Relief in Family Casework* (New York: Charity Organization Society, 1929), 45–51 and Marcus, "The Effects of Financial Dependency and Relief Giving upon Social Attitudes," NCSW, 1928, 218–225. For a review of Marcus' views see Virginia P. Robinson, "What Relief Means," *Survey* 42, no. 15 (June 15, 1929): 350–352.

43. Henry C. Schumacher, "The Influence of Relief Giving on Personality and Its Development," Sixteenth National Conference of Catholic Charities (Proceedings) (Washington, DC, 1930), 100.

44. Chambers, *Seedtime of Reform*, 96–97; Judith Trolander, *Settlement Houses and the Great Depression* (Detroit: Wayne State University Press, 1975), 36–37. Trolander rejects the view that professionalization was the primary cause of the weakening of reform sentiment among social workers in the 1920s; instead, she emphasizes the influence of financial elites located in the Community Chests.

45. Udo Sautter, *Three Cheers for the Unemployed* (Cambridge: Cambridge University Press, 1991), 141–149; Carolyn Grim, "The Unemployment Conference of 1921: An Experiment in National Cooperative Planning," *Mid-America* 55 (April 1973): 83–107; "Mr. Hoover's Conference," *Survey* 46, no. 20 (September 24, 1921): 697; William L. Chenery, "Mr. Hoover's Hand," *Survey* 47, no. 4 (October 1921): 107–109, 110; Chenery, "The President's Conference on Unemployment in the United States," *International Labor Review* 5, no. 3 (March 1922).

46. The *New York Herald Tribune* reported in March of 1928 that Democrats were attempting to make unemployment a "new political issue." In February New York governor Al Smith publicly requested a survey of unemployment, and later in the month Senator Wagner, after consulting with Smith, delivered a "carefully prepared speech" during which he outlined the reform proposals that would bear his name during the coming years. See the *New York Herald Tribune*, March 18, 1928 in Robert F. Wagner Papers, Box 234, Folder 18. See also the *New York Times*, March 6, 1928, 1, 3; May 20, 1928, 9; Sautter, *Three Cheers for the Unemployed*, 236; J. Joseph Huthmacher, *Senator Robert F. Wagner and the Rise of Urban Liberalism* (New York: Atheneum, 1968), 58–63.

47. For the National Federation of Settlements study see Trolander, *Settlement Houses and the Great Depression*, 36–37; Chambers, *Seedtime of Reform*, 143–146; Helen Hall Testimony, Senate Commerce Committee Hearings, March–April 1930, 76. The study was published by Helen Hall, *Case Studies in Unemployment* (Philadelphia: University of Pennsylvania Press, 1931) and in a popularized form by Clinch Calkins, *Some Folks Won't Work* (New York: Harcourt, Brace and Co., 1930). The *Survey* issue was entitled "Unemployment and the Ways Out—Our Stake in Steady Jobs," *Survey* 60 (April 1, 1929). For a brief discussion of the

Survey and unemployment see Clarke Chambers, *Paul U. Kellogg and the Survey* (Minneapolis: University of Minnesota Press, 1971), 116–117, 119–120. See also Paul U. Kellogg, "Unemployment and Progress," NCSW, 1929, 96–97. On employment stabilization committees in Rochester and Cincinnati see Beulah Amidon, "Three Cities Look Ahead," *Survey Graphic.* 45, no. 9 (February 1, 1931): 474–475 and C.M Bookman, "An Attempt to Meet an Unemployment Emergency," NCSW, 1930, 341–347. See also William H. Stead, "Measuring a City's Unemployment," *Survey* 63, no. 12 (March 1930): 704–705.

48. Leah H. Feder, *Unemployment Relief in Periods of Depression* (New York: Russell Sage Foundation, 1936), 304–311; "Distributing the Load: Some Suggestions as to Emergency Measures in a Period of Widespread Unemployment," *The Family* 5, no. 9 (January 1922): Section 2; Edward D. Lynde, "Unemployment— The Responsibility of the Family Case Work Agency," NCSW, 1929, 320–323.

49. Bedford, NCSW, 1931, 201–202; Julia Alsberg, "A Casework Approach to Unemployment," *Survey* 58, no. 6 (June 15, 1927): 315–316. These two essays on the St. Louis experiment may actually reveal an evolution of attitudes among social workers. Alsberg's piece, written in 1927, emphasizes the need to adapt casework methods to the unemployed cases. Bedford's 1931 National Conference on Social Work report stresses the degree to which such methods were inappropriate for unemployed cases.

50. Adelaide Henson, "Some Effects of a Period of Unemployment as Seen by a Family Society," *Smith College Studies in Social Work* 1 (September 1930): 66–67.

51. Clorinne M. Brandenburg, *Chicago Relief and Service Statistics* (Chicago: University of Chicago Press, 1932), 5–6.

52. Katz, *In the Shadow of the Poorhouse*, 156. For an analysis of unemployment and relief that rejected a division of responsibility between public and private agencies see Raymond Stockton, "The Responsibility of a Family Agency at a Time of Industrial Readjustment," *The Family* 2, no. 2 (July 1921): 22. Not only the demands of casework but the desire to experiment with new programs and policies made mass relief-giving problematic for private agencies. Robert Kelso argued in 1928 that "in the main the public agency administers relief and other public welfare measures, while the private agency experiments in the field of problems and methods not yet fully demonstrated as practicable for social legislation." Although not all social workers agreed that relief-giving should be primarily a public function, Kelso's basic formulation had, by the late 1920s, nearly become the conventional wisdom. Kelso, *The Science of Public Welfare*, 100. For other evidence of the more favorable attitudes of social workers toward public relief see Amos W. Butler, "Official Outdoor Relief and the State," NCSW, 1915, 439.

53. Useful sources on public welfare development include Kelso, *The Science of Public Welfare*; "Public Welfare in the United States," *The Annals of the American Academy of Political and Social Science* 105 (January 1923); Sophonisba Beckenridge, "Frontiers of Control in Public Welfare Administration," *Social Service Review* 1, no. 1 (March 1927): 84–85; Howard W. Odum, "Public Welfare Activities,"in *Recent Social Trends in the United States: Report of the President's Research Committee on Social Trends*, vol. 2 (New York: McGraw-Hill, 1933), 1230–1233, 1244–1255; John A. Brown, "The Organization of State and County Welfare Departments,"

NCSW, 1929, 523–530. The most detailed recent study is in Brock, *Welfare, Democracy and the New Deal*, chs. 2, 3.

54. Howard Odum, "Newer Ideals of Public Welfare," 1–2 and Robert Kelso, "The Transition from Charities and Correction to Public Welfare," 24–25, both in "Public Welfare in the United States."

55. Wilfred S. Reynolds, "Cook County Comes to Order," *Survey* 56, no. 4 (May 15, 1926): 245.

56. Kelso, *The Science of Public Welfare*, 182. See also Joseph Mayer, "Municipal Public Welfare Administration in a City of 200,000 to 750,000 Population," *Journal of Social Forces* 2, no. 2 (January 1924): 216. Mayer argued that public relief was for "destitute families and individuals who are unemployable and who cannot be cared for by private agencies. For the "unemployed and homeless . . . the tendency is to operate some form of municipal work, such as rock quarry . . . [and] to pay for such work only in the form of meals, lodgings and grocery orders for the purpose of discouraging too general a use of this form of emergency employment. . . . The modern method is to avoid shifting unemployment to charity or taxes" (216).

57. *Boston Herald*, December 11, 1926, 13; Kelso, "Recent Advances in the Administration of Poor Relief," 91–92.

58. The status of public welfare in the 1920s is difficult to evaluate. The consensus among historians has been that administrative reform proceeded at a slow pace and that social workers in the public sector were treated as second-class citizens by those in private agencies. Josephine Brown, *Public Relief, 1929–1939* (New York: Henry Holt and Co., 1940), 52–55. Even those who have stressed the expansion and modernization of public welfare have tended to emphasize the persistence of archaic local poor law practices. Katz, *In the Shadow of the Poorhouse*; Brock, *Welfare, Democracy and the New Deal*, 2, 42. Discussions by public welfare advocates in the 1920s produce similar contradictions: amazement at the growth of public activities is combined with much hand-wringing concerning the state of administrative practice, especially at the local level. One might resolve this contradiction by suggesting that the expansion of public services and agencies proceeded more rapidly than efforts to modernize their administration. This exacerbated the patchwork quality of welfare service delivery, which the reformers decried. William J. Norton, "The Philanthropic Taxpayer," *Survey* 52, no. 2 (April 15, 1924): 86–88; Brown., "The Organization of State and County Welfare Boards," 527.

59. Francis H. McClean, "National and Local Social Agencies Rendering Services to the Home and Family," *Annals* (1923): 47–51; Walker, "Privately Supported Social Work," 1186–1190; Homer Folks, "Fundamental Objectives of a Council of Social Agencies," NCSW, 1928, 295–297, Lubove, *The Professional Altruist*, ch. 6.

60. For a biography of the early career of one such administrator see June Hopkins, *Harry Hopkins: Sudden Hero, Brash Reformer* (New York: St. Martin's Press, 1999).

61. Swift, "The Relief Problem in Family Social Work," 3, 5.

62. In Cleveland, which had created the first Chest in 1914, the relief drives of the 1920s were a direct organizational extension of the Liberty Loan campaigns. Employing "sixty best sellers, a group of business and advertising men"

in the Chest changed the focus of publicity from patriotic appeals to the welfare of children." The campaign raised over $4 million between November 18 and 26, 1919. Not only was the aggregate amount significantly larger, but the number of givers tended to increase, with large numbers of small contributions from members of the middle and working classes. A report on Detroit's "patriotic fund," which raised funds for both local charity and foreign relief, estimated a tenfold increase in the number of individual givers compared with the situation prior to World War I. Mass publicity and organized "industrial appeals," where business firms solicited funds from employees, were held responsible for raising a fund of $5.2 million. William J. Norton, "Pre-War Budgets Tripled" and Carlton K. Matson, "A Full Chest," both in *Survey* 43, no. 11 (January 10, 1920): 399; Walker, "Privately Supported Social Work," 1204–1207; Lubove, *The Professional Altruist*, 184–192; Margaret Orelup, "Private Values, Public Policy, and Poverty in America, 1890–1940" (Ph.D. diss., University of Massachusetts, Amherst, 1995), 78–87.

63. Chests also may have enhanced the power of conservative local business elites over local agencies and their staffs. In the process, the Chests appear to have encouraged the tendency for social workers to avoid controversial reforms in favor of promoting individualized casework and administrative reform. Judith Trolander's classic study of the settlement houses in the Great Depression has argued that in cities where Chests predominated, social workers were less likely to support reforms such as federal relief. Trolander, *Settlement Houses and the Great Depression*, ch. 3.

64. This point is also emphasized by Katz, *In the Shadow of the Poorhouse*, 157.

65. *Survey* 53, no. 10 (February 15, 1925): 591.

66. *Survey* 51, no. 10 (February 15, 1924): 511; 58, no. 8 (January 15, 1927): 512–513. See also Paul H. Bliss, "Interpreting Standards to the Public," NCSW, 1926, 669–678.

67. *Survey* 55, no. 8 (January 15, 1926): 472.

68. Marcus, *Some Aspects of Relief in Family Casework*, 32.

69. Louise McGuire, "Trends in Relief," Sixteenth Session of the National Conference of Catholic Charities (Proceedings) (Washington, DC, 1930), 87. See also William Pear, "The Problem of Maintaining Casework Standards and Meeting Relief Requirements," NCSW, 1931, 371.

70. William E. Mullins, *The Depression and the Urban West Coast, 1929–1933* (Bloomington: Indiana University Press, 1991), 36; Leonard Leader, "Los Angeles and the Great Depression," (Ph.D. diss., UCLA, 1972), 33; Edward Shannon LaMonte, *Politics and Welfare in Birmingham, 1900–1975* (Tuscaloosa: University of Alabama Press, 1995), 97–98.

71. The speech, originally given at the National Conference on Social Work in the spring of 1930, was reprinted in the *Survey* 64, no. 12 (September 15, 1930): 502–503, 525. I stress the date of the original speech to emphasize the fact that Swift was responding to developments in the late 1920s, not the early depression relief campaigns! See also Orelup, "Private Values, Public Policy and Poverty in America, 1890–1940," 87–88.

72. Brown, *Public Relief, 1929–1939*, 55; Brock, *Welfare, Democracy and the New Deal*, 70.

73. Bogue, *The Administration of Mothers' Aid in Ten Localities*, 55; Abramowitz, *Regulating the Lives of Women*, 203.

74. Dawson, "The Significance of the Rise in Relief-Giving . . . ," 235.

75. Frank J. Bruno, "A Romance of Family Casework," *Survey* 55, no. 2 (October 15, 1925): 87–88; Marcus, *Some Aspects of Relief in Family Casework*, 6, 43, 47.

76. Swift, "Community Chests and Relief," 503.

77. Mary Barret Gibson, *Unemployment Insurance in Great Britain* (New York: Industrial Relations Counselors, 1931); *New York Times*, April 3, 1927, IX, 11. The story of the expansion of benefits to British workers during and after World War I is a good deal more complex than the account here, which is necessarily brief and reflects American perceptions. See Albert Beveridge, "Unemployment Insurance in the War and After," in Thomas Hill et al., eds., *War and Insurance* (London: Humphrey Milford, 1927); Noel Whiteside, "Welfare Legislation and the Unions during the First World War," *Historical Journal* 23, no. 4 (1980): 857–874 and Whiteside, *Bad Times* (London: Faber and Faber, 1991), 73–77; Pat Thane, *The Foundations of the Welfare State*, 2nd ed. (London: Longman, 1996), 138–139, 162–166; James Cronin, *The Politics of State Expansion* (London: Routledge and Kegan Paul, 1991), 44–48.

78. Daniel Nelson, *Unemployment Insurance: The American Experience, 1915–1935* (Madison: University of Wisconsin Press, 1969), 30. See also Lubove, *The Struggle for Social Security*, 166–167. For a defense of the British system by one American advocate of social insurance see Leo Wolman, "Unemployment Insurance in England," *Survey* 55, no. 10 (February 15, 1926): 562–563.

79. The quoted phrase is lifted from Daniel Rogers' celebrated recent study, *Atlantic Crossings: Social Politics in a Progressive Age* (Cambridge, MA: Belknap Press of Harvard University Press, 1998). Rogers, of course, stresses the more positive influences of European precedents on the American reform tradition.

80. *New York Times*, October 25, 1927, 28, January 1, 1926, 22. According to the *Times* of June 23, 1929, "all three parties [in the British Parliament] repudiate the use of the word dole as applied to unemployment insurance."

81. *New York Times*, January 27, 1926, 32; Lubove, *The Struggle for Social Security*, 167; Gibson, *Unemployment Insurance in Great Britain*, 368.

82. Rubinow, "Can Private Philanthropy Do It?," 388; Morris Mills, "Dole-ITIS," *Survey Graphic* 65, no. 9 (February 1, 1931): 487.

83. Robert Cowley, "The Drought and the Dole," *American Heritage* 23, no. 2 (February 1972): 93.

84. *New York Times*, November 13, 1929, 10.

85. Hawley, *The Great War and the Search for a Modern Order*, 126–127.

86. Jacob Billikopf, "What Have We Learned about Unemployment?," NCSW, 1931, 39. See also Helen Hall, "Shall We Stick to the American Dole?," *Survey Graphic* 65, no. 7 (January 1, 1931): 389.

Chapter 3

The Myth of Voluntarism

In early February of 1931 President Herbert Hoover, responding to demands for more aggressive federal action in the deepening economic emergency, described his view of the American system of emergency relief in the following way:

The basis of successful relief in national distress is to mobilize and organize the infinite number of agencies of relief help in the community. This has been the American way of relieving distress among our people and the country is successfully meeting its problem in the American way today.[1]

The president went on to say that local governments might provide public funds to assist the victims of economic and natural disasters. Even federal aid might be needed to prevent starvation. However, these were secondary lines of defense to be utilized only in extreme emergencies. Hoover clearly was arguing that private relief funded by voluntary contributions was the "American way" to deal with poverty and unemployment, far superior to a tax-funded "dole." Speaking before a gathering of Red Cross officials in April, the president proclaimed that "a voluntary deed by a man impressed with the sense of responsibility and brotherhood of man is infinitely more precious to our national spirit than a thousandfold poured from the treasury of the government." Several days earlier Hoover had praised Philadelphia's emergency relief committee for financing aid to the unemployed "through the private generosity of the people of Philadelphia."[2]

Hoover's relief ideology, often called "voluntarism," was once viewed by historians as perhaps the prime example of his fundamental conservatism. A substantial body of recent research, however, has shown that Hoover was not the stubborn reactionary he was once thought to be. Some historians have even come to view the Republican president as a kind of neo-Progressive. His advocacy of private, cooperative action in the pursuit of the public welfare, his aggressive support for the activities of trade associations, and his explicit rejection of versions of "rugged individualism" that left the individual at the mercy of market forces hardly seem consistent with modern laissez-faire conservatism. Several of his initiatives in response to the Great Depression, particularly his support for the Reconstruction Finance Corporation, which provided millions of dollars in government loans to failing business enterprises, represented unprecedented interventions by the federal government in the economy and paved the way for later New Deal measures.[3]

Yet this influential "Hoover revisionism," as it is sometimes called, has had less impact on accounts of Hoover's relief policy in the early depression. In part, this is because his public statements appear to show a callous disregard for the conditions faced by unemployed workers and drought-stricken farmers in 1931. It is also because Hoover's comments on the virtues of private relief echoed the rather archaic ideology of the late nineteenth-century charity movement. Public "outdoor relief," according to this perspective, tends to undermine the social fabric by breeding dependence and political corruption. Private charity is far superior to a tax-funded "dole" because it is temporary and nonpolitical and encourages the spirit of individual benevolence.[4]

Yet at the very time Hoover chose to lecture the American people on social policy, these ideas were being reevaluated (and rejected) by most of those charged with the administration of relief. "Many of us disagree with that statement [that private relief is the 'American way'] not only because it is not true, but because of its implication," argued Linton Swift, director of the Family Welfare Association, at the 1931 National Conference on Social Work. Swift pointed out that Hoover's perspective was contradicted by data collected by the president's own relief officials that showed that public funds financed nearly 60 percent of all relief. The "implication" of Hoover's analysis—that private charity was equipped to handle mass relief-giving—was also wrong: private welfare organizations, like the local family societies in Swift's organization, were designed to provide intensive casework services, not mass relief to unemployed workers. The "rising tide of relief" in the 1920s had caused some welfare officials to argue that relief should be a public function; by the spring of 1931, the resistance to public welfare had almost completely broken down, and leaders in the private field were involved in intensive efforts to generate public funds to "save" private charity from the relief burden.[5]

The observation that Hoover's relief ideology was out of touch with reality is, of course, a staple of most accounts of the early depression.

But historians need to pay closer attention to the basis of Swift's critique. There has been a tendency to view the relief policies during the Hoover period as a reflection of the president's "voluntarism." As a result, early depression relief measures, including the mass fund drives supported by the president, tend to be viewed as "traditional" social policies.[6] New developments in public and private welfare and their relationship to the relief crisis are ignored. As a result, the relief crisis that began in 1930 is seen, somewhat ahistorically, as entirely the product of the "Great Depression"—despite the fact that at this point the depression was not yet great. While mass unemployment was certainly the main factor causing the collapse of local relief, this was very much a crisis of a modernizing social welfare system: the necessity for a federal program was created not by the inadequacies of relief in rural areas and small towns but by the threatened collapse of large emergency relief organizations in cities that provided more adequate aid and that, by the spring of 1932, were being financed primarily from public funds. The goal of this chapter is to place the relief crisis of the early depression years in the context of the new institutional structures that had evolved in the 1920s—public welfare agencies, centralized private charity organizations, Community Chests, and the professionalization of social work.

Accounts of the onset of the Great Depression often depict a nation steeped in the optimism of the prosperous 1920s, blind to the realities of the economic collapse. Yet one of the most striking features of the early depression was the speed with which the issues of unemployment and relief moved to the top of the political agenda. During the winter of 1929–1930 the Hoover administration issued a series of optimistic statements on economic conditions, each one suggesting that the declines in production and employment would soon be reversed. These pronouncements were sharply attacked by reformers such as Frances Perkins, then industrial commissioner of the state of New York, Mary Van Kleeck of the Russell Sage Foundation, and New York's Senator Robert Wagner (the latter was responsible for the famous accusation that the president was promoting "prosperity by proclamation").[7] In May 1930, mass demonstrations against unemployment led by the Communist Party attracted significant numbers of workers and a good deal of press coverage.[8] These demonstrations coincided with well-publicized congressional hearings on a modest package of reform proposals by Wagner designed to deal with cyclical and technological unemployment. A parade of social workers and reformers testified on the impact of unemployment on workers and relief agencies.[9]

Developments in the spring were followed by a public controversy over the census of 1930, which had attempted to count the number of unemployed and which, according to critics of the administration, had produced a politically motivated undercount. A leading official in the Census Bureau resigned over the issue, and the administration was forced to conduct a "special census" the following winter, which showed significant increases in the unemployment count.[10] The unemployment emergency coincided with an agricultural drought, which appeared to require extraordinary relief measures. Thus, when Congress convened in the fall of 1931, leaders were confronted with an unprecedented number of proposals for federal action, including legislation for direct federal relief. Hoover, for his part, attacked such plans as if they presaged a European-style "dole."[11] The president pledged to accelerate planned federal public works and created an ad hoc committee, the President's Emergency Committee for Employment (PECE), headed by Colonel Arthur Woods. PECE sought to encourage local public works, promote private-sector job creation schemes and serve as a clearinghouse for information about local emergency relief.[12]

An emerging local relief crisis encouraged the demands for a more aggressive response from the Hoover administration. Public and private agencies, which had seen their relief caseloads increase during the late 1920s, felt the impact of growing unemployment almost immediately. The caseload of the Boston Department of Public Welfare skyrocketed to 6,000 cases. Private agencies were confronted with similar caseload increases. Fifty-one family agencies in a large sample of cities reported to the Russell Sage Foundation that their caseloads had doubled between March of 1929 and March of 1930.[13] The Philadelphia family society, according to a review of local relief by Gertrude Springer in the *Survey*, "had a hard year, receiving and quickly exhausting an appropriation from the welfare fund"; the Cleveland Community Chest increased its appropriation to the family society for relief but cut spending for social services; the St. Louis Provident Association halted intake during the summer of 1930. Springer reported that workers in private agencies, fearing that unemployment would increase during the winter, "frankly admit their lack of resources to cope alone with such a situation."[14]

The most dramatic relief crisis occurred in Detroit, where the collapse of the automobile industry caused a massive increase in the caseload of the public welfare department. The Detroit Department of Public Welfare's (DPW) expenditures increased from $156,000 in October 1929, to over $827,000 by the following spring. Helen Hall, chairman of the unemployment committee of the National Federation of Settlements, visited the city in January of 1930. "I have never confronted such misery as on the zero day of my arrival in Detroit," she wrote in the *Survey Graphic* in April. Pushing her way through the crowds filling the corridors of the welfare department, she "felt suddenly conscious of the fur lining of my coat and the good breakfast I had eaten." Long lines of men in heavy coats, soon to become one of the symbols of relief policy in the Hoover years, were featured in another *Survey* piece on conditions in New York's Bowery district. The superintendent of the Municipal Lodging House, which was using a barge to handle the overflow for the first time since 1915, reported that a new type of worker was standing in the breadlines: "there were many young men, still clean, still not too pasty of face, among the old timers."[15]

Thus, during the first year of the depression, we find a great deal of politicized controversy about the level of unemployment, a strong congressional movement for federal action and an emerging local relief crisis. Historians have tended to explain these developments as early manifestations of the "Great Depression," to which Hoover and various business elites were oblivious. But this common view is ahistorical: it tends to conflate conditions in 1930 with those at the trough of the depression several years later. All available evidence suggests that the level of unemployment in 1930 was not significantly higher than during previous recessions in the century.[16] The controversies over unemployment and the local relief crisis are better understood as the culmination of developments in the 1920s, when welfare agencies had experienced a "rising tide" of relief expenditures, when unemployment and its consequences were increasingly the concern of social reformers and when opponents of the 1920s "Republican ascendancy"—urban liberals like Wagner and Progressive Republicans like Robert LaFollette—were seeking to realign the political system around a class-based politics.[17]

We need to keep this context in mind as we examine the local relief efforts initiated in the fall of 1930, which are often described as reflecting traditional values about relief. The example frequently cited is Philadelphia's large private emergency relief organization, the so-called Lloyd committee. As described in historian Bonnie Fox Schwartz's seminal study, the committee was a typical Chest-style emergency organization composed of leading welfare officials and members of the city's business and political elite. The committee engaged in the kind of high-profile fundraising techniques that had been perfected during the 1920s—mass publicity designed to reach an ambitious funding target, solicitations through businesses and public institutions, dire warnings of impending starvation or revolution coupled with expressions of optimism in modern "American methods." Although fundraising was centralized, most aid was distributed by existing private agencies in the form of food orders to be filled by local grocers. The committee also organized a variety of special programs that may have served as models for later New Deal experiments. These included a white-collar work program, loans to the unemployed applying for relief and a breakfast program for needy children. The committee thus undertook, according to Schwartz, "the most imaginative and effective program of private community service . . . a model to other cities and a future inspiration for New Deal projects."[18]

Schwartz, while stressing the innovative aspects of the Lloyd committee's program, sees the relief effort as a prime example of traditional Hooverite voluntarism. This is certainly understandable in light of the fact that the private fund drive was consistent with the city's history of opposition to public relief, and Hoover himself praised the program, using it as a model for his national relief policy. Yet this interpretation is somewhat misleading when considered in light of the financing of the program. A number of leading welfare officials in the city, alarmed by the increasing relief budgets of private agencies, had been advocating a public relief role for several years. Their initial response to the crisis of 1930 was to call for a small appropriation from the city government.[19] When this was rejected, the Lloyd committee was organized, and a high-profile fundraising campaign was initiated.[20] The private campaign exceeded its target of $4 million, but so many of the unemployed applied for aid during the early winter months that it became clear that the fund would be exhausted by the spring. In February leaders of private charity organizations renewed the demand for a public relief appropriation. Faced with the potential collapse of a large, functioning relief organization, city officials relented, borrowed $3 million for relief and established a "Bureau of Unemployment Relief" within its welfare department. (This was essentially the Lloyd committee "in new clothes.") At the very time that Hoover was praising its relief effort as a model of "voluntarism," Philadelphia was reversing its long-standing opposition to public financing of relief.[21]

The experience of New York City also shows the ambitious nature of early local relief efforts and the willingness of welfare officials to abandon strict "voluntarism" when confronted with the potential collapse of a private emergency organization. In October of 1930, a group of business executives, led by a banker named Stewart Prosser, organized an emergency committee to finance a large work relief program. Although there was a tradition of work relief in the city, the scope of the Prosser committee's plan was unprecedented. Initially, 10,000 residents of Manhattan were to be employed in the city's parks and charitable institutions at a rate of $15 a week (a sum considerably higher than the traditional general relief allowance). The program was soon expanded to include the entire city, and, under pressure from organized labor, the wage rate increased.[22] The Prosser committee raised funds through a Liberty Loan-style campaign similar to that undertaken by Philadelphia's business elite. The effort proved highly successful as the funding target, an unprecedented $8 million, was raised by mid-December. Yet, as in Philadelphia, the publicity encouraged massive numbers of unemployed to apply for relief.[23] By the end of December, the emergency committee, with a caseload approaching 24,000, was forced to stop taking applications. Fearing that the program would have to be terminated early in the spring, Stuart Prosser approached Mayor Jimmy Walker to request a $10 million public appropriation. This represented a significant policy shift, since New York, like Philadelphia, had abolished general "outdoor relief" in the late nineteenth century. Initially, the mayor rejected this request, forcing social workers to undertake an intensive campaign for a public appropriation. As in Philadelphia, this agitation, coupled with the threatened collapse of a large and popular relief organization, led to a historic public relief appropriation from public funds. During the summer of 1931, the city financed and administered work relief as a public program.[24]

New York and Philadelphia initiated perhaps the most imaginative relief experiments in the fall of 1930. Other large cities were a good deal less ambitious and sought to avoid the publicity associated with mass fund drives. Yet nearly all of these cities established centralized unemployment committees whose policies reflected the organizational developments of the 1920s, and all were debating the need for public relief by the spring of 1931.[25] Chicago established a central coordinating committee for relief but rejected a Chest-style campaign, opting instead for a low-key fundraising approach that focused on large donations from wealthy individuals and "voluntary" payroll deductions from employed workers. The Cleveland Community [Chest] Fund simply increased the budgets of relief-dispensing agencies, again financed by a few large donations to avoid publicity, and cut social services. This was supplemented by an expanded public works program. Cincinnati expanded the work of its Committee on the Stabilization of Employment, which had been created in 1928. Subcommittees were established to encourage part-time private employment, expand the work of the local employment exchange, coordinate transient relief (a restaurant to feed transients was opened in cooperation with the city welfare department), plan public works and coordinate the activities of relief agencies. While private organizations played key roles in financing and dispensing relief in all these cities, the term "voluntarism" should be used with caution. In Cincinnati, relief was financed by both the Community Chest and the City Department of Welfare, with the former in charge of family cases and the latter focusing on transient aid and work relief. The directors of the Community Chest and the welfare department "were jointly responsible for the relief program." Although the bulk of financing came from private funds in 1930, plans were made for the city to assume virtually the entire relief burden by the end of 1931.[26] Cleveland, the pioneer Chest city, went on the "dole," in the words of the *New York Times*, in May 1931 issuing $200,000 in bonds to finance relief. In Chicago a fiscal crisis and taxpayers' revolt, which had been developing since the late 1920s, precluded a public appropriation. Still, the Cook County Bureau of Public Welfare played a key role in supplementing private relief: in 1931, the Bureau's official caseload averaged 23,450, well above that of the city's largest private relief organization.[27]

Similar modest relief efforts were implemented on the urban West Coast, as described in William E. Mullins' recent monograph.[28] Here, the depression appears to have commenced later than in the East, producing a certain complacency among political leaders and business elites. Yet the failure to aggressively address the emerging unemployment crisis could encourage radicalism and grassroots action. In Seattle there was no major emergency relief effort until the end of 1931, and existing welfare organizations were unprepared for an organized, coordinated campaign. Into the vacuum stepped left-wing activists, who organized an Unemployed Citizens League (UCL). The result was one of the most extraordinary local relief developments of the early depression years: a local emergency organization administered, in part, by the unemployed themselves. The UCL expanded rapidly, organizing committees for make-work, bartering, and the distribution of surplus commodities (activities that came to be called "self-help" in the policy jargon of the 1930s but that the Seattle workers themselves referred to as "chiseling"). The organization was so successful that when the city established its first relief fund in early 1932, the UCL played a major role distributing aid and determining eligibility. The league used the funds to purchase food and commodities in bulk and distribute them through neighborhood warehouses. Much to the dismay of local social workers, the relief program avoided strict income testing and investigations of applicants for aid.[29]

While most cities combined private and public financing, a few relied almost entirely on established public welfare departments to provide relief. The experience of Boston, which avoided a major relief crisis in 1931, seems to have encouraged the emerging view among social workers that public relief was the best solution to the unemployment emergency. The caseload of the city's public welfare department skyrocketed when the depression struck, increasing from 6,000 in October of 1930 to over 11,000 in March of 1931. The 1931 budget of the Overseers of the Public Welfare was almost double that of the previous year. But city officials, blessed with a relatively strong property tax base, were able to fund the increase by cutting other expenditures and from "voluntary" deductions from city workers' salaries. This approach was applauded by many social workers. The *Survey* commended Mayor Curley for heading off "many ill-considered and hasty schemes, including the raising of a large general fund." William Pear of the private Boston Provident Association, in a lengthy presentation to the 1931 National Conference on Social Work, compared the experience of his charity, which had avoided cuts in casework and services, with those in cities like Cleveland and Philadelphia.[30]

But the existence of a strong public welfare department did not nec-essarily preclude a local relief crisis. Detroit felt the impact of the de-pression early, and its public welfare department experienced big caseload increases during the winter of 1929–1930 (from 3,380 in October to 21,759 in April). A report by an outside consultant suggested that the welfare bureaucracy was "in a pathological condition" and "reflected and re-enacted the hysteria of its clients" (the DPW's general superin-tendent experienced a nervous breakdown in the spring of 1930). Into the emerging crisis stepped a new mayor, the populist Frank Murphy, who had been elected "on a wave of promises to find work for the idle." Murphy organized a "Mayor's Unemployment Committee" (MUC) to implement a new policy outside the existing welfare bureaucracy. Ini-tially, the MUC did not dispense relief but instead initiated a well-publicized campaign to register the unemployed and link them to new jobs in the private sector that the committee hoped to create. The Detroit program, modeled on the policies promoted by Hoover's Emergency Committee for Employment, was applauded by the mainstream press. "In no city in the country," reported the *New York Times*, "has a more systematic effort been set afoot to ameliorate economic conditions."[31]

Although the Detroit experiment did much for Mayor Murphy's na-tional reputation, it was notably unsuccessful as a relief policy. After only a few months it became clear that the job creation program, initiated with a good deal of public fanfare, would not find work for a significant number of unemployed. Meanwhile, those who had registered with the committee as unemployed and in need applied to the welfare depart-ment in increasing numbers. By the spring of 1931, the city was virtually broke. Forced to implement an austerity program to appease local bank-ers, the welfare department instituted draconian relief cuts. The average weekly food allowance for a family of five was cut from approximately eleven dollars to seven dollars, and the relief rolls were pared by nearly 50 percent over the next six months. Charges that these cutbacks pro-duced "starvation" among unemployed workers became an important issue in the debate over federal relief the following fall.[32]

These brief examples highlight the diversity of relief practices during 1930 and 1931. Yet local variation should not be allowed to obscure some important common trends. First, consistent with the data presented in Chapter 1, strict voluntarism does not really characterize local policies in 1930–1931. Even those cities that had traditionally opposed public outdoor relief were seriously considering public financing by the end of the winter. Second, the local relief programs were not "traditional" in any meaningful sense of the term. Rather, the Liberty Loan-style Chest campaigns, the employment stabilization committees, the work relief ex-periments, the centralized coordination of financing and distribution and the willingness to tap public resources reflected new developments in social policy described in the previous chapter. Finally, it was precisely the new, more "modern" features of relief policy that may well have exacerbated the local crisis so early in the depression.

The last point needs to be stressed, since it is central to the argument of this chapter. Consider, for example, the high-profile "voluntarism," which has often been criticized as long on public relations and short on assistance to the unemployed. As we have seen, such Chest-style campaigns may well have stimulated applications for aid, creating, in the end, pressures for public relief. This, indeed, had been a concern of social workers from the outset of the depression. Meeting in the fall of 1930, the officials of a number of family societies had warned against raising funds in mass public campaigns: "A tremendous single effort of this sort, with the attendant publicity about unemployment, will, it was felt, increase panic among clients, and, by over advertising relief resources, swamp any increases secured."[33] Jacob Billikopf, a leader of private social work in Philadelphia, described the Philadelphia experience to the 1931 National Conference on Social Work:

Obviously to arouse the giving public, the city fathers and our legislators to a realization of the tragedies in our midst, we were compelled to resort to considerable propaganda. The publicity given to the "human interest" stories led, in some quarters, to hysteria. That hysteria resulted in the creation of 75 bread lines and relief societies.[34]

New York City experienced similar "hysteria" in response to a public relief drive and a well-publicized work program. The Prosser committee raised nearly $8 million and registered the unemployed through the police department. But the work committee's application bureau was mobbed with unemployed workers, the majority of whom were unknown to established relief agencies. Lilian Brandt, whose study of relief measures in New York was based on questionnaires sent to front-line social workers, found that "the newspapers' stories about relief created the impression that vast sums and unlimited opportunities for work were available for the asking, thus raising false hopes [and] engendering a demanding attitude." Brandt also noted that the November police census of the unemployed "put the idea of assistance from relief funds in the minds of many to whom it had never occurred, and precipitated applications to social agencies."[35] Detroit's unemployment committee was described by the *Survey* as composed of business elites who found "satisfaction in a big, dramatic mass effort that characterized community undertakings during the war." With "loud beating of drums and fanfare of trumpets," the committee initiated effort to register the unemployed and link them to jobs in the private sector. But when jobs failed to materialize, it was only natural that those identified as being in need would apply to the welfare department for relief. According to historian Sidney Fine, social workers loaned to the MUC referred large numbers of registrants to the DPW, "with an almost catastrophic effect on its operations." Chicago attempted to avoid a centralized fundraising effort but did seek to register the jobless and conducted an unemployment census in conjunction with a state committee. One study attributed a big rise in the unemployment relief caseload to this rather modest program: "The effect of the census of unemployment conducted by the Governors commission in November, 1930 is seen in the increase in total active cases from 11,124 in October to 21,495 in November to 31,719 in December."[36]

Another factor that exacerbated the local crisis and generated demands for public appropriations was the impact of mass relief-giving on the activities of private family societies. Social work professionals found that they had to cut services and abandon casework in order to process the massive number of relief applicants. "The niceties of modern social work, the careful process of building and rehabilitation are going overboard," wrote Gertrude Springer, the *Survey*'s main relief columnist. Many local agencies began to separate unemployment cases from those that needed more intensive casework. But these compromises tended to reduce the stigma of applying for charity, encouraging more applications from low-wage workers.[37] The overall impact was to produce strong support for the view, which had been developing during the 1920s, that mass relief for the unemployed was a proper function of public agencies. As they lobbied for public appropriations to bail out private relief organizations, they came to support public welfare as crucial to maintaining "private" social work."[The] absence of public relief, the thing we have sought to avoid, has worked to the disadvantage of our casework while at the same time we have failed to meet obvious relief requirements," argued William Pear at the 1931 National Conference on Social Work. Josephine Brown's seminal study on relief policy in the 1930s called the 1931 conference "the last symposium on the pros and cons of public versus private relief."[38]

These developments help explain the rather sharp divisions between Hoover and social work leaders in the early 1930s. The problem was not so much that the president was overly optimistic about the state of the economy but that his statements about relief bore little relationship to the realities of American social policy in 1931. At the very moment that social workers were initiating difficult local campaigns for public appropriations, the president seemed determined to lecture the American people on the value of private relief. The administration lauded the drought relief efforts of the Red Cross, which most observers considered manifestly inadequate, and then put its full weight behind the mass fundraising techniques that were producing increasing skepticism in the social work community. In the late spring of 1931, Hoover's relief officials

called on the Association of Community Chests and Councils and the
Family Welfare Association to develop a plan for a national, coordinated
private relief drive in November. Then in late August, the administration
decided to coordinate the campaign itself under the auspices of a new
ad hoc federal committee.[39] The President's Emergency Committee for
Employment was transformed into the President's Organization for Unemployment Relief (POUR). Walter S. Gifford, of the American Telephone and Telegraph Company, was made chairman of the campaign,
and state-level coordinating committees were established. Localities were
encourage to set up emergency organizations modeled on Philadelphia's
Lloyd committee. The effort was portrayed as a national Liberty Loan
campaign for local unemployment relief. Hoover's central goal was to
organize a coordinated national response to the relief crisis that avoided
a federal welfare appropriation.

The specter of a federal "dole" had hovered over the earliest relief
efforts. The issue had been raised during large, communist-led unemployment demonstrations in March of 1930. The publicity generated by
these protests may have been disproportional to their size, but they
helped to put the issue of unemployment on the national agenda.[40] In
December a coalition of social democratic intellectuals and labor leaders,
led by John Dewey, called for a $500 million direct relief appropriation,
while an "Emergency Committee for Federal Public Works" lobbied for
a massive new public works program.[41] When Congress reconvened in
December 1930, the issue of federal action to address the economic crisis
was at the top of the political agenda. A flood of proposals for direct
unemployment relief, drought relief and public works was introduced
by liberal Democrats and Progressive Republicans. "It is safe to say,"
editorialized the *New York Times*, "that every Senator or Representative
returning to Washington has a bill to end the business depression and
give work to everybody."[42] As Jordan Schwarz has suggested in his
study of congressional politics in the early 1930s, these demands reflected, in large measure, the early stages of the emerging political realignment. Liberal Democrats sought to prod party leaders to take a more
partisan stance in the recession, while Republican progressives saw in
Hoover's policies the ascendancy of conservative eastern financial interests within the party. The rash of legislative proposals was not, however,
reflective of strong congressional support for federal relief, which was
not initially on the policy agenda.[43]

Ironically, the Hoover administration itself raised the relief issue most
forcefully in the context of a debate over aid to drought-stricken farmers.[44] The drought, which descended on the Midwest in the summer of
1930, at first appeared to be a political gift for the president. Hoover had
built his early reputation directing relief to Europe after the World War

I, and his 1928 presidential campaign had been energized by his work coordinating aid to victims of the great Mississippi flood the previous year. Indeed, solving big relief problems was central to Hoover's political ascendancy.[45] The drought of 1930 appeared to be a perfect opportunity to display his celebrated managerial style and promote voluntarist ideas. But the crisis, appearing in the context of Democratic victories in the 1930 congressional elections and the developing economic recession, quickly turned into a public relations disaster for the president. After appearing to agree with congressional leaders on a figure of $60 million in federal aid—itself only half the need estimated by state officials—the administration requested only $25 million from Congress. Then administration officials sought to limit aid to seed and feed for animals, arguing that direct relief to farmers would set a dangerous precedent. Not only did the administration renege on an agreement with key rural congressmen, but it seemed to take the position that federal funds could be used to feed livestock but not farm families. Democrats and "insurgent" Republicans spent the Christmas season attacking a policy that "puts hogs above humans and mules above men."[46] Administration officials, on the other hand, defended the policy by attacking direct relief to farmers as the first step on the road to a national dole. The secretary of agriculture warned that this form of aid "approaches perilously close to the dole system," while a Republican ally of the administration in the House charged that it would "establish in fact, if not in name, the dole."[47]

Such statements were no doubt designed to appeal to widespread opposition to a permanent federal welfare program, but the tactic seems to have backfired. By attacking a relatively limited and popular program as a "dole," the administration and its supporters helped legitimate federal relief. "It is all right to put a mule on the 'dole' but it is condemned, I see, to put a man on parity with a mule," commented Senate minority leader Joseph T. Robinson of Arkansas, hardly a strong supporter of European social insurance. The administration compounded the problem by warning that drought relief would produce demands for aid to the unemployed. When the secretary of agriculture, for example, argued that there was no more reason to aid farmers from the federal treasury "than any other class of people who may be in distress," and the *New York Times* editorialized that "there is no reason why the cities should not have equal standing as applicants," they unwittingly opened the Pandora's box of federal relief.[48] On January 8 an "urban bloc" in the House threatened to block a compromise drought bill unless funds were provided to assist the unemployed. Several days later, Senator Robert M. LaFollette, Jr., the influential progressive from Wisconsin, called for a national relief program.[49]

The "revolt of the cities" quickly petered out, but now it was clear that federal relief would return to the national agenda if economic conditions did not improve. Even the president, in his February 3 address attacking the drought bill, pledged that if state and local resources proved insufficient, then "I will ask the aid of every resource of the federal government." The drought debate coincided with the emerging relief crises in Philadelphia, Detroit and New York, setting social workers and reformers in opposition to the administration's relief ideology. Although no national welfare organization supported federal relief at this time, social workers at the June 1931 National Conference on Social Work were openly discussing the issue. During the summer, a number of state and local officials, including Detroit's Mayor Murphy and Governor Gifford Pinchot of Pennsylvania, threw their support behind a federal program. A *New York Times* article in August on the Chicago relief crisis reported that Pinchot's conversion to federal relief had made a "deep impression" on social workers in the city.[50]

This was the context in which Hoover's new federal relief committee, POUR, was created. There has been a tendency to minimize the importance of POUR, viewing it as simply a reincarnation of its predecessor, the President's Emergency Committee for Employment—another ineffectual response by the hapless president to the deepening economic crisis.[51] While POUR's approach to unemployment (and to the politics of relief) proved no more effective than that of PECE, important differences between the two committees had significant implications for relief policy. The earlier "employment" committee had not played a major role in the relief effort during the winter of 1930–1931, focusing instead on promoting public works and local job creation efforts. POUR's primary function, on the other hand, was to stimulate local relief organization on the model of Philadelphia's Lloyd committee and raise funds through a national publicity drive.[52] The committee was dominated by business elites with experience in Chest-style campaigns, and its activities were coordinated with those of leading national private welfare organizations.[53] It was, in effect, a national "Liberty Loan"campaign for relief, a point often made by administration officials. Advertising agencies prepared full-page ads that the committee distributed to hundreds of magazines and newspapers. Press services and newspapers donated labor and space for publicity. Committee officials estimated that 35,000 billboards throughout the country carried POUR's slogan, "Of Course We Can Do It." The Motion Picture Distributors Association encouraged local theaters to give benefits for relief. The committee reported that 131 colleges responded to its call for benefit football games. Benefit air shows were sponsored by Curtis Wright Airports throughout the country (20,000 spectators gathered at one such exhibition in Valley Stream, Long Island). Between October 19 and November 25, five national Sunday radio broadcasts featured entertainment and speeches by such notables as

Will Rogers, Charles Lindbergh, Mary Pickford, General John J. Pershing and, of course, the president himself.[54]

In hindsight, the POUR relief drive seems a rather archaic effort to provide a voluntarist alternative to federal relief. But the national relief drive was hardly "traditional" in the sense that it resembled policies implemented during previous depressions. It was, rather, typical of the kind of organizational development fostered by Hoover's brand of "voluntarism"—public officials mobilizing private resources with maximum publicity to avoid a permanent expansion of the state.[55] In the process, the POUR campaign caused an unprecedented outpouring of voluntarist effort in support of the unemployed. The data collected by the Children's Bureau shows that total private spending for relief averaged over $80 million monthly during the winter of 1931–1932, almost double that of the previous year and the highest of the Great Depression. Many cities that had not established private committees in 1930 did so under the direction of POUR, while others, such as New York and Philadelphia, saw substantial increases in private spending. The result was that most northern and western cities created large emergency organizations in the fall of 1931. These would become the main vehicles for the distribution of urban relief during the next four years, and the threat of their collapse in mid-1932 led to the first large-scale federal relief program.[56] Thus, by establishing a federal committee that focused on relief, creating new state committees and influencing local organizational developments, POUR was an important step toward the federalization of relief.

Yet the POUR campaign was also a transparent effort to undermine support for a federal relief appropriation.[57] Throughout the fall of 1931 the committee was bombarded with letters from state and local officials assuring the administration that they could take care of "their own" unemployed. These declarations were invariably linked to opposition to a federal "dole." "We Hoosiers stand unalterably opposed to the false doctrine of federal paternalism or 'dole' system," wrote the governor of Indiana. Michigan's Governor William Brucker declared that federal relief would lead to "lasting and disastrous consequences for our country as it has in other countries."[58] A key function of POUR's network of state representatives, usually business leaders who shared Hoover's relief ideology, was to assure the public that local communities had the situation well in hand. In November 1931 POUR Chairman Gifford requested information from each representative on the status of the private fund drives and "what communities, if any, consider they cannot meet unemployment needs this winter." The result was a predictable flood of telegrams assuring the administration and the nation that local funds were adequate.[59]

Such contrived assurances did little to stem the demands for federal relief. Neo-Progressives such as Robert LaFollette, Jr., and Gifford Pinchot continued to argue that unemployment was a "national problem" that required "national solutions." They attacked Hoover's emphasis on local and private relief in populist terms, linking the policy to business fears of higher federal income taxes. "The force behind the stubborn opposition to federal relief," wrote Pinchot in the *Survey*, "is fear lest the taxation to provide that relief be levied on concentrated wealth." Further to the left, a Joint Committee on Unemployment, a coalition of social democrats, labor leaders and social workers mobilized for a lobbying campaign when Congress reconvened in December, and local "councils of the unemployed" raised the issue in the context of hunger marches and rent protests.[60]

While social work leaders expressed support for the POUR campaign, they moved closer to open advocacy of federal relief. (The issue, in fact, rather sharply divided the profession in late 1931.)[61] In November a "Social Work Conference on Federal Action" was quietly organized to discuss national legislation. The group included key leaders of national welfare organizations and, according to Linton Swift, "many varieties of opinion on the subject of federal aid for public works and 'grants in aid' for unemployment relief." There was a consensus, however, that if federal aid became necessary, social workers should exert influence "to assure sound methods in the allocation and administration of such funds."[62] The emphasis on professionalism was particularly prominent in a widely publicized "open letter" to President Hoover from William Hodson, director of the New York City Welfare Council. Hodson argued that the relief crisis was far more severe than the Hoover administration had suggested and urged the administration to develop policies for the administration of a federal appropriation in case congressional action became necessary. He warned against "pork barrel" legislation and advocated grants-in-aid with strong federal controls. Reflecting the divisions among social workers, the Hodson letter did not call for legislative action but for "a rapid but objective study of the financial status of local governments throughout the country." Although far from a ringing endorsement of federal relief, the statement was generally interpreted as a rejection of Hoover's policy by a key social work leader in the private field.[63]

Despite divisions about the need for a federal appropriation, members of the social work committee began working with sympathetic members of Congress to develop legislation. In early November they approached New York's Senator Robert Wagner, who had played a key role in placing the unemployment issue at the top of the public agenda. Rebuffed by Wagner, who suggested that a large public works appropriation might still make federal relief unnecessary, they turned to Robert La-Follette, Jr., and Thomas P. Costigan, the latter a Progressive Democrat from Colorado. The result was the so-called LaFollette-Costigan bill, the first relief measure to receive substantial support in Congress.[64] The bill provided for a $375 million appropriation to aid the states, 40 percent of which would be distributed by population and the remainder according to need. Aid would take the form of grants, with the U.S. Children's Bureau initially chosen as the agency to distribute funds and monitor local relief practices. The proposal was introduced in Congress in December, hearings were held at the end of the month and the first votes on federal relief were taken in the Senate in early February 1932.[65]

The LaFollette-Costigan bill was certainly a dramatic break with the American tradition of localism in the provision of relief. It was a policy clearly at odds with the just-completed POUR campaign, which had consumed so much public energy. Many conservative Democrats, particularly within the party's southern wing, opposed the expansion of federal authority implicit in the bill. Even social workers continued to be divided over the pros and cons of federal relief.[66] Given these obstacles, the degree of support a federal welfare appropriation received in the Senate was quite remarkable. The LaFollette-Costigan bill was defeated by a margin of 45 to 38 in early February. The previous day, a "substitute" had been introduced that provided for aid in the form of "loans" to be distributed according to a population formula, thus eliminating potential federal controls. This won moderate support but lost the votes of some Progressives who, following the lead of social workers, believed that the lack of federal controls would produce a "pork barrel." As Jordan Schwarz has emphasized, a tally of the two votes shows that a majority of senators supported federal relief in some form.[67] Thus, by the end of February 1932, a consensus was emerging in Washington that a federal emergency relief program, in some form, would be necessary to prevent the collapse of local relief. By the spring, that consensus included President Hoover. On May 12 the president "shocked the capital" by introducing his own proposal for relief loans to the states.[68]

How are we to explain this dramatic breakthrough in social welfare policy? A number of historians have stressed the role of social workers who publicized the inadequacies of local relief at various congressional hearings.[69] In carefully organized testimony before the Senate Committee on Manufactures in late December key leaders of the profession challenged the central assumptions of the POUR campaign. Attacking the view that relief was adequate if it prevented "starvation," they compared prevailing standards of aid to the minimum requirements established by private social work agencies and the Mothers' Aid programs in the 1920s. Linton Swift criticized Hoover's relief ideology directly, arguing that a "dole" was not a federal relief program but rather inadequate local relief. Perhaps the testimony most damaging to the administration was that of Alan Burns of the Association of Community Chests and Councils. Burns, whose organization had played a central role in the POUR cam-

paign, implicitly challenged the view that private relief was the "American way," citing the Children's Bureau data to argue that private funds
accounted for only 30 percent of all relief expenditures.[70] To make matters worse for the Hoover administration, the testimony of POUR chairman Walter S. Gifford was a disaster. Since Hoover's allies had
persistently claimed that local efforts were adequate to meet the need,
Gifford was asked for the data used to assess local needs. The POUR
chairman admitted that he had none and responded, "I think by and
large the money spent is the money needed." His primary argument
against the LaFollette-Costigan bill was that federal relief would discourage local and particularly state appropriations then being considered
by legislatures. Although this argument raised a concern shared by many
welfare officials, it was an untenable position for the POUR leader, who
had rejected entreaties to take a strong stand in favor of state legislation,
to argue.[71]

There can be little doubt that the lobbying efforts of those closest to
the relief situation—particularly the leadership of the Community Chest
movement—seriously undermined the administration's policy, but the
impact of the social work testimony should not be exaggerated. The central question of whether local needs were being met was not an easy one
to answer. Social workers' standards of adequacy were not widely
shared, as evidenced by the widespread appeal of the slogan "no one is
starving." When Connecticut senator Hiram Bingham, an outspoken opponent of federal relief, polled governors in March as to whether there
was evidence of starvation in their states due to low relief payments,
thirty-nine of forty responding answered in the negative. In April of
1932, a time when Congress was rapidly moving toward agreement on
the need for federal aid, an informal survey of local opinion reported in
the *Survey* showed almost universal opposition or indifference to a federal program.[72] Part of the problem, as Karl DeSchweinitz told the National Conference on Social Work, was that actual cases of starvation
were relatively rare: "This is because people live on inadequacies and
because they live on inadequacies the thing does not become dramatic
and we do not hear about it." Attitudes toward relief also reflected class
divisions, exacerbated by the uneven impact of the depression. A representative of the American Association of Public Welfare Officials, writing in November of 1931, explained why this made it so difficult to get
a consensus on the relief situation:

One seems to receive very similar answers to questions concerning the depression and unemployment in any particular community from people in similar
circumstances. Questioning bankers, mayors and members of committees or
those in comfortable circumstances, one finds a note of optimism and the stere-
otyped remark "we shall take care of the situation all right. We shall not let

anyone suffer." Replies from those who are unemployed or those who are at the mercy [*sic*] of charitable groups or unemployment committees almost invariably are that the situation is desperate.[73]

What abruptly tipped the scales in favor of federal relief in early 1932 was not a generalized recognition that Hoover's voluntarism had failed to meet needs but, as Frances Fox Piven and Richard A. Cloward have argued, a local relief crisis that made the debate over adequacy problematic. By the spring of 1932, the large relief organizations created during the POUR campaign, now often bankrolled by public funds, were bankrupt, and thousands of workers were about to be cut off relief. The relief emergency in Chicago was particularly acute, and it is possible that the situation in this city forced the hand of the Hoover administration and Congress. The reports and telegrams in the files of Rowland Haynes, a POUR field representative, indicate the administration was closely monitoring the relief crisis in the city. Chicago had raised an unprecedented $10 million during the fall POUR campaign, approximately double the amount raised for private relief the previous year. But the relief caseload in the city exploded during the early winter, with monthly relief expenditures exceeding $3 million. "The situation in Chicago is extremely serious," Haynes wrote to new POUR director Fred Croxton on January 29. "Mr. Ryerson [Illinois POUR representative] had two weeks ago said that private funds would last until February 15 or March 1. It is now apparent that the funds will be exhausted by February 1."[74] Although some of the expenditures for relief were coming from public funds, allocated through the Cook County Bureau of public welfare, the collapse of the city's property tax base precluded a public borrowing for relief.[75] The only solution was a state relief appropriation. But the state constitution appeared to prohibit borrowing for relief purposes, and the rural legislators opposed a state fund that would mainly benefit the unemployed in Chicago. By late January the crisis in Chicago was so acute that Ryerson, with the support of national POUR officials, convinced the governor to call a special session of the legislature. The result was a $20 million appropriation for relief financed by "tax anticipation" warrants, a form of borrowing that stipulated that the local aid would be offset by reductions in state county road funds (a convoluted financing mechanism designed to avoid the appearance of a state relief program similar to the one soon to be incorporated into the federal relief bill).[76]

Thus, by the end of February, relief to Chicago's 120,000 families was being financed by a state appropriation administered by a new agency, the Illinois Emergency Relief Commission, through the Cook County Public Welfare Bureau. In theory, the state fund was designed to last for a year, an estimate that represented, at best, wishful thinking, since Chicago alone was spending over $3 million per month for relief. In April the State Relief Commission estimated that the fund would be exhausted by August 1 and that the state would need approximately $7 million to furnish relief through September 30. On April 6 Haynes wired Croxton that "Funds for Chicago will be gone before October 1 and probably by August and Mr. Ryerson is at a loss where to get additional tax funds for relief."[77] By the beginning of May, the president and congressional leaders had determined that federal relief aid, in some form, was required to avoid the collapse of relief in cities like Chicago. Throughout the summer, as Congress debated proposals for relief and public works, local officials lobbied hard for federal aid. On June 2, for example, a group of the city's "bankers and civic leaders" telephoned the president warning that thousands of recipients faced "starvation" unless federal funds were made available. Three weeks later Mayor Cermac told a Senate committee that the collapse of relief would provoke open rebellion among the unemployed: "It is a case of relief or use of troops in what would follow unless relief is assured.[78] When federal relief was finally approved at the end of July, Illinois was the first state to receive funds. The Reconstruction Finance Corporation, which administered the appropriation, did not even require the state to make a formal application for aid.

A similar sequence of events occurred in Philadelphia. A successful POUR relief drive in the fall of 1931 (raising $10 million) was followed by massive applications that threatened to bankrupt the emergency committee, precipitating demands for a state appropriation. Earlier in the fall, Pennsylvania's governor, Republican Progressive Gifford Pinchot, had called for an ambitious public employment and relief program, to be financed by both tax increases and a special bond issue. Pinchot's program was opposed in the legislature by both regular mainline Republicans and Democrats, who instead engineered a $10 million direct relief appropriation with uncertain financing and administration. Pinchot, considering the measure an irresponsible pork barrel, challenged the law in court.[79] A state court eventually found the law constitutional, but not before the Lloyd committee in Philadelphia was forced to discontinue aid entirely for two weeks in early April. Social workers publicized the impact of these cuts to counter the "no one is starving" argument of the opponents of federal relief. (Karl deSchweinitz told a Senate committee one woman lived on stale bread and a family subsisted on dandelions for several days during the relief stoppage.)[80] A court decision in mid-April freed $2.5 million of the state fund for Philadelphia, but by this time, the city was spending at a rate of $1 million per month. On June 20, the emergency relief committee ceased to function, discontinuing aid to most recipients and handing the responsibility for relief over to the city's welfare department. Philadelphia, according to a "leading citizen" quoted in the press, was passing "from civilization to barbarism."[81]

Because they had been the great success stories of the POUR campaign, Chicago and Philadelphia may have received the most attention from federal officials, but the sense of impending crisis, with warnings that cuts in relief would produce social disorder, appears frequently in the agency's files. Alice Stenholm reported from Little Rock, Arkansas, that "the city and county are literally broke" and that the largest private welfare agency had implemented a policy of not accepting unemployment cases. "I suppose the next four to six weeks will be the severe testing point as to whether riots are really to break out in this part of the country," a representative of the American Friends Service Committee wrote to Croxton from the Southwest. "Cincinnati will have exhausted its resources April 1," Rowland Haynes reported. "Cleveland about as bad." In June he telegrammed Fred Croxton: "Situation in St. Louis much more serious than anticipated three months ago. They have stopped taking new cases [which were] averaging four hundred per day and if added funds not available will have to eliminate forty percent of relief families."[82] A number of cities were able to avoid the collapse of local relief either by cutting standards of aid to recipients or by reducing other city services to fund relief. Detroit had been forced to implement draconian cutbacks in mid-1931, and by January only 22,000 families were being aided. At the same time, allowances were lowered to a "survival basis." By the end of July 1932, the city had stopped reimbursing local grocers for food orders, and many recipients had been reduced to an "iron ration" of bread and milk. Meanwhile, the Public Welfare Commission had threatened to cut all unemployment cases from the public rolls, warning that this policy could produce "chaos and violence." (According to Sidney Fine, Mayor Frank Murphy dramatically rushed back to Detroit from the Democratic National Convention to countermand the department's order and call for the passage of federal relief legislation to prevent imminent "starvation.") Boston continued to finance aid to the unemployed by channeling private funds through the public welfare department, cutting other municipal expenditures, and collecting "voluntary contributions" from city workers. Although the city's relief program was generally considered to be the most stable in the county, Alice Stenholm reported "much distress and need for relief in Boston and outer Boston and in mill cities along the eastern part of the state. . . . The private agencies have exhausted their funds for relief and the public welfare department has exceeded its appropriation."[83]

At first glance, New York City would appear to be the exception to the gloomy story of local relief in early 1932. The city was able to avoid the collapse of its emergency committee through public borrowing and a state program initiated in the fall of 1931 by Governor Franklin D.

Roosevelt. Responding to the appeals of social work leaders, the governor had called a special session of the legislature in September, which appropriated $20 million for relief. The New York program presented a striking contrast to those of other states during this period: funds were initially raised through tax increases, most of the local aid was earmarked for work relief and the new state agency, the Temporary Emergency Relief Administration (TERA), attempted to exercise some control over local administration of state funds.[84] A precursor to New Deal's Federal Emergency Relief Administration, the TERA was certainly a pioneering agency, and its approach to relief has frequently been stressed by historians emphasizing the contrasts between the policies of Roosevelt and Hoover. But the impact of state aid on local relief in New York should not be exaggerated. In New York City, battles over relief appropriations, accompanied by abrupt cuts or threatened cuts in aid to the unemployed, were frequent during the first six months of 1932. Relief for 20,000 families was suspended in the second week of January, as local bankers and the city comptroller negotiated the terms of an emergency loan. Later in the month the city's Home Relief Bureau stopped intake for two weeks. In mid-April, the *New York Times* estimated that 50,000 families were in need but not receiving aid. Social workers criticized the city's relief program as wholly inadequate, and there were calls on the mayor to lead a march on Washington for federal aid.[85]

These brief examples show the dimensions of the crisis of early 1932, which, to one degree or another, was experienced by most urban relief programs: mass unemployment, exceeding the levels of previous recessions, compounded by the length of the depression; local fiscal crises produced by the collapse of property tax bases; the drying up of private sources of relief financing; resistance to state appropriations from rural-dominated legislatures. But another side to the collapse of local relief in early 1932 should not be ignored: in a sense, the effectiveness of the public and private relief financing mechanisms created the conditions for the crisis. The POUR fund drive, local public funds and new, state-level appropriations had created large, new urban relief organizations. But the publicity associated with these efforts, the creation of new centralized committees and the opening of new local districts for dispensing aid tended to encourage applications from the unemployed. Several observers had warned the administration that the POUR tactics might prove counterproductive. "I have been interested in noting the press assertions that one of the President's objectives in creating your organization, however, has been to lessen the demands for direct federal aid," an administration supporter wrote to Gifford in September 1931. "Certainly a worthy motive, but . . . one could fear that publicity might defeat its accomplishment." Jacob Billikopf, a leader of the Philadelphia emergency committee, had warned Gifford that the POUR relief campaigns might well cause "hysteria . . . another reason why it might be cheaper for the federal government to make a subvention." When asked by a member of the Senate Committee on Manufactures whether Chicago's massive caseload increases were caused by the level or duration of unemployment, Edward Ryerson replied that both were important factors. But he went on to stress another dynamic that influenced applications for relief:

A community like Chicago cannot raise $10,000,000 from private contributions without making a lot of noise about it. We carried on an intensive campaign for two months and obtained more money than anybody thought possible from private subscriptions, but, as a result, we created an interest in the participation and the proceeds on [the part of] a large number of people.[86]

Many fund drives relied heavily on "industrial solicitations," quasi-voluntary requests for donations from workers by employer groups, and public financing often involved similar "contributions" (i.e., payroll deductions) from public employees. Both of these financing mechanisms tended to create the feeling that the relief fund was, in Linton Swift's words quoted in the previous chapter, "insurance against [workers'] own future needs."[87]

Caseload increases were also encouraged by the fact that the expansion of relief required the reorganization of existing relief machinery, a disruptive process that made the careful investigation of recipients nearly impossible. In Seattle, an extreme case, the leftist Unemployed Citizens League played a central role in administering the city's first large relief fund, virtually dispensing with the means test at the public commissaries that it operated. In Chicago social workers dominated the relief program but had to dispense with traditional methods of determining eligibility. Jeanette Elder, a student in social work at the University of Chicago who wrote a master's thesis on relief in one Chicago district, described the situation at the Grovehill relief station. Grovehill was created as a new public agency in December of 1931 to dispense aid raised by the POUR drive and, beginning in February, the new state appropriation. In January thousands of recipients on the rolls of private agencies were abruptly dumped on the district (3,500 cases in one week alone).With so many recipients suddenly being assisted by the public agency and no commensurate expansion of its staff, Grovehill "had little or no control of its intake."[88]

In these ways, the expansion of relief undermined the mechanisms that traditionally discouraged low-wage workers from applying for aid, exacerbating the crisis caused by mass unemployment. What was the role of disorder and protest by the unemployed in this process? This question needs to be addressed because of the influential work of Frances Fox Piven and Richard A. Cloward, who have argued that the expansion of relief has historically been a response to disruptive protest by the poor and unemployed (their work dovetails with a good deal of literature that sees the modern welfare state as a response to protest and class-based politics). One can easily find evidence for the influence of protest in the frequent warnings by public officials lobbying for private donations and new public appropriations. Philadelphia's Mayor Mackey warned that the "militia will be needed if the rich ignore the relief appeal." "I say to the men who may object to this public relief because it will add to the tax burden on their property that they should be glad to pay it for it is the best way of insuring that they will keep that property," warned Chicago's Mayor Cermac during the debate over state relief legislation. Six months later, as federal relief legislation was stalled in the Senate, he told reporters that "[i]t is a case of relief or the use of troops in what would follow unless relief is assured."[89] Such comments might be passed off as hyperbole, coming as they did from local officials seeking funds. But there is a good deal of evidence in the POUR files that officials in the Hoover administration were concerned about potential disorder. A representative of the American Public Welfare Association, whose reports appear in the files of POUR's Fred Croxton, noted a sense of "desperation and frequently rebellion [among the unemployed] that they will go to any extremes to get food for themselves and their families and that they will probably have to take what they can from 'those people who are hanging on to all they have got" or 'from those who are storing all the money and are keeping it out of circulation.' "[90] POUR representative Rowland Haynes was dispatched to the scene of a well-publicized "riot" at the Ford motor plant in Dearborn, Michigan. Haynes assured Croxton that workers' protests were directed at the auto company, not the local relief program, and that the violence was a product of the "stupidity" of the local police. But his quick visit to the site of violence and subsequent lengthy report show that federal officials were on edge about potential disorder caused by local relief conditions.[91]

On the other hand, instances of mass protest were relatively rare, and the image of unemployed workers demanding relief from resisting local officials, which Piven and Cloward's work occasionally conjures up, cannot be sustained.[92] The large emergency relief organizations created in the early winter of 1931–1932 do not seem to have been a response to demanding workers but were produced by a genuine desire to "prevent starvation" and a somewhat optimistic belief that the "American way" could resolve the crisis without a European-style "dole." The impending collapse of these local organizations created a context in which relatively small protests, even rumors of protest, had an impact on skittish officials. In applying for federal aid in September of 1932, the Joint Relief Committee of Cuyahoga County (Cleveland), noting that approximately 100,000 persons in the Cleveland area were dependent on relief, warned:

Interruption of these relief services for even a few days would cause additional, untold hardship. In this connection, we feel we should mention the occasional disturbances already encountered, attributable to radical organizers seeking an opportunity to precipitate widespread commotion. The Joint Relief Committee feels keenly its responsibility for protecting this community against the perils of starvation and, also, against the disruption of law and order through lack of material relief requirements.

Officials in Birmingham, Alabama, sounded a similar warning in their initial application for federal aid: "Unless relief is immediately forthcoming, the relief agencies in the city of Birmingham and Jefferson County will be forced to suspend their relief work and no alternative can be expected other than wholesale starvation or disorder." Reporting on the relief situation in Chicago, the *New York Times* noted that the unemployed had shown "patience and endurance": "There have been a few demonstrations, but none of an alarming measure. There is much under-surface mulling, however, and if the relief machinery breaks down, grave trouble may follow."[93]

These concerns no doubt help explain the timing of the end of congressional gridlock on the relief issue. In February, it will be recalled, the Senate had deadlocked over methods of financing and allocation, with Progressives refusing to endorse relief loans to the states and moderates opposing the federal controls implicit in the LaFollette-Costigan bill. By mid-April it was clear that a national relief crisis was imminent. Citing surveys of local relief conducted by *Business Week* and the *Survey*, the *New York Times* reported on April 17 that "the huge unemployment relief funds raised throughout the Untied States have been unequal to the serious burden placed upon them and a crisis in unemployment relief in the United States is imminent." The Joint Committee on Unemployment, a coalition organized to lobby for federal relief, reported to its members that

the opposition to federal relief of the unemployed and the other items in our program is rapidly breaking down. At our conference last Saturday, April 30, we learned that both the Administration and Congress now realize that cities and smaller communities are exhausting their resources and are utterly unable to save the unemployed from destitution and starvation.[94]

On May 11, Joseph T. Robinson, the Senate Democratic leader, unveiled a program for relief and public works prepared with the assistance of financier Bernard Baruch. The proposal called for issuing $2 billion in bonds to finance aid to the states and federal public works. Two days later, Hoover shocked observers in the capital by calling for a $1.5 billion program for relief and public works, to be financed and administered by the newly created Reconstruction Finance Corporation. Both the Rob-

inson and Hoover proposals included virtually identical provisions for
$300 million in direct relief aid. The relief funds, according to a provision
devised by Senator Robert Wagner, would be in the form of "loans" to
be deducted from future highway grants. Although Progressives in Congress and social workers disliked this approach, they temporarily
dropped their opposition to get a relief bill passed.[95]

There followed a politically charged debate over the public works provisions of the bill and the role of the Reconstruction Finance Corporation,
which was designated to distribute loans to the states. From the outset,
Hoover opposed a Democratic plan for a $500 million bond issue for
federal public works. Then John Nance Garner, the House Speaker and
a contender for the Democratic presidential nomination, proposed that
RFC loans be provided directly to "any person" who needed aid, not
just corporations and states.[96] The conflict over these issues, which
dragged on through July, has created the impression that Hoover continued to resist a federal relief program. This is not the case. Both sides
had agreed on the relief formula in May; the delay in passing a bill was
as much the product of political posturing by the Democrats as by re-
calcitrance on Hoover's part.[97] Finally in late July, with relief having been
discontinued in Philadelphia and on the verge of collapse in Chicago
and with recipients subsisting on bread and milk in Detroit, Hoover
signed the Emergency Relief and Construction Act of 1932. The bill contained compromise provisions for federal and state public works, but the
most important element, for our purposes, was $300 million in federal
aid for local relief. Despite the fig leaf that these were temporary "loans,"
the reality was that the federal government had permanently entered the
field of means-tested relief.

NOTES

1. Hoover press statement (February 3, 1931), in *The State Papers and Other
Writings of Herbert Hoover*, William Starr Myers, ed. (Garden City, NY: Doubleday, Doran and Co., 1934), 497. Hoover's statement was a response to a congressional appropriation for drought relief. David Hamilton has called the
February 3 press release "perhaps [Hoover's] most important statement on relief
issues during his term in office." David E. Hamilton, "Herbert Hoover and the
Great Drought of 1930," *Journal of American History* 68, no. 4 (March 1982): 871.
It is important to note that Hoover's statement did not reject federal relief if state
and local resources failed to "prevent starvation." Thus, the administration's official position was not that an emergency program was, a priori, a violation of a
fundamental constitutional principle but rather that it was unnecessary and dangerous.

2. *The State Papers of Herbert Hoover*, 499; *New York Times*, April 8, 1931, 4;
April 14, 1931, 1, 12.

3. Joan Hoff Wilson, *Herbert Hoover: Forgotten Progressive* (Boston: Little,

Brown, 1975); Ellis Hawley, *The Great War and the Search for a Modern Order* (New York: St. Martin's Press, 1992), 188; Hawley, "Neo-Institutional History and the Understanding of Herbert Hoover," in Lee Nash, ed., *Understanding Herbert Hoover: Ten Perspectives* (Stanford, CA: Stanford University Press, 1987), 67–68; Gary Dean Best, *The Politics of American Individualism: Herbert Hoover in Transition, 1918–1921* (Westport, CT: Greenwood Press, 1975), 93. On Hoover's rejection of "rugged individualism" see William E. Mullins, *The Depression and the Urban West Coast, 1929–1933* (Bloomington: Indiana University Press, 1991), 3–4. For Hoover's response to the depression see the essays in J. Joseph Huthmacher and Warren Susman, eds., *Herbert Hoover and the Crisis of American Capitalism* (Cambridge, MA: Schenkman, 1973). For a critique of the "Hoover revisionism" see Arthur Schlesinger, Jr., "Hoover Makes a Comeback," *The New York Review of Books* (May 8, 1979): 10–16.

4. Hamilton, "Herbert Hoover and the Great Drought of 1930," 853–854; Walter I. Trattner, *From Poor Law to Welfare State*, 2nd ed. (New York: Free Press, 1979), 225; Michael Katz, *Improving Poor People* (Princeton, NJ: Princeton University Press, 1995), 37.

5. Linton Swift, "The Future of Public Social Work: From the Point of View of the Private Agency," *Proceedings of the National Conference on Social Work* [hereafter NCSW] (Chicago: University of Chicago Press, 1931), 451–452; William W. Bremer, *Depression Winters: Social Workers and the New Deal* (Philadelphia: Temple University Press, 1984), 35.

6. Mullins, *The Depression and the Urban West Coast*, 4, 30; Bonnie Fox Schwartz, "Unemployment Relief in Philadelphia, 1930–1932: A Study of the Depression's Impact on Voluntarism," in Bernard Sternsher, ed., *Hitting Home: The Great Depression in Town and Country* (Chicago: Quadrangle Books, 1970), 60, 62; Lizbeth Cohen, *Making a New Deal* (New York: Cambridge University Press, 1990), 223; Bremer, *Depression Winters*, 31–32, 35; William R. Brock, *Welfare, Democracy and the New Deal* (New York: Cambridge University Press, 1987), 86. Bremer sees the social workers in New York expressing traditional opposition to public outdoor relief in the fall of 1930 but suggests that the events of the following winter produced a dramatic reversal in the direction of support for public aid. While Brock stresses the modernizing reforms of the 1920s, he does not emphasize the ways they influenced the relief efforts of 1930–1931.

7. *New York Times*, January 22, 1930, 1; January 23, 1930, 11; January 25, 1930, 3; February 9, 1930, 1; February 11, 1930, 7; March 1, 1930, 11. For an account of Perkins' role in the controversy over the level of unemployment see George S. Martin, *Madam Secretary: Frances Perkins* (Boston: Houghton Mifflin, 1976), 213–214.

8. *New York Times*, March 7, 1930, 1; Daniel Leab, "United We Eat: The Creation and Organization of the Unemployment Councils in 1930," *Labor History* 8 (Fall 1967): 306–307; Irving Bernstein, *The Lean Years* (Baltimore: Houghton Mifflin, 1960) 427. Charles H. Trout, *Boston, the Great Depression, and the New Deal* (New York: Oxford University Press, 1977), 55–58.

9. Jordan A. Schwarz, *The Interregnum of Despair* (Urbana: University of Illinois Press, 1970), 23–31.

10. John A. Garraty, *Unemployment in History* (New York: Harper and Row,

1978), 169; Mary Van Kleeck, "The Federal Unemployment Census of 1931," *Journal of the American Statistical Association* (Supplement) 26 (March 1931): 189–201.

11. Schwarz, *The Interregnum of Despair*, 32–35; *New York Times*, December 3, 1930, 20; December 4, 1930, 10; December 8, 1930, 2.

12. "Brief Outline of Community Organizaiton in Unemployment Emergencies" [undated memo re PECE relief activities], Files of the President's Emergency Committee for Employment/President's Organization for Unemployment [hereafter POUR Files], National Archives Record Group 73, Box 253, File: Cities 2; "The President's Committee for Employment," *Survey* 65, no. 10 (February 15, 1931): 542–543.

13. "Annual Report of the Boston Overseers of the Poor [Public Welfare]," Documents of the City of Boston (1929–1930); Wendell F. Johnson, "How Case Working Agencies Have Met Unemployment," NCSW, 1931, 190; Seattle Community Fund, "The Last Word" 1, no. 6 (March 16, 1931), University of Washington–Pacific Northwest Collection.

14. Gertrude Springer, "The Burden of Mass Relief," *Survey* 65, no. 4 (November 115, 1930): 200.

15. James H. Hannah, "Urban Reaction to the Great Depression, 1929–1933" (Ph.D., diss., University of California, 1963), 104. Also Charles R. Walker, "Down and Out in Detroit," in Beard, *America Faces the Future* (Boston: Houghton Mifflin, 1932), 75–80; William J. Norton, "The Relief Crisis in Detroit," *Social Service Review* 7, no. 1 (March 1933): 3; Helen Hall, "When Detroit's Out of Gear," 9; "Hall, New Faces on the Bowery," 15, both in *Survey* 64, no. 1 (April 1, 1930).

16. As noted in Chapter 1, Stanley Lebergott has estimated an unemployment rate for 1930 at 8.9 percent, as compared with 8.5 percent for 1915 and 11.7 percent in 1921. Stanley Lebergott, *Manpower in Economic Growth* (New York: McGraw-Hill, 1964), 512.

17. Caroline Bedford, "The Effect of an Unemployment Situation in Family Societies," NCSW, 1931, 201. The political aspects of Wagner's unemployment proposals are emphasized in the *New York Times*, March 6, 1928, 1, 2.

18. Schwartz, "Unemployment Relief in Philadelphia," 63, 68–75.

19. William Pear, "The Problem of Maintaining Casework Standards and Meeting Relief Requirements," NCSW, 1931, 377; John F. Bauman, "The City, the Depression and Relief: The Philadelphia Experience, 1929–1939" (Ph.D. diss., Rutgers University, 1969), 86–87.

20. Schwarz, "Unemployment Relief in Philadelphia," 66–67; Jacob Billikopf, "What Have We Learned about Unemployment?," NCSW, 1931, 35–37.

21. Schwartz, "Unemployment Relief in Philadelphia," 78–80; Bauman, 97–98. The city continued to distribute aid through private charities and in the fall of 1931 returned to private financing. Five million dollars was raised in a relief drive that dovetailed with a national "Liberty Loan"–style campaign coordinated by the Hoover administration. Once again the Lloyd committee had to be bailed out by public funds, this time coming from the state. By mid-1932, the Lloyd committee was almost entirely dependent on public funds, a fact that generated a great deal of pressure for a federal relief program (Bauman, "The City, the Depression and Relief," 136–141).

22. *New York Times*, October 16, 1930, 1; November 6, 1930, 19; November 7, 1930, 1; November 12, 1930, 15; November 15, 1930, 1. Gertrude Springer, "The Job Line," *Survey* 65, no. 9 (February 1, 1931): 496–497. This private relief program was supplemented by the periodic distribution of food boxes, organized by a separate mayor's committee and financed by "voluntary" contributions from city employees. Finally, teachers in the public schools raised a small fund to provide lunches for needy children. Social workers in the New York Welfare Council, created in the late 1920s, attempted to coordinate these efforts.

23. *New York Times*, November 18, 1930, 1; November 30, 1930, 1; December 5, 1930, 1; Springer, "The Job Line," 498. For the impact of the work program on the morale of the unemployed, see William E. Mathews, "Helping the Unemployed Man: Lessons for Another Winter," *New York Times*, August 16, 1931, IX, 5. See also the report of the Prosser committee in the *New York Times*, August 11, 1931, 23.

24. *New York Times*, January 6, 1931, 1; January 7, 1931, 1; February 1, 1931, 2; March 1, 1931, 3; March 28, 1931, 11; April 8, 1931, 12; April 18, 1931, 5. The city took over the Prosser committee's work relief program in May, but the caseload was reduced to below 15,000. Bremer, *Depression Winters*, 35–36.

25. For a general overview of local relief in the fall of 1930 see *New York Times*, October 28, 1930, 15.

26. C.M. Bookman, "Community Organization to Meet Unemployment Needs," NCSW, 1931, 388–398; *New York Times*, April 6, 1930, X, 1. Bookman estimated that during the winter of 1930–1931, $460,000 was spent from private funds and $200,000 from public funds for "direct unemployment relief."

27. Cleveland: *New York Times*, May 10, 1931, 5; Pear, "The Problem of Maintaining Casework Standards and Meeting Relief Requirements," 375; St. Louis: E.G. Steger, "Public Money through Private Agencies," *Survey* 66, no. 2 (October 15, 1931): 98–99; Chicago: Clorinne Brandenberg, *Chicago Relief and Service Statistics* (Chicago: University of Chicago Press, 1932), 8–17, 35, 68; *New York Times*, June 19, 1931, 14; July 12, 1931, III, 5.

28. Mullins, *The Depression and the Urban West Coast*, ch. 3. Despite the moderate levels of unemployment, social agencies on the West Coast did experience significant caseload increases in 1930. The Los Angeles County Department of Charities increased from an average of approximately 6,000 per month, to 10,784 in March 1930, to nearly 17, 000 in January 1931. Private charities reported large increases as well. In the late spring of 1931 the city initiated a work relief program financed by a $5 billion bond issue. In San Francisco, where private agencies financed by the Community Chest handled most unemployment relief in early 1930, the expanding caseload led to publicly funded work relief program in the fall of 1930. Leonard Leader, "Los Angeles and the Great Depression" (Ph.D. diss., UCLA, 1972); Emily P. Huntington, *Unemployment Relief and the Unemployed in the San Francisco Bay Area* (Berkeley: University of California Press, 1939), 8–11.

29. The UCL's role in distributing aid to the unemployed made it a force in city politics but also a locus for factional disputes among left-wing organizers. This, along with the increasing hostility of the social work establishment, con-

tributed to its demise as a relief-dispensing organization by the end of 1932. Arthur Hillman, *The Unemployed Citizens League of Seattle*, the University of Washington Publications in the Social Sciences, vol. 5, no. 5 (Seattle: University of Washington Press, 1934). See especially ch. 3 on the role of the league in administering relief. John Arthur Hogan, "The Decline of Self-Help and the Growth of Radicalism among Seattle's Organized Unemployed" (Master's thesis, University of Washington, 1934); Tom Jones Parry, "The Republic of the Penniless," *Atlantic Monthly* 150, no. 4 (October 1932): 449–457.

30. *Boston Globe*, November 18, 1930, 14; Gertrude Springer, "Well Advertised Bread Lines," *Survey* 65, no. 10 (February 15, 1931): 545; Pear, "The Problem of Maintaining Casework Standards and Meeting Relief Requirements," 377; Trout, *Boston, the Great Depression and the New Deal*, 30–33, 66–68. Milwaukee was another example of a city which relied on public relief. See Hannah, "Urban Reaction to the Great Depression," 108; *New York Times*, December 19, 1931, 3.

31. *New York Times*, December 14, 1930, III, 6. A detailed account of the MUC can be found in Sidney Fine, *Frank Murphy: The Detroit Years* (Ann Arbor: University of Michigan Press, 1975), 261–292. The description of relief conditions in Detroit in early 1930 is from Fine, 205, 260. See also Beulah Amidon, "Detroit Does Something about It," *Survey* 65, no. 10 (February 15, 1931): 540–542.

32. Fine, *Frank Murphy*, 305–306, 325–339; Norton, "The Relief Crisis in Detroit," 5; *The New Republic* 68 (October 7, 1931): 191–192; Wilhelmina Luten, "A Survey of 1200 Families, Detroit Department of Public Welfare," *Family* 13, no. 4 (June 1932): 127–130.

33. Joanna Colcord, "Facing the Coming Winter," NCSW, 1931, 207.

34. Billikopf, "What Have We Learned About Unemployment?," 37–38. See also Springer, "Well Advertised Breadlines," 545.

35. New York: *New York Times*, January 7, 1931, 5. See also *New York Times*, August 16, 1931, X, 5; Lilian Brandt, *An Impressionistic View of the Winter of 1930–31 in New York City* (New York: Welfare Council of New York City, 1932), 43, 53.

36. Detroit: Amidon, "Detroit Does Something about It," 540–541; *New York Times*, December 14, 1930, III, 6; Fine, *Frank Murphy*, 265, 303; Chicago: Brandenberg, *Chicago Relief and Service Statistics*, 49–50.

37. Springer, "The Burden of Mass Relief," 199.

38. Pear, "The Problem of Maintaining Casework Standards," 374; Bremer, *Depression Winters*, 36–37; Josephine Brown, *Public Relief, 1929–1939* (New York: Henry Holt and Co., 1940), 80–82.

39. On the origins of POUR see material in POUR files, Box 186, File: New York—Local Organizations, and in E.P. Hayes Files, "Relief." See also Gertrude Springer, "Where Is the Money Coming From?," *Survey* 67, no. 2 (October 1931): 71.

40. *New York Times*, March 7, 1930, 1; Leab, "United We Eat," 306–307.

41. *New York Times*, December 8, 1930, 2; December 15, 1930, 4. The emergency public works appeal was signed by mayors of forty-one cities, including Mayor Curley of Boston and Mayor Murphy of Detroit.

42. *New York Times*, December 1, 1930, 1; December 2, 1930, 26; December 3, 1930, 20; December 4, 1930, 18; December 8, 1930 2; December 9, 1930, 26.

43. Schwarz, *The Interregnum of Despair*, 32–33, 63–65; *New York Times*, December 8, 1930, 2; December 11, 1930, 1, 2.

44. The following analysis relies heavily on Hamilton, "Herbert Hoover and the Great Drought of 1930," and Robert Crowley, "The Drought and the Dole," *American Heritage* 23 (February 1972): 16–19, 92–99.

45. Hamilton, "Herbert Hoover and the Great Drought," 850–851. For an account of the 1927 Mississippi flood that argues that Hoover's relief role was central to his capture of the 1928 presidential nomination see John M. Barry, *Rising Tide: The Great Mississippi Flood of 1927 and How It Changed America* (New York: Simon and Schuster, 1997), 395.

46. *The New York Times*, December 20, 1930, 2; Hamilton, "Herbert Hoover and the Great Drought," 867–868. Hamilton argues that Hoover's decision to ask for only $25 million in federal loans was "one of the great blunders of his Presidency" (865).

47. *New York Times*, December 9, 1930, 1; December 13, 1930, 2; April 14, 1931, 12; David Hamilton, *From New Day to New Deal* (Chapel Hill: University of North Carolina Press, 1991), 156–157; Hamilton, "Herbert Hoover and the Great Drought," 856, 867.

48. *New York Times*, December 9, 1930, 1; December 18, 1930, 1; January 7, 1931, 28.

49. *New York Times*, January 9, 1931, 16; January 10, 1931, 1; Hamilton, "Herbert Hoover and the Great Drought," 869.

50. Gertrude Springer, "The Challenge of Hard Times, *Survey* 66, no. 8 (July 15, 1931): 382; Harry Lurie, "The Drift to Public Relief," NCSW, 1931, 221; "Petition of the Mayors Unemployment Committee (July 29, 1931)," POUR Files, Box 255, File: Relief; *New York Times*, August 2, 1931, 17; August 14, 1931, 16; "Unemployment Leadership," *Survey*, 66, no. 12 (September 15, 1931): 537.

51. Arthur M. Schlesinger, *The Crisis of the Old Order* (Cambridge, MA: Houghton Mifflin, 1957), 172–174; Albert Romasco, *The Poverty of Abundance* (New York: Oxford University Press, 1965), 163; Robert S. McElvaine, *The Great Depression* (New York: Times Books, 1993), 78.

52. Hoover had apparently attempted to create a similar committee the previous winter to deal with the drought but was rebuffed by the social work leadership and some of his own relief officials. Hamilton, "Herbert Hoover and the Great Drought," 863.

53. The relationship between POUR and the private welfare organizations was not an easy one. In May of 1931 PECE had encouraged the Chests to organize a national campaign the following fall. However, soon after POUR was created in August, it became clear that the president's committee would play a more important role in the publicity campaign. This created a good deal of confusion among Chest officials. Furthermore, the Chests were in the process of agitating for local and state public appropriations, and it was hoped that POUR would more aggressively support public relief. The Gifford committee was virtually silent on the need for public appropriations until the La Follette Costigan federal relief bill generated support for a federal appropriation. Then POUR officials began to argue against federal relief on the basis that it would undermine state appropriations. For sources on the origins of the POUR fund drive see, especially, Fred Croxton to J. Herbert Chase, May 1, 1931, Box 186, File: New York—Local

Organizations; Minutes of Relief Meeting with Leaders of Various National Organizations, June 4, 1931, Box 255, E.P. Hayes Files: "Relief"; "Memorandum to Community Chest Executives" (September 1931), File 60.2: Assoc. of Commmunity Chests and Councils; Gertrude Springer "Funds for Another Bleak Winter," *Survey* 66, no. 6 (June 5, 1931): 302; Springer, "Where Is the Money Coming From?," *Survey* 67, no. 2 (October 15, 1931): 71. For POUR and local public relief see the exchange of letters between Joanna Colcord and Walter S. Gifford in late August 1931, Box 186, File: Local Organizations. See also Haynes Memos to Fred Croxton, August 17, 1931, Box 221, File: Rowland Haynes memos.

54. Owen D. Young, "Report to the Director of the President's Organization on Unemployment Relief" (November 27, 1931), Box 210, File: Committee on Mobilization of Relief Resources; full-page advertisement describing POUR campaign in the *St. Louis Daily Globe-Democrat* (October 27, 1931), Box 246 (Croxton State Reports File: Missouri City Information, both in POUR Files; Gifford Testimony, Sen. Manuf. Hearings, 311; *New York Times*, October 15, 1931, 1; October 18, 1931, II, 4; November 16, 1931, 4; December 8, 1931, 2.

55. Hawley, *The Great War and the Search for a Modern Order*, 83–84. On Hoover's use of publicity see Barry, *Rising Tide*, 1269–1270, and especially Craig Lloyd's excellent monograph *Aggressive Introvert: A Study of Hoover and Public Relations Management* (Columbus: Ohio State University Press, 1972).

56. Emma Winslow, *Trends in Different Types of Public and Private Relief in Urban Areas, 1929–1935* (Washington, DC: Government Printing Office, 1937, 69–71; *New York Times*, October 2, 1931, 43; December 8, 1931, 32; December 9, 1931, 3; December 11, 1931, 19; William Ryerson to Walter S. Gifford, December 22, 1931, POUR, Box 180, File: Illinois—Local Organizations; Schwartz, "Unemployment Relief in Philadelphia," 75–76. Detroit, on the other hand, avoided a POUR-style campaign, with the result that the city's "Emergency Relief Fund" fell far short of its $3.5 million goal. See Fine, *Frank Murphy*, 336–337.

57. "The new set-up [POUR] has been generally accepted by political leaders and by the press as a move to forestall a flood of socialist legislation and a widespread demand for federal unemployment insurance when Congress meets," editorialized the *Survey* 66, no. 12 (September 15, 1931): 537.

58. Harry Leslie [government of Indiana] to Herbert Hoover, September 9, 1931, Government William W. Bruckner to Herbert Hoover, August 21, 1931, both in Box 209, Gifford State Reports File.

59. See Gifford telegram dated November 17, 1931, and response, POUR, Box 209, File: State Reports. While POUR did not oppose local or state public appropriations, Gifford refused to endorse local relief legislation and studiously avoided mentioning that public expenditures were key to maintaining the stability of local relief. This stance was ironic, since Gifford had helped lobby for New York City's historic relief appropriation in the spring of 1931. The *New York Times* called Gifford the "chief proponent" of a special $20 million public appropriation for relief in the city. *New York Times*, August 22, 1931, 4.

60. Gifford Pinchot, "The Case for Federal Relief," *Survey* 68, no. 7 (January 1, 1932), 349; *New York Times*, November 2, 1931, 2; December 8, 1931, 8. See also Joint Committee on Unemployment, "The Fight for Direct Relief of the Unemployed" Box 187, File: New York City Committee; "*Chicago Hunger Fighter*," January 23, 1932, Box 180, File: Illinois State Committee, both in POUR files.

61. A December 2, 1931 request from the *Survey* for a short statement by Walter S. Gifford, to be printed in a pro-and-con symposium on federal relief, noted that the "30,000 readers" of the magazine had not taken a stand on the issue and that "they want their thinking cleared up." Arthur Kellogg to Walter S. Gifford, December 2, 1931, POUR, Box 235, File 020: General.

62. Linton Swift to Walter S. Gifford, November 12, 1934, and Family Welfare Association of America, "The Social Work Conference on Federal Action," tentative draft statement (November 10, 1931), both in POUR, Box 186, File: New York—Local Organizations. Swift defined that the purpose of the group "at this time is not to agitate for federal action, but to make available any ideas, knowledge and experience which we may have on the administrative aspects of the problem in case such legislation is passed."

63. William Hodson, "An Open Letter to the President on Federal Relief Appropriations," *Survey Graphic* 67, no. 3 (November 1, 1931): 144–145.

64. For a description of the origins of the LaFollette-Costigan bill see Fred Greenbaum, *Fighting Progressive: A Biography of Edward P. Costigan* (Washington, DC: Public Affairs Press, 1971), 122–124; Joanna C. Colcord, "Social Work and the First Federal Relief Program," NCSW, 1943, 382–394. For Wagner's position in November and December of 1931 see his letter to the *Survey* 67, no. 6 (December 15, 1931): 331.

65. For the provisions of the LaFollette-Costigan bill see Sec. 3045, 72 Cong., 2nd sess. January 15, 1932; *Survey* 67, no. 6 (December 15, 1931): 331. For more detailed accounts of its legislative history see Schwarz, *The Interregnum of Despair*, 150–155; Brock, *Welfare, Democracy and the New Deal*, 134–138. The bill actually created a new Federal Board for Unemployment Relief, but this agency, despite representatives from the Agricultural Extension Services and the federal Board for Vocational Rehabilitation, would clearly be dominated by the Children's Bureau. See Brown, *Public Relief, 1929–1939*, 103.

66. Schwarz, *The Interregnum of Despair*, 151.

67. Ibid., 154–155. J. Joseph Huthmacher, *Senator Robert F. Wagner and the Rise of Urban Liberalism* (New York: Atheneum), 95, discusses the origins of the loan provisions, which were eventually incorporated into the federal relief bill. Initially, the loan formula was opposed by social workers and progressives supporting the LaFollette–Costigan bill. See "Federal Relief," *Survey* 67, no. 12 (March 15, 1932): 659, which suggested that the Wagner substitute "appears within striking distance of being a $375,000,000 pork barrel."

68. *New York Times*, May 13, 1932, 1, 11; Huthmacher, *Robert F. Wagner*, 95–97.

69. This view is particularly prominent in accounts that draw on social work sources from the 1930s. See Edward A. Williams, *Federal Aid for Relief* (New York: Columbia University Press, 1939), 36–41; Brown, *Public Relief, 1929–1939*, 106–110; Clarke Chambers, *Seedtime of Reform* (Minneapolis: University of Minnesota Press, 1963), 246–250; Harris Gaylord Warren, *Herbert Hoover and the Great Depression* (New York: Oxford University Press, 1959), 199–204; Trattner, *From Poor Law to Welfare State*, 224–225.

70. U.S. Congress, Senate Committee on Manufactures, *Unemployment Relief*, Hearings on Sec. 174 and 262, 72nd Cong., 1st sess., December 28, 1931–January 9, 1932, 32, 99–102, 116–117, 125–126, 131. See also *New York Times*, December

29, 1931, 1; December 30, 1931, 1. The *Survey* reprinted portions of the testimony in vol. 67, no. 9 (February 1, 1932), 465–467.

71. Senate Committee on Manufactures, *Unemployment Relief*, 312–313, 319; *New York Times*, January 9, 1932, 1.

72. "How the Cities Stand," *Survey* 68, no. 2 (April 15, 1932): 71–75; Jacob Billikopf Testimony, 1931 Sen. Manuf. Hearings, 116–117.

73. A.E. Howell, "Report on Unemployment Situation in Certain Cities Visited, Nov. 20, and 21, 1931," POUR Files, Box 245, "Kansas" Folder. See also Alice Stenholm, "Report on Trip to Columbia, South Carolina, Oct. 15 and 16, 1931," POUR Files, Box 246, File: South Carolina. Stenholm told Croxton that "it was not possible . . . to get a true picture of the Charlestown situation in the short period of time spent there. Most outstanding was conflicting reports received." The optimistic view of the executive secretary of the Community Chest contrasted sharply with the opinion of the head of the Bureau of Social Welfare.

74. Haynes to Croxton, "Report on Visit to Chicago, January 29, 1932," dated February 1, 1932. This and other memos on Chicago relief appear in POUR, Box 210, Illinois-Cities File. See also *New York Times*, August 8, 1931, III, 4, October 2, 1931, 43; Frank Z. Glick, "The Illinois Emergency Relief Commission," *Social Service Review* 7, no. 1 (March 1933): 32.

75. *Financial and Economic Position of Chicago* (unsigned pamphlet), Reconstruction Finance Corporation-Relief Division (National Archives Record Group 234 [hereafter RFC Files], Box 26, Illinois-Loan no. 1 Document File; David Beito, *Taxpayers in Revolt* (Chapel Hill: University of North Carolina Press, 1989), ch. 2.

76. Rowland Haynes, "Report on Visit to Chicago, Illinois, February 4, 1932, POUR, Box 245, Illinois-Cities File; *New York Times*, February 4, 1931, 14; February 6, 1931, 2; February 7, 1932, III, 5; Glick, "The Illinois Emergency Relief Commission," 23–24, 32–33; and Glick, *The Illinois Emergency Relief Commission* (Chicago: University of Chicago Press, 1940), 16–28.

77. "First Interim Report of the Illinois Emergency Relief Commission," April 15, 1932, 38–39, Box 180, File: Illinois State Committee; Haynes to Croxton, April 6, 1932, Box 245, File: Illinois Cities, both in POUR files.

78. *New York Times*, June 3, 1932, 10; June 22, 1932, 2.

79. For the legislative confllict over Pinchot's relief program see E.R. Phelps to Gifford, POUR Box 190, File: Pennsylvania State Reps.; *New York Times*, September 18, 1931, 2; November 10, 1931, 13; November 11, 1931, 16; December 13, 1931, III, 6; December 24, 1931, 38; Brock, *Welfare Democracy and the New Deal*, 106–109.

80. U.S. Congress, Senate, Committee on Banking and Currency, Unemployment Relief, Hearings on Senate 4632, 4727, 4755 and 4822, 72nd Cong., 2nd Sess., June 2–13, 1932, 21; *New York Times*, January 18, 1932, 3, February 8, 1932, 18; April 14, 1932, 20; Schwartz, "Unemployment Relief in Philadelphia," 76–78.

81. Jacob Billikopf Testimony, U.S. Congress, Senate Committee on Manufactures, *Federal Aid for Unemployment Relief*, Hearings on Sec. 5125, 72nd Cong., 2nd sess., January 3–February 13, 1933, 8; *New York Times*, July 3, 1932, II, 6; Bauman, "The City, the Depression and Relief," 141–142.

82. Alice Stenholm, "Report on Field Trip, December 13 to 17," Box 244, File: Arkansas; Clarence E. Pickett to Croxton, May 17, 1932, Box 217, File: American Friends Service Committee; Haynes to Croxton (undated telegram), Box 246, File:

Ohio; Haynes to Croxton, June 20, 1932, Box 221, File: Rowland Haynes, all in POUR files.

83. Detroit: *New York Times,* March 13, 1932, III, 6; April 26, 1932, 32; June 6, 1932, II, 6; August 2, 1932, 7; Fine, *Frank Murphy,* 336–339; Norton, "The Relief Crisis in Detroit," 6–7. Boston: Alice Stenholm, "Summary of Relief Situation in Massachusetts," January 22, 23, 25, 1932 and other materials in Box 245, File: Massachusetts; Trout, *Boston, the Great Depression and the New Deal,* 85–89.

84. The tax increase for relief proved extremely unpopular, and Roosevelt was forced to continue TERA financing through a $30 million special bond issue. The TERA was also forced to retreat on its emphasis on work relief, due to the expense. On the origins and financing of New York's state relief program see *New York Times,* August 22, 1931, 4; August 29, 1931, 1; September 10, 1931, 1; October 8, 1931, 4; October 17, 1931, 17; January 11, 1932, 1; February 8, 1932, 25; March 9, 1932, 1; Haynes to Croxton, March 21, 1932, POUR, Box 26, New York File Octavia O. Lundberg, "The New York State Temporary Emergency Relief Administration," *The Social Service Review* 6 (1932): 545–566; Gertrude Springer, "The Lever of State Relief," *Survey* 67, no. 8 (January 15, 1932): 407–408; Brock, *Welfare, Democracy and the New Deal,* 92–100.

85. *New York Times,* January 1, 1932, 1; January 9, 1932, 4; January 12, 1932, 1; January 15, 1932, 2; January 28, 1932, 12; April 10, 1932, 1; April 27, 1932, 1; April 28, 1932, 23; April 30, 1932, 11.

86. Robert C. McMarsh to Walter S. Gifford, September 9, 1931, Box 210, File: Gifford; Jacob Billikopf to Gifford, August 27, 1931, Box 190 File: Local Organizations, both in POUR files; Ryerson testimony, Senate Manuf. Hearings (1930–1931), 263.

87. *Survey* 64, no. 12 (September 15, 1930): 502–503, 525; E. Wright Bakke, *The Unemployed Worker: A Study of the Task of Making a Living without a Job* (New Haven, CT: Yale University Press, 1940), 317–318, 321.

88. Jeanette Elder, "A Study of One Hundred Applicants for Relief in the Fourth Winter of Unemployment" (Master's thesis, University of Chicago, 1933), 9–11.

89. Bauman, "The City, the Depression and Relief," 118.

90. Howell, "Report on Unemployment Situation in Certain Cities."

91. Haynes to Croxton, March 14, 1932, POUR, Box 245 File: Michigan; James J. Lorence, *Organizing the Unemployed: Community and Union Activists in the Industrial Heartland* (Albany: State University of New York Press, 1996), 38–43.

92. Frances Fox Piven and Richard A. Cloward, *Poor People's Movements* (New York: Random House, 1977), 60–61, 64. In other sections of this important monograph, Cloward and Piven present a much more complex analysis of the relationship between protest and institutional disruption. Their views have strongly influenced the argument presented here. See *Poor People's Movements,* 11–13.

93. "An Application for RFC Relief Funds Submitted by the Cuyahoga County Joint Relief Committee," September 14, 1932, RFC Files, Box 79, File: Ohio Document File Loan no. 3; supporting statement with Alabama loan request in RFC Files, Box 1, Alabama Loan no. 1 Document File; *New York Times,* February 7, 1932, III, 5.

94. *New York Times,* April 17, 1932, 1, 3; Letter from Joint Committee on Unemployment, May 3, 1932, POUR, Box 187, File: New York City Committee.

95. Schwarz, *The Interregnum of Despair*, 161–163; *New York Times*, May 12, 1932, 1; May 13, 1932, 1; May 14, 1932, 8; May 21, 1932, 2.

96. *New York Times*, May 21, 1932, 2; May 23, 1932, 1; May 27, 1932, 1, 4; May 28, 1932, 1.

97. Schwarz, *The Interregnum of Despair*, 164–169; *New York Times*, July 7, 1932,

Chapter 4

The National Dole

The Emergency Relief and Construction Act of 1932 created a national "dole," a term that had many of the negative connotations now embodied in the word "welfare."[1] The dole, however, was a somewhat more elastic concept that could be used to justify a range of contradictory positions. Although its notoriety derived from public criticism of the British system of unemployment compensation, it came to be used to disparage whatever one didn't like about American relief policy. Hoover and those to his right generally used it when referring to federal, as opposed to local or state, and public, as against private, relief. Critics, particularly in the social work community, frequently noted that this was an artificial distinction of little use to either the unemployed workers or the beleaguered local agencies dispensing aid to them. Franklin D. Roosevelt and liberals in Congress also attacked doles, but their implicit definition focused on the issue of work: to them, the dole was a degrading and inadequate general relief payment not linked to employment. Public works and work relief programs such as WPA were seen as alternatives to the "direct dole."[2] Social workers, despite efforts to avoid using the term, often applied it to so-called poor law relief, inadequate aid rationed by politically connected local officials without casework.[3] The unemployed themselves, or at least those who spoke for them in protest organizations, often equated the dole with "charity relief" administered by stingy social workers who, in applying the means test, "snooped" in the homes of working-class recipients.[4]

Yet despite the almost universal opposition to such a policy, a distinctive American "dole" appeared to emerge in response to the fiscal crisis of 1932. In July Congress, without a great deal of enthusiasm, had appropriated $300 million for direct relief to the unemployed, and Hoover, with even less, approved it. Although an effort was made to disguise the new federal welfare role by distributing aid in the form of "loans" to states, most public officials knew this was a national relief program.[5] The Hoover administration hoped to limit the scope of the program by distributing aid through the Reconstruction Finance Corporation, rather than a federal welfare agency, and requiring states to show that they were virtually bankrupt as a precondition for receiving funds. But mass unemployment and the local relief crisis made this policy untenable. By the time the New Deal was inaugurated in March of 1933, federal funds were financing most relief nationwide. The Roosevelt administration ended the discredited loan policy, appropriated $500 million for grants to the states and established a new federal agency, the Federal Emergency Relief Administration. The FERA stabilized the relief financing and aggressively sought to improve standards of aid and relief administration. Federal relief "czar" Harry Hopkins quickly established himself as a charismatic public official—an ardent defender of the relief program and the unemployed who applied to it. But the New Deal was almost as hostile to the "dole" as the Hoover administration and sought to phase it out as quickly as possible. Initially, the administration hoped its recovery program, coupled with pressure on the states to accept a larger share of the relief burden, would eliminate federal relief. When this approach appeared to fail, Hopkins convinced Roosevelt to embark on the first of a series of work relief experiments, the Civil Works Administration, which would come to symbolize New Deal social policy

The origin of federal relief is certainly not a new story, but this crucial period in the history of the American welfare state is still not well understood. For many years, the contrasts between the policies of Hoover and Roosevelt seemed to provide a relatively satisfactory explanation for most policy developments. It was generally assumed that a vast new federal relief program was initiated under the New Deal's Harry Hopkins; the earlier federal program of the RFC was either ignored or quickly discounted as inadequate.[6] In recent years, both the influential "Hoover revisionism" and new approaches to the expansion of the "administrative state" have had some impact on interpretations of national relief policy. Several specialized studies have stressed the importance of the RFC's program and the early New Deal's hostility to the federal dole.[7] This research has worked its way into a number of general accounts. But in the absence of an alternative framework for interpreting federal welfare policy during 1932 and 1933, the contrasts between the Hoover and Roosevelt administrations continue to be emphasized in most general studies, creating the impression that the federalized welfare state was a product of New Deal policy.[8]

It was not. Although the New Deal was far more willing to defend the national relief program than its predecessor, both administrations were attempting to cope with a "dole system" that had been forced upon them. Each initially sought to limit the scope of the federal program by withholding funds until states agreed to accept a greater share of the financing burden. The Hoover administration quickly abandoned this approach because it did not wish to be held responsible for local relief crises. In the process, the RFC's relief division was drawn into aspects of administration and financing that were not envisioned in the original law. The New Deal, assuming a more aggressive administrative role from the outset, was somewhat more successful in forcing states to share the relief burden. But as the winter of 1933–1934 approached, it appeared that its "emergency" program was well on its way to becoming a permanent federal welfare policy. This reality created an opening for those in the administration who sought to implement a public employment program as an alternative to the "dole"—the result was the Civil Works Administration, one of the most ambitious policy experiments of the New Deal era. The real contrast between the policies of the New Deal and the Hoover administration was not in their attitudes toward a federal relief but in their vastly different approaches to eliminating it.

The program initiated by the Emergency Relief and Construction Act (ERCA) of 1932 and implemented by the Reconstruction Finance Corporation was the direct antecedent to our contemporary federal welfare policy. This fact is rarely emphasized in histories of American social policy or of the Great Depression itself. This rather striking omission is certainly understandable in light of the legislative history of the ERCA and the controversies surrounding its early implementation. Key provisions of the 1932 law were designed to placate the Hoover administration and moderates in Congress by creating the fiction that this was not really a federal relief program. Since federal aid was to be deducted from future highway grants, these were, according to the logic, really state funds temporarily "loaned" from the federal government. Second, the program was to be administered by the Reconstruction Finance Corporation, hardly the model for a federal social welfare organization. The RFC's primary objective was to assist failing business enterprises, particularly banks, with federal funds, and its board was dominated by business leaders largely unsympathetic to the plight of the states in need of relief funds. The RFC's small relief division was staffed by holdovers from Hoover's earlier "voluntarist" committees.[9]

The policies initially adopted by the RFC board appeared to be a continuation of the Hoover administration's opposition to federal relief. Applicants were required to show that all state and local funds had been completely exhausted, a "pauper's oath" that seemed to discourage applications. "The attitude of the RFC to date has been that [states] must practically go with their hats in their hands, drop on their knees and confess bankruptcy before they will get any [of the ERCA funds]," according to one informed observer.[10] The agency's initial loan policies seem to have been designed to stretch the federal appropriation well beyond the winter of 1932–1933. Hoping that economic conditions would improve, the corporation loaned states funds on a month-to-month basis (a policy apparently adopted over the objection of former POUR chairman Walter S. Gifford, who had advocated six-month loans). The agency also believed, no doubt correctly, that a liberal federal loan policy would discourage state action. In the midst of what most informed observers believed was an acute national relief crisis, the RFC's Rowland Haynes told a delegation from Louisiana that federal officials "intended to go slowly and carefully." In September RFC chairman Atlee Pomerene told a group of welfare officials that the ERCA appropriation was "not intended ... [to] be expended all at once or allocated to a state upon the ipso dicta of its government." Pomerene was reported to have suggested that the intent of Congress was that the appropriation should last for two years.[11]

Such comments infuriated supporters of federal relief, who argued that the ERCA fund was designed to aid local relief during the coming winter and should be distributed as quickly as possible. Senator Robert F. Wagner, a key author of the Emergency Relief and Construction Act, believed that the Hoover administration was trying to undermine the law by tying up relief and public works funds with "red tape. In September 1932 he demanded that the funds appropriated by Congress be released immediately, or the nation would face a winter of "unspeakable cruelty." The Joint Committee on Unemployment, a lobbying coalition that had helped generate public support for the ERCA, attacked the RFC's policies as a continuation of Hoover's opposition to federal relief. The committee urged governors to bombard the agency with applications for aid.[12] Similar criticisms were heard when Senator LaFollette's Committee on Manufactures reconvened in January of 1933. Building support for new legislation to provide federal relief in the form of grants with stronger federal controls, social workers and public officials launched sharp attacks on the RFC for the pauper's oath, the short-term loan policies and its cavalier attitude toward low standards of relief prevailing throughout the country. The social workers' critique has tended to dominate historical accounts of the early implementation of the ERCA.[13]

The RFC's historical reputation has not been enhanced by a dispute with Pennsylvania governor Gifford Pinchot. In mid-August, Pinchot, a sharp critic of the Hoover administration's relief policy, filed an application for $45 million, the maximum amount allowed an individual state under the ERCA. The request created a dilemma for the RFC. Just prior to the application, Pinchot had worked with the RFC board to pressure the legislature into passing a new tax bill for relief.[14] Clearly, the state had done its part, and the continuing crisis in Philadelphia showed that Pennsylvania needed supplemental federal aid. Yet if the agency acceded to Pinchot's request for a large, lump-sum loan, the ERCA appropriation would quickly be exhausted before all states had a chance to apply. To complicate matters, Congress had not included a distribution formula in the law, nor had it provided guidelines for loans beyond the vague requirement that states receive federal aid as a last resort. On what basis could the board reject the state's application, particularly given the assumption of the relief law that these "loans" were really state, not federal, funds? The relief division rejected Pennsylvania's application on what appeared to be a technicality: the state had not presented data on spending, caseloads, and sources of future relief financing for every county applying for aid. This provided an opening for Pinchot to accuse the bankers on the RFC board of "splitting hairs while children starve." A standoff between the governor and the RFC quickly produced a major relief crisis in Philadelphia. The impending collapse of relief in the city forced the RFC to grant Pennsylvania aid without the data, but the funds were sufficient only until the end of September. At that time Pinchot, "hat in hand," had to apply for a new short-term loan.[15]

The Pinchot controversy, a public relations disaster for the RFC, has strongly influenced historical accounts of the implementation of the ERCA. But focusing on the disputes between the corporation and its most vocal critics distorts the impact of federal aid on local relief in late 1932. The Children's Bureau series shows that relief spending increased from approximately $20 million in August, when the first relief "loans" were made, to over $30 million in December. While we do not know how much of this money was ERCA funds, the condition of state and local financing, as shown on applications to the RFC files, suggests that most of the increase was a product of federal aid. Data collected by the Federal Emergency Relief Administration, discussed in Chapter 1, shows that 60 percent of all relief expenditures nationwide was accounted for by federal funds in January of 1933.[16] Critics of the RFC have frequently noted that only a small percentage of the original ERCA fund (approximately $80,000 of the $300 million appropriation) was distributed during the last three months of 1932.[17] But they ignore the fact that this level of expenditures was consistent with the seasonal trend of relief during previous depression winters. The RFC approved loans totaling well under $20 million per month from August through November; aggregate loan authorizations jumped to $36 million in December and reached nearly $50 million in January.[18] Whatever the intent of the agency's board of directors in September, the federal aid bankrolled relief nationally during the winter of 1932–1933, and the $300 million appropriation was exhausted by the following May. In essence, the local relief crisis that led to the passage of the ERCA made the RFC's conservative approach to federal aid untenable. Even when it was theoretically possible to argue that states could do more, the RFC could simply not withhold federal aid from states without being held responsible for massive cutbacks in relief.

Loan applications in the files of the RFC's relief division show this process at work. Chicago, whose relief crisis played a key role in the demand for federal relief, is a case in point. By July of 1932, total relief expenditures in the city exceeded $3 million per month, the city was broke and state funds appropriated the previous January had been exhausted. Immediately after the ERCA was passed, Illinois applied for $10 million to finance relief in Chicago and a number of downstate counties. Although the state was able to provide only limited supporting data on its application, the situation in Chicago (Cook County) was so serious that the RFC was willing to loan $3 million immediately. The board requested that the state file another application later in the month with more extensive documentation for local political units seeking federal aid. In mid-August, the state was granted an additional $6 million to last until the end of September. Although the state relief commission had requested substantially more, the reduced loan covered a shorter time period and thus did not produce a cut in relief.[19] Illinois was required to apply for aid on a monthly basis in late 1932, as RFC officials attempted to make federal aid contingent upon state action. In October the RFC, hoping to force the state to pass an emergency relief appropriation, reduced federal aid by approximately 25 percent. The decision, which led to a significant cut in the monthly food ration in Chicago, elicited bitter criticism from social workers and produced a mass protest movement among unemployed workers in the city. The RFC quickly backed off, restoring aid to previous levels the next month, but the October relief cut has understandably contributed to the agency's historical reputation for "penny-pinching." Such criticisms, however, mask the enormous impact of the federal relief program on Chicago. According to data on applications in the RFC files, Illinois was loaned over $25 million between August and December of 1932, a sum that financed nearly all of Chicago's relief bill. The RFC files also reveal that federal funds financed most relief in smaller urban areas, towns, and downstate rural counties in Illinois in late 1932.[20]

Detroit was another city whose relief crisis had helped to force the passage of federal legislation and where the RFC financed virtually the entire relief bill during these months. On August 4, the board approved a loan to the city of $1,800,000, designed to last for two months. These funds were loaned under section E of the new relief law, a provision that allowed local governments to borrow directly from the corporation at fixed interest rates without applying through state governors.[21] This was necessary because Michigan's Governor William Brucker, a vocif-erous opponent of federal relief, refused to establish a state relief pro-gram or an administrative mechanism for the distribution of federal funds. Under Section E, the RFC essentially bought municipal bonds that Detroit could not sell in the private markets. Federal officials were less than enthusiastic about Detroit's relief program, which they considered too liberal in its relief standards and treatment of the unemployed, but federal aid was the only mechanism for avoiding the collapse of relief in the city. In October the RFC reduced aid to well below Detroit's re-quest because the city appeared to be using federal funds to pay bills incurred before the relief program was passed (the Relief Division's Row-land Haynes accused Detroit of attempting to "unload eighty-five per-cent of its costs" for the previous fiscal year on the federal government). Still, federal aid financed virtually the entire relief bill in the city between August and December of 1932. During this period Detroit's relief case-load rose from 24,000 to over 38,000 families, and family allowances averaged over $30 per month. Although certainly well below prevailing social work standards, this was a significant improvement over the "iron ration" that the city had been forced to implement before the passage of the ERCA.[22]

Perhaps the most controversial loan approved by the RFC was the one that bailed out Philadelphia's relief organization. The deadlock between Governor Pinchot and the RFC board during August and September exacerbated the city's chronic relief crisis. Faced with potential collapse or relief, the RFC loaned the state $2.5 million in September. At the same time Pinchot was forced to retreat from his demand for a large, lump-sum loan and applied for federal aid on a monthly basis. Critics found the RFC's demands on the state burdensome and its short-term loan policy disruptive.[23] But this should not obscure the role federal aid played in Pennsylvania in late 1932. Applications in the RFC's files show that federal allocations to the state totaled over $12 million during the last three months of 1932. During this period, federal funds financed nearly 40 percent of Philadelphia's relief bill and well over half of that in Pittsburgh. The Pennsylvania files also show that federal aid played a key role in financing relief in rural areas and impoverished mining regions during these months. For example, in early October, the agency approved a loan of over $3.3 million, which financed aid to numerous smaller counties that had provided little emergency relief prior to the advent of the federal program.[24]

These loans reveal an aspect of the RFC's relief program that has not been widely appreciated—the impact of federal aid on small cities and rural areas with relatively undeveloped relief organizations. The RFC's first loans to Ohio, for example, were earmarked for Akron, Warren and Niles. From August to December the Corporation approved twenty sep-

arate loans to cities and towns in the state. In October 1932 the RFC
began funding relief in Michigan's Upper Peninsula, a chronically de-
pressed mining and lumbering region. Applications in the files of the
RFC's relief division reveal that the situation was much the same in West
Virginia, Kentucky and "downstate" Illinois.[25] By the end of 1932 every
state in the Old South was receiving federal funds. In late September,
for example, the RFC granted $1,200,000 to thirty-five parishes in Loui-
siana, that reported only small amounts of Red Cross aid in previous
months. When Virginia applied for aid in late August, it reported spending $48,000 in the applying counties during the first eight months of
1932. The RFC loaned these political units $283,367 for the last four
months of the year.[26] A similar trend can be seen on loan applications
from the plains states. The corporation loaned South Dakota $150,000 at
the end of August for seven counties that reported no locally funded
relief. Oklahoma received a large loan for twenty counties despite the
fact that the state could not provide data on the levels of local relief
"owing to the lack of records for the preparation of reports to the Governor."[27]

Thus, while the ERCA was created in response to the relief crises in
major urban centers, the law produced a flood of applications from
regions that the welfare modernization process of the 1920s had barely
touched. In these localities, the federal relief program absorbed large
numbers of recipients whose chronic poverty was not entirely the product of the depression. This was certainly the case in the Michigan's Upper
Peninsula, where, by the spring of 1933, a number of counties showed
over half the population receiving federal relief. A similar situation prevailed in the South. An April 1933 report in the *Survey* noted that more
than 75 percent of the population in some southern counties was on
relief: "These have been in plantation areas where in previous years the
planters have carried their field hands through the winter months, but
where, with an RFC-financed work program, a certain shift of responsibility has occurred."[28]

The lure of federal aid in these localities helps explain why, despite
the efforts of the RFC board, the Emergency Relief and Construction Act
quickly blossomed into a full-fledged federal relief program. Beginning
in January 1933, levels of federal aid increased substantially. By this time
the RFC had been using a standardized application form for several
months and could evaluate the trend of local relief with some accuracy.
Projected caseload increases consistent with the seasonal trend of relief
were generally financed even where the state and local relief effort was
minimal. Several populous states that had not previously applied for
RFC funds did so. California first applied for aid in January of 1933,
receiving large loans for Los Angeles and San Francisco. New York,
which had refused to take the "pauper's oath" while Franklin D. Roo-

sevelt was governor, was loaned $6 million in January. The RFC financed approximately 40 percent of relief in New York City from February through May 1933, a larger share of the city's relief bill than financed by the state's famous relief program.[29]

One of the main criticisms of the RFC's relief program has been that the federal agency made no effort to improve the abysmal standards of relief that prevailed in most parts of the country in late 1932. It is certainly true that federal officials explicitly stated that they would not impose a national standard and appeared to adopt an attitude of benign neglect toward monthly allowances, which, in many cases, were below ten dollars per month.[30] In some cases, the relief division rejected requests for loans based on big increases in relief allowances. One application from Louisiana, for example, indicates that an RFC official systematically lowered benefit levels used to calculate the request for federal aid. When a staff member of the Children's Bureau recommended that recipients in West Virginia be paid twenty-six dollars per month, Rowland Haynes, of the RFC's relief division, commented that she was attempting to "jump them too quickly to northern standards of relief."[31] RFC pressure on the states to appropriate funds for relief could produce cuts in standards of aid. In one of the most notorious cases, the RFC, attempting to force the Illinois legislature to appropriate more state funds for relief, reduced federal aid to Illinois. This led to a cut of 25 percent in the standard food allowance in Chicago. While federal aid was restored in response to local protests, the relief division appeared to show a callous disregard for the unemployed on relief.[32]

The RFC's "penny-pinching" attitude toward relief standards appeared to have encouraged one of the most controversial policy developments in late 1932—the "commissary system," in which local officials replaced the standard food order filled by local grocers with mass distribution of food from warehouses. Social workers argued that the policy not only stigmatized recipients but was a serious retreat in social policy, eliminating casework and encouraging "dependency" among clients.[33]

Yet despite the official policy of the RFC, the overall impact of the federal relief program was probably an improvement in relief standards. Federal aid created greater stability in relief financing, virtually eliminating the draconian cuts that had occurred in the earlier years of the depression. We have already noted that the "iron ration" in Detroit was abandoned with the advent of federal aid. In Philadelphia recipients who had suffered through two relief stoppages during the summer of 1932 received steady aid at the rate of over $25 per month during the fall. Administrative and financial stability led to incremental increases in benefits. The director of the Illinois Emergency Relief Commission estimated that relief standards per family had increased "slightly," from $18.99 in February 1932 to $26.76 in February 1933. One relief administrator explained increases in relief standards in St. Louis by noting that under the federal relief program "the agencies [in the city] are better organized to do adequate work among the families who are actually in need and to discover their needs."[34] This tendency was most pronounced in rural areas, whose applications to the RFC consistently provided for higher relief payments.

While RFC officials did not always adopt the policies advocated by social workers, they were dismayed at the levels of relief in many localities. Thus, Rowland Haynes refused to endorse an increase in West Virginia that provided for rates above the national average, but he also called the relief allowance provided by the Charleston commissary "tragically low" and recommended that federal aid provide for a substantial increase. Robert Kelso, preparing applications for Texas, recommended allowances of twelve dollars per month for a number of counties that reported previous levels of aid well below five dollars. It also appears that the relief division became more amenable to requests based on higher standards of aid after sharp criticisms of prevailing allowances at Senate hearings in early 1933. In January the RFC actually approved a loan to Rhode Island that was based primarily on the need to raise benefit levels, a significant departure from the policy which had initially required that all loans be justified on the basis of the exhaustion of state resources.[35]

Thus, it would appear that the existence of a large federal fund created a dynamic that—the intent of the law and attitudes of RFC board members notwithstanding—improved standards of aid. A similar generalization can be made about the role of federal aid in fostering local and state administrative development. The legislative history of the Emergency Relief and Construction Act shows strong congressional opposition to federal controls, particularly those supported by advocates of public welfare reform: this, indeed, was one of the main reasons for the defeat of the original LaFollette-Costigan bill and the decision to distribute aid through the RFC. The corporation's relief division bore little resemblance to a federal social agency. The division employed a small staff consisting of director, Fred Croxton, and four "field representatives." In terms of "administrative capacity" this did not represent a significant expansion over Hoover's earlier voluntarist relief committees. Federal officials did not issue formal guidelines for applying for aid or for the administration of federal funds. The limited administrative role conformed to the notion that federal aid, in the form of "loans," was, in reality, state funds: the "rules and regulations" that would accompany federal grants simply did not apply.[36] RFC funds could not be used for local relief administration, and the RFC board issued no guidelines concerning the kinds of agencies that could dispense federal aid. As a result, aid was channeled through a hodgepodge of local relief agencies, and many state relief administrations were dominated by business elites or bureaucrats with little experience in welfare policy. This situation greatly agitated social work leaders, who had hoped the federal relief program would be a vehicle for the expansion and modernization of state welfare administration.[37]

Yet as implementation of the federal program proceeded, there developed strong incentives to encourage state and local administrative development. First, officials in the RFC relief division were social workers who, despite their rather conservative orientation, could not ignore the fact that the local relief crisis had overwhelmed the existing relief machinery, creating chaotic conditions that made control of caseloads virtually impossible. Without stability in the administration of relief, the existence of a large federal relief fund might actually exacerbate the local crisis, encouraging a rush to the relief rolls. Second, RFC officials, hoping to conserve the federal appropriation, demanded that applying states provide supporting data on caseloads and spending data to justify requests for aid. Faced with an "avalanche" of requests for large loans in late July 1932, the relief division issued an elaborate questionnaire requiring states to provide detailed data on past expenditures, caseloads and projected future needs for every local unity applying for aid.[38] Local chaos and the primitive level of state administrative development made record keeping nearly impossible. In some cases, RFC staff members had to help local officials assemble the required data.[39] This was obviously not a realistic way to administer a federal relief program, so the RFC quickly found it necessary to encourage the expansion of local and state administrative capacity.

From the outset, the RFC loaned undeveloped states funds to set up new administrative machinery. Louisiana received $55,750 in August of 1932 to create a new state relief organization. Croxton told the RFC board that the committee would use the funds to employ "trained executives in social organization and accounting work to help in the organization of each of the sixty-four political subdivisions of the state." The pattern was repeated in other rural states with little in the way of public welfare organization. South Carolina's first loan from the RFC, for example, included $3,600 to establish a new "state relief council"; in February Croxton recommended that the federal agency give the state $20,000 to help cover administrative expenses.[40] In Texas the RFC not only allocated funds for administrative purposes but played an active role in the reorganizing the state relief committee. Initially, federal aid was channeled through an organization consisting of three regional directors of the state Chamber of Commerce. Federal officials came to oppose this arrangement, and RFC director Fred Croxton called on the governor to create a new state welfare organization. A $5,000 loan for state administrative development in January of 1933 was made contingent on "the approval of the field representative of the Emergency Relief Division of plans for further state administrative activities and subject to approval by the corporation."[41]

Another factor that, somewhat paradoxically, encouraged federal intervention in state-level policy making was the much-criticized "pauper's oath"—the RFC's demand that federal funds be approved only after states could show that they had exhausted their resources. In practice, this meant that federal aid to wealthier states, necessary to avoid the collapse of local relief, was accompanied by demands that state legislatures meeting in the fall of 1933 appropriate funds to aid the unemployed. After approving applications from a number of cities in Ohio, for example, the board stated that it would "hesitate to consider such an application [in the future] until every effort was made to secure the needed funds from state and local sources." When Detroit applied for its initial loan, state officials were questioned at length about potential new revenue sources, including taxes on income, gasoline and luxuries. In some cases, the potential for new revenues led to more direct forms of federal pressure. The RFC board initially worked closely with Pennsylvania's Governor Pinchot to exert pressure on the state legislature, making federal aid contingent on passage of a new state sales tax for relief. Federal demands on states intensified during the winter of 1932–1933, when many legislatures met in regular session. The RFC prodded Michigan's Governor Bruckner to support an appropriation to assist the unemployed. When the state refused to act, Fred Croxton approved a loan for one month only: "This should be taken as a final warning that action by the state is absolutely essential to meet relief needs."[42] Other states were more cooperative. In a number of cases governors and welfare officials worked closely with the RFC to force legislatures to act. Minnesota initially sought a large loan for several months but, after consultation with the RFC, applied for aid for February only "in view of the possibilities of local relief." Governor Floyd Olson then prepared a relief program that provided for new local bond issues and a state relief fund. In his efforts to secure legislative approval of the package, Olson was reported as "very appreciative . . . of the backing given by the RFC." In Texas the RFC field representative worked closely with state officials, drawing up a plan for a $20,000 bond issue. Governor Miriam Ferguson requested that the RFC representative address several committees of the legislature in support of the proposal.[43]

RFC's impact on local administrative development and financing was indirect. While ERCA aid technically could not be used for local administration, federal aid could free local funds to expand the staffs of relief agencies. The relief division of the RFC does not appear to have discouraged this trend. An analysis of relief in Chicago's Grovehill district, discussed briefly in the previous chapter, suggests that the federal relief program that began in August stabilized local administration. In early 1932 the district was swamped with new applicants and suffered through several funding crises caused by political conflicts over state financing. In July of 1932, the month before the first federal aid was received, Grovehill employed 85 relief workers, including staff and administration. By February of 1933 the total number of staff members had grown to 150, and nearly half of these were listed as "professional workers." As a result, according to Jeanette Elder, relief administration had stabilized despite the fact that the district's caseload had nearly doubled under the federal relief program.[44] In Pennsylvania the RFC program not only stabilized relief financing but provided the impetus for a direct challenge to the local poor law relief machinery, according to John Bauman. The original state program, passed in late 1932, had channeled funds through the traditional politically controlled poor boards, much to the consternation of social workers in the state. During the RFC period, new relief districts were created that bypassed the boards and served as spearheads for the reform of local relief.[45]

As the Pennsylvania example suggests, political interference and corruption in the administration of relief were a major concern of federal officials. The RFC's willingness to provide funds for relief administration in Louisiana, for example, reflected fears that federal aid might be used to bankroll the political machine of Huey Long. In New Orleans, a federally financed work program was the focus of labor agitation and charges of political corruption. The RFC monitored the situation closely, as evidenced by lengthy reports from local welfare officials and undercover agents in the RFC files.[46] In Los Angeles the RFC intervened directly in the local relief policy. Here, federal funds had been used to finance a work relief program that provided the political base of the populist mayoral candidate Frank Shaw (the comedian Will Rogers was reported to have quipped at a post-election celebration that "we're all here by the grace of the Reconstruction Finance Corporation"). Three weeks before the election, RFC field representative A.W. McMillen visited the city, ordering Shaw's "Employment Stabilization Bureau" discontinued and its 100,000 registrants cleared by the local social service exchange. The RFC then demanded that local relief be reorganized so that the city's welfare department could play a more active role in screening applicants.[47] In Rhode Island, RFC field representative Robert Kelso became embroiled in conflict between the state relief director and the state legislature over the appointment of local relief officials. In the case of Michigan, where a conservative Republican governor had refused to create a state relief organization, the RFC was receiving applications from a bewildering array of local political units. RFC officials believed the state could not properly account for federal funds received, a problem compounded by evidence that Detroit had used federal aid for institutional care prohibited by the RFC. In March of 1933 the RFC demanded that the state undertake a special survey of local relief expenditures. The federal agency not only loaned the state funds to hire staff but even required that appointees be approved by RFC field representative Rowland Haynes.[48]

The greater administrative and financial stability of local relief under the new federal program goes a long way toward explaining the relative lack of protest during the winter of 1932–1933. To be sure, the hunger marches and rent strikes continued. Abrupt relief cuts, as in Chicago during October 1933, could produce a mass reaction from the unemployed. But, in general, one senses that there was a decline in organized protest activity during the winter of the greatest unemployment in all the depression years. Some observers explained this phenomenon as a product of the exhaustion of the unemployed, a passivity produced perhaps by extreme poverty. But a better explanation for the relative lack of protest during these months is that the federal grant program expanded relief and strengthened local administration.

A good example of the impact of the RFC's relief program on grassroots action can be seen in Seattle. Here, the radical Unemployed Citizens League, a protest organization of the unemployed, had played a key role in administration of relief through the operation of commissaries that distributed "in kind" aid to the unemployed. Responding to both the radicalization of the league in late 1932 (workers linked to the American Communist Party had taken control of the organization) and the need to administer state and federal relief appropriations, mainstream welfare officials seized control of the relief machinery, eliminated the commissaries controlled by the UCL and began the process of implementing standard social work procedures for administering aid. This led to an abrupt and rapid decine in the influence of the UCL during the early months of 1933.[49] A similar development occurred in Chicago. Here, the Chicago Workers Committee, an organization created by the socialist League for Industrial Democracy, had been recognized as the "negotiating agent" for workers applying for relief during the summer of 1932. By the end of the year the organization claimed a membership of 35,000 in 63 "locals." Then in January of 1933, the city abruptly discontinued coordinating relief with the committee and established a centralized Public Relations Bureau to handle recipients' complaints. The league's influence declined precipitously. In explaining the declined of organized protest in the city, one observer emphasized that "the unemployed no longer fear so greatly the periodic halting of relief funds in municipalities. Federal appropriations have gone a long way to insure steady funds."[50]

The implementation of the ERCA abounds with ironies and unintended consequences. Loans without formal federal controls—a policy designed to disguise the federal welfare role—encouraged political corruption, which, in turn, produced an expanded federal relief role. The policy of distributing federal aid as a last resort led the relief division to pressure states to pass new legislation. The experience of the RFC's relief program suggests we need to look beyond legislative intent and the goals of administrators to explain the expansion and federalization of public welfare in the United States. Certainly, the increasing level of federal activism was partly a product of the fact that those administering the law in the relief division—professional welfare administrators like Fred Croxton, Rowland Haynes and Pierce Williams—supported professional standards of administration and norms of adequacy that prevailed in the social work community. But growing federal influence in state and local policy should not be seen primarily as a product of the influence of well-placed bureaucrats, who, at least initially, appear to have been quite willing to live within the restrictions imposed by the ERCA. The urban relief crisis forced RFC officials to expand the federal relief role well beyond what had originally been envisioned; the existence of a large federal fund served as a magnet for undeveloped regions with limited relief programs; and the need to encourage state relief appropriations and a more stable administration produced a more active federal welfare role.

By the time Franklin D. Roosevelt was inaugurated in March of 1933, every state, with the exception of Massachusetts, was dependent on federal aid for relief. Federal funds financed aid to roughly 5 million cases in March of 1933, the month when depression-induced unemployment peaked at nearly 13 million. Although benefit levels were wholly inadequate, the federal program had stabilized relief financing to the extent that abrupt cuts in caseloads and benefits were rare. While public and private organizations continued to distribute aid, the trend was clearly toward public agencies staffed by professional social workers. Local private financing, the essence of voluntarism, had virtually disappeared. Although the level of state funding was disappointing to RFC officials, the state relief role had expanded significantly since the previous years: most states had established emergency relief organizations to serve as conduits for federal aid. Perhaps most importantly, the ERCA appropriation was nearly exhausted, and the fiction that federal aid could be dispensed as "loans" to the states had virtually collapsed. Criticisms of the federal program at congressional hearings the previous winter—and the ad hoc activism of the RFC's relief division—had produced a consensus that federal aid should be distributed in the form of grants, with a federal welfare agency playing a more explicit regulatory role.[51]

Although the New Deal was less than enthusiastic with the "dole" it had inherited, the Roosevelt administration did not make reform of fed-

eral welfare policy a central goal of the "first 100 days." The RFC's relief
division continued to distribute aid to the states for two months while
new relief legislation worked its way through Congress. The Federal
Emergency Relief act, appropriating $500 million for relief grants to the
states, was delayed by a jurisdictional dispute within Congress over
which chamber should originate relief legislation.[52] After the law was
finally passed on May 10, Roosevelt waited nearly two weeks before
appointing a new administrator, a delay that produced a desperate appeal from the RFC's Fred Croxton for quick action. Harry Hopkins, the
new FERA director, faced a major relief crisis in May because the funds
from the earlier federal appropriation were exhausted, not because local
relief had collapsed, as is often supposed. The first grants approved by
Hopkins were based on agreements between the RFC's Fred Croxton and
the states.[53] The story of Hopkins' cutting through red tape to save local
relief with big new grants, which still frequently appears in histories of
the period, is highly misleading.

The mythology surrounding Hopkins' early days at FERA headquarters—he is often depicted dispensing large sums in federal aid from an
office cluttered with unopened file boxes—accurately reflects his style as
an aggressive, no-nonsense relief administrator. But it seriously distorts
the New Deal's relief philosophy and its early approach to federal aid
to the states. While FDR, as governor of New York, had initiated the
most ambitious state relief program in the nation, he had not been an
outspoken advocate of federal relief in late 1931. During the 1932 campaign he had spoken vaguely of the "forgotten man"—presumably the
unemployed worker—but did not attack Hoover's relief policy directly.
In the interregnum between the election and his inauguration he had
failed to endorse the grant approach to relief despite appeals from Progressives like LaFollette.[54] Although Roosevelt was eventually convinced
to support grants, the federal program inherited from Hoover was
clearly distasteful to him. Indeed, as president his initial pronouncement
on relief could barely be distinguished from that of his Republican predecessor:

The federal government, of course, does have to prevent anyone from starving,
but the federal government should not be called upon to exercise that duty until
all other agencies fail. The primary duty is that of the locality, the city, county,
town. If they should fail and cannot raise enough to meet the needs the next
responsibility is on the states and they have to do all they can. If it is still proven
that they cannot do any more and the funds are still insufficient, it is the duty
of the federal government to step in.[55]

Of course, the comparisons with Hoover should not be carried too far:
Roosevelt's attitude may have reflected benign disinterest, more than

ideological opposition, to federal programs for the unemployed. He spoke enthusiastically of the Civilian Conservation Corps (CCC), the agency that put unemployed youth to work in rural settings. "We can take a vast Army of these unemployed out into healthful surroundings," he told Congress, "[and] can eliminate to some extent at least the threat that enforced idleness brings to spiritual and moral stability."[56] One can detect, here, the values that produced the larger public employment experiments later in the New Deal. But the CCC, never designed to assist more than a small fraction of the national relief caseload, was something of a diversion from the crisis that was brewing in the existing federal relief program.

Unlike Roosevelt, new FERA administrator Harry Hopkins had endorsed grants and an expanded federal welfare role during congressional hearings the previous winter.[57] But his initial pronouncements as FERA administrator emphasized his personal distaste for relief as a response to unemployment. On the day he became administrator, Hopkins told a reporter that his primary goal was to do away with relief for the unemployed: "We will begin with the premise that direct relief is a bad thing." The administration, according to the *Survey*, considered relief "a miserable business necessary to tide people over an emergency but not to be continued a moment longer."[58] Eventually, these attitudes would lead to pioneering experiments with work relief, but during the spring and summer of 1933, the FERA's main goal seemed to be reducing the national relief caseload and the federal welfare role. New Deal officials did not believe such an approach would necessarily entail denying aid to needy recipients: there was a sincere belief that the New Deal's recovery program, embodied in the National Industrial Recovery Act, would significantly reduce unemployment. Furthermore, Hopkins believed that states could pick up a good deal more of the tab for relief. "Many of the states have plenty of money or could have sold bonds," he told the National Conference on Social Work. "The only reason for their not doing so is that they thought they could get money out of Washington."[59]

Thus, while the observation that the New Deal disliked relief would not surprise most historians, the degree to which these attitudes influenced the early policies of the FERA is not widely appreciated. Furthermore, even if Hopkins had wanted to expand federal relief, provisions of the Federal Emergency Relief Act would made such a policy problematic. Most informed observers considered the $500 million inadequate to finance the caseload inherited from the Hoover administration. Hopkins estimated that if federal spending continued at its present rate, the relief fund would be exhausted before Congress reconvened the following winter.[60] Furthermore, the formula for distributing aid was designed to encourage a reduced federal spending role. According to the relief law, half the appropriation was to be distributed by to a formula whereby each state would automatically receive quarterly grants equal to one-third of its relief expenditures. The remaining $250 million was held in a "discretionary fund" to be distributed according to need as determined by the relief administrator. The intent of the law appeared to be that the one-third matching grants should be distributed first, with the remainder to be held back for emergencies and to induce states to appropriate their own funds.[61] Yet this policy, if rigidly implemented, would have produce massive relief cutbacks since in most states federal funds financed well over half of the relief bill by the spring of 1933.

The first grants approved by Hopkins were made under the matching section of the Federal Emergency Relief Act. The FERA immediately made available to each state a sum equal to one-third of all public relief expenditures, including RFC "loans" for the first two months of 1933. States were requested to certify the dollar value of all relief distributed in March 1933, at which time the federal agency would release the remainder of the matching grant. No mention was made of loans from the discretionary fund at Hopkins' disposal.[62] The fact that the federal government was now providing only one-third of all relief expenditures could have produced an immediate relief crisis. This did not occur because states used the federal aid, calculated as a percentage of spending for two winter months, to finance relief in June only. Yet this level of federal reimbursement could not continue through the summer without producing massive cutbacks. To maintain relief at existing levels, matching funds would have to be supplemented either by grants from the "discretionary fund" or by new state appropriations. FERA officials informed states that applications in excess of the matching formula would not be approved unless they agreed to do more. Hopkins told a meeting of state relief officials that states "would not get a dime" from the discretionary fund unless they put up more of their own money. "Some states are due for a rude shock in the near future, if they do not come through with action," Hopkins warned in July. He later suggested that the FERA's goal during the coming months was for state appropriations to match the $500 million approved by Congress. To this end he called on governors to call legislatures into special session to provide funds for relief. Pierce Williams, a former RFC staff member employed by the FERA, explained the "new situation with respect to federal aid" to a relief administrator in Washington State: "I said that I believed it might be difficult for any state to convince the FERA of the justifiability of a grant out of the unrestricted fund unless it was prepared to do much more in its own behalf than had been done during the past ten months."[63]

Thus, the FERA, rather than opening the federal money spigot, hoped to take a harder line regarding state appropriations than the RFC. As a

result, Hopkins and other FERA officials spent most of the summer bick-
ering with the states over grants and appropriations. When Ohio applied
for a large grant from the discretionary fund in June, for example, the
FERA rejected the request because no state spending was listed on the
application. Providing funds under these conditions, Hopkins noted,
would mean that the FERA would be funding three-quarters of the
states' relief bill. FERA demands eventually forced a special session of
the legislature, which passed a $9 million relief bill, but not before federal
pressure nearly caused a major state relief crisis. Similarly, Hopkins
threatened Kentucky with a cutoff of relief after August 15, demanding
a special session of the state legislature. Washington State had passed a
relief appropriation the previous January, but the governor had earmarked the funds for public works, not relief. FERA field representative
Pierce Williams spent much of the summer and fall of 1933 attempting
to get the money directed to local relief.[64] Michigan, on the other hand,
passed a 3 percent sales tax to finance relief, and the Texas legislature
approved a bond issue for relief, subject to the approval of voters in a
statewide referendum. They were the first two states to receive grants
from the discretionary fund at Hopkins' disposal.[65]

Closely linked to the policy of increasing state funding was an effort
to reduce the national relief caseload. FERA officials hoped New Deal
recovery measures—particularly the National Industrial Recovery Act
and its offspring, the Public Works Administration—would jump-start
the economy, reducing unemployment and the need for relief. In the late
spring Hopkins told reporters that the "peak of relief needs is past" and
that the federal relief program would soon be supplanted by public
works. On June 10 the FERA administrator ordered all state relief administrations to "scrutinize their lists of relief cases classifying them by
occupations" in preparation for the start-up of the public works program.[66] The desire to reduce the role of relief eventually led the New
Deal to bold experiments in public employment and work relief, but
during the spring and summer of 1933 the FERA relied on more traditional mechanisms to cut the caseload: strengthening local relief administration, strict investigations of applicants and rigid application of the
means test. On June 14 Hopkins told state relief officials gathered in
Washington that New Deal recovery measures "will render it unnecessary for many on the relief rolls to continue receiving relief. This means,
and requires, frequent re-investigation of cases. The federal money will
not last through the coming winter if the load is permitted to rise from
its present peak."[67] Directives from the FERA to the states stressed the
need to strengthen local administrative machinery. To this end the federal agency issued detailed guidelines on local and state administration
during the summer of 1933. Local relief agencies were required to employ at least one "experienced" investigator and, for every twenty work-

ers, a supervisor, "trained and experienced in the essentials of family casework." Although a maximum caseload level was not established, staffing levels were to be sufficient to "insure reasonable investigation procedures." The FERA even issued guidelines concerning the investigation of recipients. Investigations were to include prompt and frequent home visits, a report on all assets and an interview with at least one recent employer.[68]

When states applied for grants during the summer of 1933, federal officials scrutinized the caseload data on applications. On June 19, for example, Hopkins wrote the head of the Ohio ERA about caseload increases in Cleveland during May 1933. Expressing concern that the number of relief recipients increased despite a decline in unemployment, he urged "that the relief lists be reviewed in order to be sure that persons obtaining employment at adequate wages are removed from the relief lists." Indeed, some of the policies encouraged by the FERA would appear, in retrospect, rather draconian. In supporting Pennsylvania's application for federal aid, field representative Robert Kelso reported that the hiring of new administrative personnel in one county had led to a dramatic decline in the caseload: 818 families had been removed from relief in two months, and new applications had declined 44 percent. In Philadelphia, he reported, thousands of applicants had been rejected "through effective interviews at application and thousands more following further investigation." A similar development was reported in Seattle, where federal aid allowed the city to replace its "volunteer service" with an expanded staff of professional home visitors. Here, the relief caseload was reduced from over 20,000 in April 1933, to approximately 11,000 by September. The head of the Illinois Emergency Relief Administration reported that "a great deal has been accomplished in Chicago and Cook County during the summer months in reducing the case load."[69] In Louisiana, on the other hand, federal officials saw caseload increases in the early fall as evidence that local relief administration was lax. "I am asking [the state ERA] to adopt an affidavit form such as we are using in Arkansas and Oklahoma," Aubrey Williams told Hopkins, "as a means of eliminating persons from the relief rolls and this is being done." Comparing Ohio's low percentage of unemployed receiving relief with the higher numbers in Kentucky, Pierce Atwater concluded that "the personnel standards insisted upon by Ohio has [sic] been the thing which has kept the caseload within reason and the lack of such standards in Kentucky is one of the reasons why it has gone as high as it has."[70]

Thus, early FERA appeared intent on strengthening what New Deal officials like Hopkins believed was one of the most objectionable aspects of the "dole"—the means testing and the resulting investigations of applicants by social workers. On the other hand, a central goal of the new policy was to raise standards for those on relief. The attitude of FERA officials, common among social workers, was that the stricter application of the means test would, in fact, benefit recipients: scarce funds could then be used for raising standards of aid. Hopkins' statements nearly always reflected this connection. At times, it is difficult to tell whether his frequent criticisms of the relief system reflected opposition to the large federal welfare role or to low standards of aid prevailing throughout the country. In June he told reporters that while the federal dole should be eliminated, those on relief were getting "woefully little": "We are not going to get all the 18,000,000 people in this country off relief this year. It seems to me that our job is first and foremost to see that these people continue to get relief."[71] At the same July conference at which he urged states to reduce their caseloads, he also demanded that they provide more adequate relief:

It will be the fixed policy of the federal organization to give relief which is adequate to the needs of those receiving it. While federal funds are not to be wasted, they are also not to be spent at a rate so low as to degrade the recipients thereof. No federal funds will be made available to States, for instance, which choose to expend them at the rate of $1.00 per family per week under a pretense that it is in accord with local standards. There is no place for miserable relief of that sort.[72]

In a 1935 report to Roosevelt on the history of the federal relief program, Hopkins suggested that the problem of adequacy was the "most important issue" facing New Deal officials when they took over the relief program of the RFC.[73]

The same "Rules and Regulations" that required strict investigation of applicants also defined adequacy of relief in terms consistent with the approach of more enlightened social workers. Adequacy was described as "sufficient relief to prevent physical suffering and to maintain minimum living standards." Although a national relief standard was not adopted, the memo explicitly stated that allowances should include funds for "shelter, the provision of fuel for cooking and for warmth when necessary, medical care and other necessities." On the controversial issue of rent, the FERA advised not only that rental payments be included in the relief budget but also that taxes or mortgage interest payments be considered in determining need.[74] To monitor the implementation of these guidelines, field statisticians employed by state relief administrations were directed to include detailed information on budgets and forms of relief in applications for federal aid. FERA officials showed a great deal of concern over inflation and its impact on food budgets. In September a Hopkins memo to the state ERAs expressed alarm at a survey that showed that retail food prices had increased 18 percent and called for a thorough review of food orders and costs. An October memorandum, which called on states to reinvestigate relief caseloads in preparation for the winter relief program, also directed that "a study should be made to determine whether [relief allowances] are sufficient to carry the unemployed through the coming months."[75]

The FERA's detailed directives on relief standards represented a significant change from the approach of the RFC's relief division. Yet the bottom line was money: how were real increases in benefits to be financed? In some cases FERA officials were willing to use federal dollars to raise local standards of aid. This was particularly true in rural states with benefits below $10 per month. Aubrey Williams' reports from the South reflect the concerns of FERA officials and their determination to improve standards of aid. Williams reported from Alabama that relief, averaging $8 to $9 per month, was "far from adequate measured by any decent standards." In recommending a bigger FERA grant, Williams stressed inadequate clothing, lack of basic medical care and the failure to pay rent. In October Williams wrote Hopkins that the governor of Louisiana would request an additional $125,000 "due to the increase in the [case]load and to putting in the standard of adequacy which we are insisting upon."[76] But in most cases the FERA's attitude was that funds to raise relief standards would have to come from new state appropriations and savings from caseload reductions. Ohio's June application for federal aid was based, in part, on the need to raise the average monthly allowance in the state from $15.55 to $20 but was initially rejected because the state contribution was not sufficient.[77] Thus, despite the more liberal federal policy, providing more adequate relief was primarily a state responsibility during the early months of the New Deal. As C.M. Bookman told the National Conference on Social Work in 1934, states "hesitated to apply the standard of relief set up by the FERA, because to do so would have been to increase the amount of money necessary to be raised by state taxes." Thus, despite increases in relief allowances in some states as a result of federal action, the average benefit was "still below any reasonable standard of relief."[78]

Implementation of the key FERA policies—reducing dependence on the "dole," encouraging a larger state welfare role and improving standards of aid—led to an unprecedented level of federal intervention in state and local policy making. The agency issued a steady stream of "rules and regulations" in early 1933 concerning the administration of relief funds. The first of these required that only "public" agencies distribute federal funds. Confusion over what precisely constituted a public agency—local ad hoc emergency committees continued to distribute relief through private agencies, some with religious affiliation—produced more detailed guidelines in July. The FERA stated that although a relief agency did not have to be a public welfare department, emergency committees had to be officially approved by state ERAs; workers borrowed from private agencies had to be city employees; buildings, records and forms had to bear the name of the relief agency and all bills were required to be paid directly by the relief organization, rather than channeled through existing private welfare organizations.[79] To many social workers, it appeared that FERA was using its temporary role as a grant-giving agency to modernize state and local relief in line with the goals of the public welfare movement. We have seen how the agency issued regulations defining adequate assistance and professional administration.

Another example is the FERA's "rules and regulations" covering the use of federal funds for transient relief. During the early years of the depression aid to this group—primarily homeless single men—had been characterized by the most archaic practices associated with "poor law relief" (work tests, unsupervised flophouses and breadlines). In July the FERA issued detailed regulations on the kinds of projects eligible for federal aid. The various categories of "homeless persons" were described, and a basic program of assistance and rehabilitation was outlined. The directives for the provision of shelter provide a good example of the regulatory role assumed by the federal agency:

Shelter of good quality for unattached males implies that casework service shall be available to all clients; that beds, bedding, balanced diet, medical service, work, recreation, laundry, bathing, barbering, and clothing shall be included in the program and that there shall be a proper segregation of men according to age, etc. Shelter for families, unattached women and girls and boys should be individualized according to need.[80]

The administrative role assumed by the FERA represented a significant advance over the policies of the relief division of the RFC; according to the agency's historian, Edward A. Williams, "the FERA attempted to assume a higher degree of control over state administration than had prior grant agencies." In retrospect the FERA was a crucial link in the expansion of federal administrative capacity in the public welfare field, a process that began with the Children's Bureau and culminated in the cabinet-level Department of Health and Human Services.[81] But a permanent federal welfare role was explicitly not the goal of Hopkins in 1933. "Our job is to see that the unemployed get relief," he told the 1933 National Conference on Social Work, "not to develop a great social work organization throughout the United States." "[Hopkins'] idea," according to a news report in the FERA files, "is that federal relief aid for the destitute should be mere makeshift pending enactment of a broad public works program so that those now receiving aid can get real constructive jobs."[82] Somewhat paradoxically, the FERA sought to use federal power to strengthen state and local relief administration so that it could get out of the picture. These attitudes produced a certain ad hoc quality to the FERA's operations. The FERA's "field representatives," most of them inherited from the RFC, did not initially have defined regions. Hopkins would send them into the field to resolve immediate crises, explain federal policies and report on local conditions. Although the agency expanded its staff of statisticians and required states applying for aid to fill out detailed forms, grants were often based on informal agreements between Hopkins and state officials.[83] The agency's free-wheeling approach to administration reflected the pragmatic, no-nonsense public image Harry Hopkins was cultivating. It also encouraged the abrupt policy shifts and the experimentalism for which the New Deal's relief program was famous. "I am for experimenting with this fund in various parts of the country, trying out schemes which are supported by reasonable people to see if they work," he told the 1933 National Conference on Social Work, adding that he didn't think anyone clearly understood this "relief business."[84]

But behind Hopkins' casual, shoot-from-the-hip style were central policy goals—eliminate the federal dole by cutting the national relief caseload and forcing a large state relief role, while improving standards of aid and strengthening relief administration. How successful was the early New Deal in achieving its goals? The biggest success, if we are to rely strictly on statistical policy measures, was the reduction of the national relief caseload, which fell from approximately 5 million recipients at the beginning of the New Deal to well under 4 million in September. Much of this decline can probably be explained by the reduction in unemployment during the summer of 1933, but there is a good deal of evidence that FERA policy encouraged local caseload reductions as well. In Washington, to take an extreme example, the caseload fell from 91,245 in June to under 50,000 in September due to federally induced cuts.[85]

Since total spending for relief did not decline during the summer, the caseload reductions appear to have freed funds for higher standards of aid. According to the FERA data, average benefits rose to over twenty-five dollars per month in September, an increase of approximately 25 percent. But these standards remained well below levels advocated by social work leaders who had lobbied for federal grants. Furthermore, the statistical increase in benefits was offset by inflation, as commodity prices increased significantly during the recovery of the summer of 1933.[86]

Problems in raising relief standards help explain why the FERA, somewhat grudgingly, began to distribute surplus agricultural commodities in September of 1933. Responding to a public outcry over the mass slaughter of pigs, part of the Agricultural Adjustment Administration's program to raise agricultural prices by limiting production, the New Deal established he Federal Surplus Relief Corporation (FSRC) as an adjunct to the FERA. The FSRC began distributing pork in the fall of 1933, and its program eventually expanded to include other forms of "in kind" relief (including providing materials for production in FERA workshops). The commodity program proved to be an inexpensive and effective way to both raise relief standards and subsidize agriculture. But for relief officials and social workers who had waged a strong campaign against public commissaries during the RFC period, this was a retreat to the worst form of "in kind" relief.[87]

Another key goal of FERA policy, increasing the level of state relief expenditures, showed mixed results. State financing increased during the summer and early fall of 1933, from approximately $8 million in May to over $14 million in November. But the federal relief role was not reduced significantly.[88] The increase in state funding was offset by a decline in local expenditures and was far short of the amount needed to allow states to assume half the relief funding burden, Hopkins' goal at the beginning of the summer. FERA demands on states were undermined by precisely the same problem that had confronted the RFC: efforts to force state appropriations by withholding funds produced a major crisis for which federal officials would be held responsible. In Washington, the FERA, confronted with the potential collapse of local relief, was forced to give a section C (discretionary) grant for August and September despite the limited state relief role. Other states were slow to implement legislation that had been passed under federal pressure, and tax revenues were often disappointing. Michigan, for example, agreed to finance a large portion of its relief bill through state sales and "weight" taxes, but by November 1933 the funds had "not materialized."[89] Obstacles to increased funding for relief were even more formidable in rural states. The agency sent an expert in public finance to Louisiana to evaluate the state's "ability to bear a reasonable cost of relief work" but was forced to send discretionary funds to the state because preliminary reports indicated the state was in "a very difficult financial situation." In early August the FERA approved a discretionary grant of $1.5 million to Alabama, which had appropriated virtually no state funds for relief, with the warning that "further grants of federal funds will depend on action taken by Alabama."[90] Thus, while the FERA was somewhat successful in using federal power in the form of discretionary grants to increase the state spending for relief, this did not have the effect of reducing the federal welfare role. Quite the contrary, federal officials, like their predecessors in the RFC's relief division, were drawn into state-level political conflicts over relief as a result of their financial demands on the states.[91]

A similar generalization would seem to apply to the effort to modernize administrative capacity. The FERA's rules and regulations led to the hiring of more social workers; professional administrators replaced politically connected poor law officials; localities that had resisted the trend toward public welfare were required to create new public agencies to handle FERA funds. State emergency relief organizations, although maintaining their "temporary" status, began to function more like welfare departments and exercised much more control over local policies. The use of grants greatly accelerated trends that had begun under the RFC. Most social workers viewed the early months of the FERA as a great advance for public welfare movement (Gertrude Springer, the *Survey*'s relief columnist, later called this period a "social worker bull market").[92] But the expansion of state and local administrative capacity does not appear to have reduced the federal relief role. On the contrary, there developed a phenomenon that William R. Brock has astutely called "parallel government," whereby the informal relationships between state and local officials and the FERA made the former appear as extensions of federal authority:

In the operation of parallel government, personal ties and assumptions were more important than official relationships. Many of the key officials in state and county relief agencies were trained social workers. Shared experiences and identical sympathies bound them to their federal counterparts and separated them from the old breed of locally elected poor law officials.[93]

But "parallel government" was not the welfare policy of the New Deal. Thus, by the late summer, although FERA officials could certainly see significant improvements over the program inherited from the RFC, there was little evidence that federal relief was in the process of being phased out. Recovery had been sluggish, and few recipients were finding jobs in the public works program (Harold Ickes' PWA). The relief caseload threatened to increase significantly during the coming winter, wiping out the gains made during the FERA's early months. Key elements of the New Deal's recovery program exacerbated relief problems. The National Recovery Administration's (NRA) price guidelines tended to encourage inflation, which reduced the real value of increases in relief standards; the Agricultural Adjustment Administration's efforts to raise agricultural prices by reducing acreage threw many poor tenant farmers off the land (and onto the relief rolls).[94] Furthermore, although the FERA had pressed states to eliminate ineligible cases through strict investigation of recipients, federal officials, like many social workers in 1933, were uncomfortable with the policy of subjecting unemployed workers to the means test. The detailed application forms, interviews and frequent investigations that FERA guidelines promoted were clearly among the worst features of the existing "dole."[95] Equally demoralizing was the absence of employment in a culture that valued work. This point had been frequently emphasized by Hopkins, but even among more conservative social worriers and welfare officials a consensus was developing that protracted unemployment and dependence on relief undermined workers' self-esteem and threatened family stability.[96]

One solution to this problem was work relief—the policy of providing employment to recipients, with "wages" calculated to conform to relief allowances. Hopkins had been associated with this approach to unemployment relief throughout his career, from his first job administering work relief in New York during the recession of 1914, to his tenure at New York's Temporary Emergency Relief Administration. There had been unprecedented experimentation with work relief during the Hoover years, and the FERA encouraged this trend from the outset.[97] A work division, directed by Jacob Baker, had been created during the summer to encourage local work experiments and find employment for recipients in other federal agencies. Fiscal constraints limited the impact of Baker's program—the FERA simply did not have the funds to bankroll a significant expansion of work relief—but there was now a constituency within the FERA for public employment. By October, tentative plans were being developed by the work division to expand work relief during the coming winter. The division increased its staff, began to issue guidelines for local projects and more aggressively sought funding for projects in federal agencies. In October Jacob Baker's assistant, Tex Goldschmidt, convinced Rexford Tugwell, then a close adviser to Roosevelt, that PWA funds might be used to finance supervision on federal projects.[98]

But the real breakthrough was a plan and rationale developed by Aubrey Williams, one of Hopkins' "field men." A savvy, articulate, southern liberal who had been a field representative of the American Public Welfare Association during the RFC period, Williams' outspoken advocacy of more generous relief payments and his impatience with the traditionalists in the social work community led to a close relationship with Hopkins at the top of the FERA.[99] By the early fall of 1933 Williams had developed the view that federal funds should finance work relief and that direct relief should be returned to state administration. By creating a full-fledged public employment program, the New Deal could at once raise relief standards for most recipients and eliminate the direct dole. Such a program, which would involve a big increase in federal spending, would also provide an economic stimulus during the winter of 1933–1934 and serve as a transition to employment in public works. Expanding on Goldschmitd's proposal to Tugwell, Williams suggested that the program could be funded by the large, unexpended balances held by Harold Ickes' slowly moving Public Works Administration; workers would then be paid according to public works wage rates, rather than relief allowances. Unemployed workers would essentially be pulled out of the existing relief system.[100] The beauty of Williams' proposal was that, while it represented a significant expansion of federal aid to the unemployed, it appeared consistent with the central goal of New Deal policy articulated by Hopkins in May—the elimination of federal relief. An added benefit was that the plan could be implemented without immediate congressional action simply by transferring funds from the PWA.

In late October Williams prevailed on a somewhat skeptical Hopkins to propose the plan to Roosevelt. A rather sketchy outline of a program employing 4 million workers was prepared during a trip to the Midwest; Hopkins returned to Washington and presented it to Roosevelt on October 29. To the FERA administrator's apparent shock, FDR immediately accepted the plan and agreed to finance it with public works funds. (Hopkins later told a biographer that he left the meeting with Roosevelt "walking on air.")[101] The result was the CWA, one of the most radical and dramatic public policy experiments of the New Deal era.

NOTES

1. For important discussions of the evolution of the term "welfare" see Linda Gordon, *Pitied but Not Entitled* (New York: Free Press, 1994), 1–2; Michael Katz, *Improving Poor People* (Princeton, NJ: Princeton University Press, 1995), 19–20, 24.

2. On the Hoover administration's use of the term see *New York Times*, December 13, 1930, 2; December 18, 1930; April 14, 1931, 12; Josephine Brown, *Public Relief, 1929–1939* (New York: Henry Holt and Co., 1940), 105. Harry Hopkins, in a report to Roosevelt in late 1935 on the history of the FERA, noted that "the greater part of relief [in May of 1933] was extended as direct relief, or the dole." New Deal officials avoided the term in the early months of the FERA but used it more frequently as justification for the transition from federal relief to the work program (WPA) in 1934. Hopkins to Roosevelt, "Genesis, History and Results of the Federal Relief Program," August 23, 1935, FERA Files, Box 2, same File as title. See also " 'Relief Can't Last,' Hopkins Warning," Press Clip: May 23, 1933, Federal Emergency Relief Administration—Old Subject File.

3. Thus, for example, Robert Kelso reported that the governor of Rhode Island was "determined in the application of these federal relief funds to keep it out of the 'pauper aid' channel and free from the ruts and dole-like processes of that kind of aid." RFC Files, Box 93, Rhode Island Correspondence File. See also Gertrude Springer, "The New Deal and the Old Dole," *Survey Graphic* 22, no. 7 (July 1933): 347.

4. Organizations of the unemployed.

5. Edward A. Williams, *Federal Aid for Relief* (New York: Columbia University Press, 1939), 48–49; Brown, *Public Relief 1929–1939*, 126; Donald S. Watson, "The Reconstruction Finance Corporation," in Clarence E. Ridley and Orin F. Woltin, eds., *The Municipal Yearbook* (Chicago: International City Manager's Association, 1937), 375.

6. See, for example, Clarke Chambers, *Seedtime of Reform: American Social Service and Social Action, 1918–1933* (Minneapolis: University of Minnesota Press, 1963), 202; Charles H. Trout, "Welfare in the New Deal Era," *Current History* 65 (July–December 1973): 11; Walter I Trattner, *From Poor Law to Welfare State*, 6th ed. (New York: Free Press, 1979), 280–284; Frances Fox Piven and Richard A.

Cloward, *Regulating the Poor: The Functions of Public Welfare* (New York: Random House, 1971), 56. The negative view of the RFC's relief program is based on accounts of federal relief policy by former employees of the New Deal's FERA. See in particular Brown, *Public Relief, 1929–1939*, 126; Williams, *Federal Aid for Relief*, 49–57. See also Springer, "The New Deal and the Old Dole," 348–349.

7. The best recently published account of the RFC's relief role is William R. Brock, *Welfare, Democracy and the New Deal* (Cambridge: Cambridge University Press, 1986), ch. 4. See also Jeff Singleton, "Unemployment Relief and the Welfare State" (Ph.D. diss., Boston University, 1986). My dissertation is digested in Udo Sautter, *Three Cheers for the Unemployed* (Cambridge: Cambridge University Press, 1991), 311. For an account of early New Deal relief policy that stresses Harry Hopkins' efforts to reduce the federal relief role see George McJimsey, *Harry Hopkins, Ally of the Poor and Defender of Democracy* (Cambridge, MA: Harvard University Press, 1987), 53–54. Searle F. Charles' older account of early New Deal relief policy also stresses Hopkins' efforts to force states to share the relief burden but creates the impression that the FERA was the first federal relief program. Searle F. Charles, *Minister of Relief: Harry Hopkins and the Depression* (Syracuse, NY: Syracuse University Press, 1963), ch. 2.

8. Roger Biles, *A New Deal for the American People* (De Kalb: Northern Illinois University Press, 1991), 97; Robert S. McElvaine, *The Great Depression*, 2nd ed. (New York: Times Books, 1993), 151; Gordon, *Pitied but Not Entitled*, 187–189; Katz, *Improving Poor People*, 51–52; James T. Patterson, *America's Struggle against Poverty*, 3rd ed. (Cambridge, MA: Harvard University Press, 1994), 57.

9. "The RFC Goes Democratic," *Literary Digest* 114, no. 6 (August 13, 1932): 6; Williams, *Federal Aid for Relief*, 56; Springer, "The New Deal and the Old Dole," 349.

10. Henry Root Stern to Charles Stuart Guthrie, September 19, 1932, RFC Files, Box 70, File: New York State Correspondence, Part 1. The problems caused by this requirement were compounded by the fact that the loans were to be deducted from highway funds, which tended to benefit rural areas. Since relief money primarily benefited urban areas, state legislatures were often split over the need to apply for federal aid. See the testimony of Paul Betters in U.S. Congress, Senate, Committee in Manufactures, *Federal Aid for Unemployment Relief*, Hearings on Sec. 5125, 72nd Cong., 2nd sess., January 3–February 13, 1933, 204–205.

11. Unemployment Committee of the State of Louisiana, "Minutes of Meeting with Rowland Haynes," August 5, 1932, RFC Files, Box 39, File: Louisiana Loan 1 Document File; RFC Minutes, July 30, 1932, 1208; *New York Times*, January 20, 1933, clip in RFC Files, Box 70, File: New York Correspondence, Part I; Gertrude Springer, "How Federal Relief Gets into Action," *Survey* 58, no. 14 (October 15, 1932): 506–507. Atlee Pomerene, chairman of the RFC, denied that the agency had ever had a policy of stretching the ERCA appropriation to last for two years on the Senate. See Senate Committee on Manufactures, *Federal Aid for Unemployment Relief* (1933), 305.

12. *New York Times*, September 4, 1932, 8; October 10, 1932, 11; October 19, 1932, 34; Joint Committee on Unemployment, "Dear Friend" Letter (Undated), RFC Files, Box 38, Louisiana Correspondence File, Part 2.

13. Senate Committee on Manufactures, Federal Aid for Unemployment Re-

lief (1933), 26 (Frank Bane), 133 (Prof. Sumner H. Slichter), 205, 209 (Paul Betters). *New York Times*, January 4, 1933, 9; January 11, 1933, 6; January 12, 1933, 2. On the social work effort to transform the federal relief role see Gertrude Springer, "A Platform for Public Relief," *The Survey* 68, no. 12 (December 15, 1932): 681.

14. RFC Minutes (August 2–4, 1932); *Philadelphia Ledger*, August 6, 1932, in Box 91, Pennsylvania News Clips File and Pinchot to Pomerene, August 19, 1932, Box 88, Pennsylvania Correspondence, Part 1, both in RFC Files; *New York Times*, August 3, 1932, 2; August 5, 1932, 1; August 8, 1932, 1.

15. For Correspondence re Pennsylvania's Loan see RFC Files, Box 88, Correspondence, Part 1 File. For documentation on the state's first loan see Box 89, Loan no. 1, Document File. For local news clips on the Pennsylvania controversy and the relief crisis in Philadelphia see Box 91, Pennsylvania News Clips File (particularly *Philadelphia Enquirer*, September 9, 1932, and *Philadelphia Ledger* editorial, September 22, 1932).

16. See Chapter 1, Tables 1 and 2. For raw data see Emma A. Winslow, *Trends in Different Types of Public and Private Relief in Urban Areas, 1929–1935* (Children's Bureau Publication no. 237) (Washington, DC: Government Printing Office, 1937), 69–71; Federal Works Agency, *Final Statistical Report of the Federal Emergency Relief Administration* (Washington, DC: Government Printing Office, 1942), 88.

17. Brown, *Public Relief*, 126; Williams, *Federal Aid for Relief*, 49.

18. Reconstruction Finance Corporation, *Quarterly Report* (April 1–June 30, 1933): 26–27.

19. Reconstruction Finance Corporation, *Minutes*, vol. 7 [hereafter RFC Minutes] (July 27, 1932), 1067 and (August 18, 1932), 897–903; RFC Files Box 26, Illinois Loan no. 1, Document File.

20. Illinois Loans 3–4 Document Files. Box 26, RFC Files. See especially Croxton recommendation for November (dated October 27) in Loan no. 4, Document File. He estimated that 98 percent of the funds for relief of the city's 146,000 recipients in September came from the RFC.

21. For sharp critique of Section E Loans see Paul Betters Testimony, Senate Committee on Manufactures, Federal Aid for Unemployment Relief (1933), 206–207.

22. All data re Detroit is on applications and supporting documents in RFC Files, Unnumbered "Michigan" Box, Detroit Correspondence File. See also Senate Committee on Manufactures, *Federal Aid for Unemployment Relief* (1933), 207; Sidney Fine, *Frank Murphy: The Detroit Years* (Ann Arbor: University of Michigan Press, 1975), 366–370.

23. For documentation on the first RFC loan to Pennsylvania see RFC Files Box 89, Pennsylvania Loans 1–4, Document File. For a critique of RFC short-term loan policy see *Philadelphia Ledger*, October 29, 1932, in same file. See also Box 91, Pennsylvania News clips File, especially *Philadelphia Enquirer*, September 9, 1932, and *Philadelphia Ledger*, September 22, 1932.

24. Estimates of the percentage of federal relief in Pittsburgh and Philadelphia based on data on Loans no. 5, Document File in Pennsylvania Box 89; for the October loan see RFC Minutes, vol. 9, part 1 (October 7, 1932).

25. Ohio: RFC Minutes, vol. 7, part 1 (August 3, 1932), part 2 (August 18, 1932); RFC Files, Boxes 78–83, Loans 1–20, Document Files. Michigan: RFC

Minutes, vol. 8, part 2 (September 24, 1932), vol. 9, part 2 (October 15, 1932). West Virginia: RFC Files, Box 120, Loan no. 1, Document File. Kentucky: RFC Minutes, vol. 7, part 2 (September 23, 1932); Illinois: Box 26, Illinois Loan no. 1 Correspondence File.

26. Louisiana: RFC Minutes, vol. 7, part 2 (August 16, 1932), vol. 8, part 2 (September 30, 1932); RFC Files Box 39, Louisiana Loans 1–3, Document Files. Virginia: RFC Minutes, vol. 8, part 1, (September 1, 1932).

27. South Dakota: RFC Minutes, vol. 7 part 2, August 25, 1932. Oklahoma: RFC Minutes, vol. 9, part 2, (October 15, 1932). Edward Shannon LaMonte, *Politics and Welfare in Birmingham, 1900–1975* (Tuscaloosa: University of Alabama Press, 1995), 119.

28. RFC Files, Box 48, Michigan Loan no. 28, Document File; Box 53, Loans 42 and 44, Document File; Joanna Colcord and Russell Kurtz, "Unemployment Relief in the South," *Survey* 69 (April 1933): 168–139. See also RFC Minutes, vol. 8, part 2 (September 16, 1932), 617.

29. For example, out of approximately $8.8 million estimated as expenditures for relief in the city in February, the RFC financed over $3.3 million, the city government provided $3 million and the state share was estimated at $758,100. The remainder was listed under the category "contributions" on the application to the RFC. RFC Files, Box 70, New York Loans 1–3, Document File. For California's first application see Box 11, California Loans 1–2, Document Files. California's initial application, approved on January 13 for $281,372, was to provide funds for transient relief in so-called state labor camps. This was an unprecedented loan, and the agency does not appear to have required the state to use the normal application form. Loan no. 2, on January 27, was for 1.8 million and was used primarily in Los Angeles County.

30. Croxton to Major E.O. Braught, February 6, 1933, RFC Files, Box 77, File: Ohio Correspondence Part 2; Croxton Testimony, Senate Committee on Manufactures, Federal Aid for Unemployment Relief (1933), 322.

31. Louisiana: RFC Files, Box 40, Louisiana Loan no. 2, Document File, Part 1. W. Virginia: see Neiburg Memos on relief budgets in West Virginia Counties, RFC Files, Box 120, Loan no. 1, Document File and Haynes to Croxton, August 29–30; Box 121, W. Virginia Correspondence File.

32. Croxton Memo, RFC Files, Box 26, Illinois Loan no. 4 Document File.

33. The RFC did not have an official policy on the form local relief should take, but the relief division appears to have been sympathetic to the statewide experiment in Pennsylvania. See Robert Kelso to Croxton, December 22, 1932, RFC Files, Pennsylvania Loan Correspondence File: February–March; News Clips on Commissary Debate in Pennsylvania, Box 91, Loans 1–3 News Clips File; Q and A on Commissaries, January 30, 1933, Box 79, Cleveland, Alliance and Niles Correspondence Files, both in RFC Files. For social work critiques of commissaries see Margaret Wead, "Penny-Wise Relief," *Survey* 68, no. 12 (September 15, 1932): 419–420; Julius Amberg, "Scrip-Wise and Pound Foolish," *Survey* 68, no. 16 (November 15, 1933): 597. For a defense of commissaries see A.M. Luntz, "Canton's Commissary Store," *Survey* 68, no. 16 (November 15, 1932): 588. On the demise of the commissary movement see *Survey* 69, no. 10 (October 15, 1933): 348, 361.

34. Philadelphia: estimate of relief standards made on Pennsylvania Loan no.

3 (November 4, 1932), Document File. Cook County: Wilfred Reynolds, *Proceedings of the National Conference on Social Work* [hereafter NCSW] (Chicago: University of Chicago Press, 1933), 511. St. Louis: memo from Walter Burr re St. Louis County, December 21, 1932; RFC Files Box 60, Missouri Loan no. 9, Document File.

35. West Virginia: Haynes to Croxton, August 29–20, 1933, Box 120, Loan, no. 1, Document File. Texas: see memo by Robert Kelso, RFC Files, Box 103, Texas Correspondence File. Rhode Island: Box 93, Rhode Island Loan no. 1, Document File.

36. Brown, *Public Relief, 1929–1939*, 128–131; Williams, *Federal Aid for Relief*, 56; Brock, *Welfare, Democracy and the New Deal*, 139.

37. For a critical analysis of state relief organization under the RFC see Margaret Klein to Emma Winslow, April 6, 1933, Children's Bureau Files, Box 538, File 12-7-4 (0) "General." For an example of the RFC's official hands-off attitude toward local relief organization see exchange of letters between Vincent Stevens of the Akron Chamber of Commerce and Fred Croxton in RFC Files, Box 76, Ohio Correspondence File, Part 1.

38. *New York Times*, July 20, 1932, 1; August 3, 1932, 1; RFC Minutes, vol. 6, part 2 (July 30, 1932); Unemployment Relief Committee of Louisiana, Minutes of Meeting with Rowland Haynes (August 5, 1932), Box 39, Loan no. 1 Document File; Williams, *Federal Aid for Relief*, 53–55; Brown, *Public Relief, 1929–1939*, 125.

39. For example, Fred Croxton reported that a number of counties in West Virginia applying for federal aid in January had "never organized for relief work" and that "records showing what has been done for relief are almost nonexistent." Box 121, West Virginia Loan no. 7, Document File. On October 15, 1932, Robert Kelso wired Fred Croxton that he had examined thirty-eight applications from Texas counties: "Will work all day today and tomorrow on West Texas data," Box 102, Texas Correspondence File, Part 1.

40. Louisiana: RFC Minutes, vol. 7, no. 2 (August 16, 1932), 792–794; South Carolina: RFC Files, Box 94, Loans 1, 3, Document Files.

41. RFC Files, Box 106, Loan no. 9, Document File.

42. Michigan: Croxton recommendation on Michigan loan, RFC Files, Box 50, Loan no. 34, Document File, Part 1.

43. Minnesota: RFC Files, Box 53, Minnesota Correspondence File [quote is from Ewing to Croxton, February 25, 1933]. Texas: Mirriam W. Fergeson to A.W. McMillen (February 27, 1933) in RFC files, Box 103, Correspondence File, Part 2. See also Box 108 Loans 11–13, Document Files.

44. Jeanette Elder, "A Study of One Hundred Applicants for Relief in the Fourth Winter of Unemployment" (Master's thesis, University of Chicago, 1933), 9–11. Elder considered the number of professionally trained workers in the district "pitifully small," despite the increase. According to a memo in the RFC Files, 1,195 workers and caseworkers in Cook County were being paid by federal funds in September of 1932, a development that does not appear to have been in accordance with RFC policy. See RFC Files, Box 2, Illinois Loan no. 4, Document File.

45. John F. Bauman, "The City, the Depression and Relief: The Philadelphia Experience, 1929–1939" (Ph.D. diss., Rutgers University, 1969); Brock, *Welfare, Democracy and the New Deal*, 142, 146.

46. Rowland Haynes, "Visit to New Orleans, August 7, 1937," Box 41, Loan no. 5, Document File.

47. "Report of Los Angeles County, California" (July 30 1934), Federal Emergency Relief Administration Files, Box 26, California Field Reports File; see also Croxton loan recommendation (May 1, 1933) in RFC files, Box 11, California Loan no. 7, Document File; Bonnie Fox Schwartz, "Social Workers and New Deal Politicians in Conflict: California's Brannon–Williams Case, 1933–1934," *Pacific Historical Review* 43 (February 1973): 55–56.

48. Rhode Island: see letters in RFC, Box 93, Rhode Island Correspondence File. Michigan: RFC Files, Box 51, Michigan Loan no. 39, Document File. Fred Croxton also demanded that, as a precondition for its March 1933 loan, the "supervisory and investigatory staff of the Detroit Welfare Department be materially strengthened." The salaries of trained caseworkers, selected "without regard to the civil service restrictions as is set up by the City of Detroit," were paid by RFC funds. "Memo from Ballinger, February 25, 1933, Box 51, Loan 35, Document File.

49. Undated news clip on history of relief in King County, FERA [not RFC] Files, Box 306, Washington Field Reports 2, File; John Arthur Hogan, "The Decline of Self-Help and the Growth of Radicalism among Seattle's Organized Unemployed" (Master's thesis, University of Washington, 1934), 43–44; Bruce Blumell, *The Development of Public Assistance in the State of Washington during the Great Depression* (New York: Garland, 1984), 89–91. In both Washington and Pennsylvania the effort to reform local relief began in response to a state relief appropriation and preceded the receipt of federal aid.

50. Eleanor Kahn, "Organizations of the Unemployed as a Factor in the American Labor Movement" (Master's thesis, University of Wisconsin, 1934), 67.

51. On attempts to amend the ERCA during the congressional session that began in December 1932 see *New York Times*, January 1, 1933, II, 11; January 23, 1933, 1; February 7, 1932, 7; February 17, 1933, 6; J. Joseph Huthmacher, *Senator Robert F. Wagner and the Rise of Urban Liberalism* (New York: Atheneum, 1968), 127–129; Fred Greenbaum, *Fighting Progressive: A Biography of Edward P. Costigan* (Washington, DC: Public Affairs Press, 1971), 133; Brock, *Welfare, Democracy and the New Deal*, 161–169.

52. On the legislative history of the FERA see *New York Times*, March 15, 1933, 1. For a good discussion of the origins of the FERA see John Joseph Wallis, "Work Relief and Unemployment in the 1930s" (Ph.D. diss., University of Washington, 1981).

53. *New York Times*, May 10, 1933, 4; May 20, 1933, 5; May 23, 1933, 21; May 30, 1933, 13. For Croxton appeal to FDR re the new FERA administrator see Memo re Telephone Call from Croxton, May 15, 1933, and FDR Telegram to Hopkins, May 19, 1933, both in Hopkins Papers, Official File 444, FERA, January–August 1933. See also Springer, "The New Deal and the Old Dole," 347. On Hopkins and the RFC grants see "Don't Quote Me," undated U.P. news clip in FERA (Old Subject Series), Box 17, Hopkins Press Clips File: "Mr. Hopkins immediately recognized emergency conditions, however, and accepted the decision of Fred Croxton, who was making the relief advances for the Reconstruction Finance Corporation, that a total of $5,336,317 be made available immediately."

54. At a meeting with LaFollette and Bronson Cutting, Roosevelt gave the

senators' bill, which called for grants and an emergency relief board to replace the RFC, "a very attentive and sympathetic hearing. So far as his general attitude was concerned, it was very gratifying." *New York Times*, January 23, 1933, 1. For a discussion of FDR's relief philosophy that stresses the similarities with that of Hoover see Charles, *Minister of Relief*, 19–21.

55. Franklin D. Roosevelt, "Address before the Governors Conference at the White House" (March 6, 1933), in Samuel L. Rosenman, ed., *The Public Papers and Addresses of Franklin D. Roosevelt*, vol. 2 (New York: Random House, 1938), 19–20. As William Brock notes, Edith Abbott called Roosevelt's statement "[P]robably the most reactionary pronouncement that has come from the White House since the New Deal was inaugurated." Brock, *Welfare, Democracy and the New Deal*, 172.

56. Franklin D. Roosevelt, "Three Essentials for Unemployment Relief" (March 21, 1933), in *The Public Papers and Addresses of Franklin D. Roosevelt*, vol. 2, 80–81. This was FDR's message to Congress on the Public Works Administration, the CCC and the FERA.

57. McJimsey, *Harry Hopkins*, 51; Brown, *Public Relief*, 140–141.

58. *New York Times*, May 23, 1933, 1; Russell Kurtz, "Two Months of the New Deal in Federal Relief," *Survey* 69, no. 8 (August 1933): 284.

59. Harry Hopkins, "The Developing National Program of Relief," NCSW, 1933, 68; Springer, "The New Deal and the Old Dole," 350–351; Charles, *Minister of Relief*, 32–43.

60. During the congressional debate over the new relief measure, LaFollette had argued that the relief bill for the coming year would be close to $1 billion. Hopkins, in his review of the FERA's history, made a similar estimate, noting that the "$500,000,000 made available [under the Federal Emergency Relief Act], was thus adequate only for a period of six months." The *Survey*'s Paul Kellogg, noting that the relief law fell short of the expectations of social workers, reported "no sound basis" for assuming that the fund would last any longer than the ERCA appropriation. Costigan Testimony in U.S. Congress, House, Committee on Banking and Currency, *Unemployment Relief*, Hearings on HR4606, April 11–18, 1933, 49; "Federal Emergency Relief Grants to the States," FERA-OSF, Box 2, File: same as title; Paul U. Kellogg, "Get Help Through," *Survey* 69, no. 6 (June 1933): 211; Hopkins, "The Developing National Program of Relief" NCSW, 1933.

61. Williams, *Federal Aid for Relief*, 183–184; Kurtz, "Two Months of the New Deal in Federal Relief," 285. Alan Burns, of the Association of Community Chests and Councils, had told a congressional committee that the relief administrator "would require that [states] come in with matching money before they come in with their discretionary money. I feel that the states will be compelled in the best way that the federal government has found of compelling states, to make appropriations to share the burden." House Committee on Banking and Currency, *Unemployment Relief*, 73rd Cong., 1st sess., April 1933, 90.

62. Doris Carothers, *Chronology of the Federal Emergency Relief Administration*, WPA Research Monograph no. 6 (Washington, DC: Government Printing Office, 1937), 2–3; *New York Times*, May 30, 1933, 13; June 4, 1933, 24.

63. Executive Committee of the Board of Directors of the Louisiana Emergency Relief Administration, Report of Meeting with Hopkins (June 22, 1933);

Pierce Williams to Hopkins, June 1, 1933, FERA Files, Box 306, File: Washington Field Reports; Kurtz, "Two Months of the New Deal in Federal Relief," 285.

64. Ohio: See exchange of letters between Hopkins and Ohio officials in FERA, Box 222, File: Ohio May–December 1933; David Maurer, "Public Relief Programs and Politics in Ohio" (Ph.D. diss., Ohio State University, 1962), 126–129. Washington: Pierce Williams to Harry Hopkins, July 25, 1933, and October 18, 1933, in FERA Files, Box 306, Field Reports 2 File; Blumell, *The Development of Public Assistance in the State of Washington*, 122–143.

65. See letters in FERA, Box 137, File: Michigan Field Reports 2; Kurtz, "Two Months of the New Deal," 285–286.

66. "Don't Quote Me"; Springer, "The New Deal and the Old Dole," 352.

67. Executive Committee of the . . . Emergency Relief Commission of the State of Louisiana, Report of Meeting with Hopkins June, 14, 1933, 1. In October Hopkins sent a memo to state ERAs calling on them to "have every case on your lists reviewed to the end that every family or person not entitled to unemployment relief be dropped." Hopkins memo to ERAs, October 20, 1933, FERA, Box 12, File: January–November.

68. FERA Rules and Regulations no. 3 (July 11, 1933), FERA Old Subject File, Box 12. See also Carothers, *Chronology of the Federal Emergency Relief Administration*, 7–8.

69. Ohio: Hopkins to General F.D. Henderson, June 19, 1933, FERA, Box 222, File: Ohio May–December 1933. Pennsylvania: Robert Kelso Report to Hopkins re Pennsylvania, June 29, 1933. Seattle: Claude Arnold, "Review of Emergency Relief Activities of King County [Seattle] Welfare Board," University of Washington Library–Pacific Northwest Collection, 7–8, 30–31. Illinois: Wilfred S. Reynolds [Illinois ERA director] to Hopkins, October 25, 1933.

70. Louisiana: Aubrey Williams to Hopkins, October 19, 1933, FERA, Box 114, "Field Reports" File. Ohio: Pierce Atwater to Hopkins, March 9, 19344, FERA, Box 224, "Ohio" Field Reports. FERA official Robert S. Myers made a similar observation comparing the high percentages of the population on relief in some poorly organized, downstate Illinois counties with Chicago, where relief was on a "scientific basis." Myers to Corrington Gill, April 12, 1934, FERA Files, Box 76, File: Illinois, January–May 1934.

71. *New York Sun*, June 23, 1933, in FERA-OSF, Box 17, File: Newspaper Accounts of Dinner Given in Honor of Mr. Hopkins.

72. Louisiana State Relief Committee, "Report of Meeting with Hopkins."

73. H.H. to the President, "Genesis, History and Results of the Federal Emergency Relief Program" (August 23, 1935), FERA 69, Old Subject File, Box 2 File: same as title. See also transcript of speech to Millbank Memorial Fund, April 16, 1934, FERA Old Subject File, Box 17, File: Hopkins, H.L.; Williams, *Federal Aid for Relief*, 87.

74. FERA Rules and Regulations no. 3, July 11, 1922, FERA, Old Subject File, Box 12, File: Forms January–November 1933. See also Carothers, FERA Chronology, 7.

75. "Questions to be submitted to Field Men" (Undated), Box 10 File: Field Statistician; FERA Rules and Regulations no. 3 and Memo on Reinvestigation of Relief Caseload (October 20, 1933), both in Box 12, File: Forms: January–Novem-

ber 1933 in FERA-OSF. On the issue of inflation: Hopkins to State Relief Admin-istrators, September 6, 1933, Box 76, File: Statistical Division-Requests.

76. Alabama Field Report, September 13, 1933, Box 3, File: Alabama Field Reports; Aubrey Williams to Harry Hopkins, October 19, 1933, October 19, 1933, Box 114, File: Field Reports, both in FERA Files.

77. Hopkins linked the issue of adequacy directly to the need for higher state expenditures in a memo to the states on July 20, 1933, FERA OSF, Box 12, File: January–November 1933. On Ohio application see Governor George White to Hopkins, June 6, 1933, and Hopkins to White, June 8, 1933, both in FERA Box 222, File: May–December 1933.

78. Charles M. Bookman, "The Federal Emergency Relief Administration: Its Problems and Significance," NCSW, 1934, 17, 25.

79. "Rules and Regulations no. 3 (July 11, 1933), FERA OSF, Box 12, File: Forms January–November. Some local relief organizations were able to tempo-rarily avoid the policy with a mere face-lift. In Seattle, for example, "deputized" private social workers could administer relief from the offices of private agencies, but the name of the King County Welfare Board "should appear on [the] door of each private agency in addition to the name of the private agency." In one extremely controversial case, the FERA was forced to compromise with the Chi-cago relief organization and provide federal aid to the Catholic Relief Bureau. But in most cases, the FERA was able to enforce the federal regulations, in large part because the policy was consistent with the trend toward public welfare and with the goals of local social workers. In many cases, local welfare reformers associated with private charity were able to dominate the new local public agen-cies created by the FERA directives. Russell Kurtz and Joanna Colcord, "Private Agencies Go Public," *Survey* 69, no. 9 (September 1933): 133; Joanna Colcord and Russell Kurtz, "San Francisco Relief Survey," *Survey*, 69, no. 11 (November 1933): 390. Regarding the Seattle compromise see Pierce Williams to John F. Hall, June 11, 1933, FERA Box 306, File: Washington Field Reports 2. For the Chicago relief controversy see C.M. Bookman to Hopkins, August 28, 1933, FERA OSF, Box 27, File: Hopkins Memoranda to Staff; Lizbeth Cohen, *Making a New Deal* (Cam-bridge: Cambridge University Press, 1990), 269.

80. Carothers, *Chronology of the Federal Emergency Relief Administration*, 13–14; Joan M. Crouse, *The Homeless Transient in the Great Depression: New York State, 1929–1941* (Albany: State University of New York Press, 1986), 132–139.

81. Williams, *Federal Aid for Relief*, 150.

82. Hopkins, "The Developing National Program of Relief, 71; "Don't Quote Me."

83. Williams, *Federal Aid for Relief*, 71–72. See, for example, the August FERA grant to Alabama, which was made before members of the Division of Research and Statistics could investigate the state's financial condition. Hopkins to Gov-ernor B.M. Miller, August 2, 1933, Box 1, File: Alabama, May–September 1933, FERA Files.

84. Hopkins, "The Developing National Program of Relief," 69.

85. Federal Works Agency, *Final Statistical Report of the Federal Emergency Re-lief Administration*; Blumell, *The Development of Public Assistance in the State of Washington*, 165.

86. On food price increases see Maude Barrett to RB Pixley (Louisiana State

Relief Official), August 5, 1933, FERA Files, Box 111, File: Louisiana, May–December 1933.

87. The best account of the origins of the FSRC is Janet Poppendeick, *Breadlines Knee Deep in Wheat: Food Assistance and the Great Depression* (New Brunswick, NJ: Rutgers University Press, 1986, ch. 7. See also "Eating the Surplus," *Survey* 69, no. 11 (November 1933); "The Federal Surplus Relief Corporation," *FERA Monthly Report* (July 1935). Hopkins appears to have initially opposed the distribution of surplus commodities. See his August 3, 1933, memo on the subject and the September 23 FERA press release announcing the distribution of 85 million pounds of surplus pork, in FDR Papers, Official File 444, File: FERA January–August 1933. By October, however, Hopkins was suggesting that states raise relief standards via commodity distribution. See Wilfred S. Reynolds to Hopkins, October 25, 1933. For a social work critique of commodity relief see Joanna Colcord, *Cash Relief* (New York: Russell Sage Foundation, 1936), 20–26; Brown, *Federal Aid for Relief*, 255.

88. Federal Works Agency, *Final Statistical Report*, 88.

89. Michigan: see material in Box 137, Files: Field Representatives Report, especially Rowland Haynes, July 2, 1933, report and memo on finances dated November 13, 1933. Washington: see Pierce Williams August memoranda in Box 306, Washington Field Reports File. For a detailed discussion of the conflict over relief funding in Washington see Blumell, *The Development of Public Assistance in the State of Washington*, 136–148.

90. Louisiana: FERA Press Release (August 12, 1933), Box 111, File: Louisiana, May–December 1933. Alabama: Hopkins to Governor B.M. Miller, August 2, 1933, Box 1, File: Alabama, May–September 1933, both in FERA Files.

91. *Survey* 69, no. 9 (September 1933): 33. For a seminal account of the New Deal and its relationship to the states that emphasizes state resistance to federal policies see James T. Patterson, *The New Deal and the States* (Westport, CT: Greenwood Press, 1981), ch. 3.

92. Gertrude Springer, "Social Workers—What Now," *Survey* 71, no. 10 (October 1935): 293; Kurtz and Colcord, "Private Agencies Go Public," 133. For a general discussion of the FERA's methods of influencing state and local personnel selection see Williams, *Federal Aid for Relief*, 154–158. On the impact of the early FERA on state and local relief in Ohio see Maurer, "Public Relief Programs and Politics in Ohio," 75–76.

93. Brock, *Welfare, Democracy and the New Deal*, 173; Williams, *Federal Aid for Relief*, 80–81.

94. Aubrey Williams, Field Report from Louisiana, September 13, 1933, FERA, Box 114, File: Field Reps. Reports.

95. Harry Hopkins, *Spending to Save: The Complete Story of Relief* (New York: W.W. Norton, 1936), 117. The FERA issued a sample application form designed to produce much information about sources of income and family life but increasingly sought to simplify investigatory procedures for the increasing numbers of unemployed on its work relief program.

96. William W. Bremer, "Along the American Way: The New Deal's Work Relief Programs for the Unemployed," *The Journal of American History* 62 (December 1975): 636–637.

97. McJimsey, *Harry Hopkins*, 21, 45–49; June Hopkins, *Harry Hopkins: Sudden Hero, Brash Reformer* (New York: St. Martin's Press, 1999), 65–70; Joanna Colcord,

William Koplovitz and Russell Kurtz, *Emergency Work Relief* (New York: Russell Sage Foundation, 1932).

98. On early FERA work program see material in Box 84, File: Work Relief—First Federal Work Projects, especially Hopkins' memo on federal projects (July 8, 1933), and Jacob Baker to Sherrard Ewing (undated list of army projects); Carothers, FERA Chronology, 15. The best accounts of work relief in the early months of the FERA and the poorly documented process that produced the CWA are Bonnie Fox Schwartz, *The Civil Works Administration: The Business of Emergency Employment in the New Deal* (Princeton, NJ: Princeton University Press, 1984), 31–38 and McJimsey, *Harry Hopkins*, 56–59. On the use of PWA funds to expand work relief see the recollections of Tex Goldschmidt in Kate Louchheim, ed., *The Making of the New Deal: The Insiders Speak* (Cambridge, MA: Harvard University Press, 1983), 187–188. Goldsmith's recollections are cited in McJimsey, *Harry Hopkins*, 57.

99. Schwarz, *The Civil Works Administration*, 27–28; John Salmond, *Southern Rebel: The Life and Times of Aubrey Williams* (Chapel Hill: University of North Carolina Press, 1983), 51–52, 54–56; Williams, "The New Deal—A Dead Battery," unpublished manuscript in Aubrey Williams Papers, Box 44, FDR Library.

100. Aubrey Williams to Harry Hopkins, "Memo on Reemployment of the Unemployed," October 30, 1933, Aubrey Williams Papers, Box FDR Library.

101. Schwartz, *The Civil Works Administration*, 38; McJimsey, *Harry Hopkins*, 58; Robert E. Sherwood, *Roosevelt and Hopkins* (New York: Bantam Books, 1950), 62–63.

Chapter 5

Work Relief

The CWA began the odyssey that led the New Deal to withdraw from the "business of relief," replacing the federal grant program with public employment (the WPA).[1] It was, as Hopkins later described it, a "precocious child in a family of slower-growing but more substantial children."[2] Historians have tended to explain the New Deal's turn toward work relief as a product of the values of Roosevelt and Harry Hopkins. The CWA, according to one of the president's biographers, was "rooted in a profound aversion to direct 'handout' relief ('the dole') to men and women able and willing to work, an aversion Harry Hopkins shared with Franklin D. Roosevelt." Hopkins' biographer, George McJimsey, explains the origins of the WPA by noting that Roosevelt and Hopkins "believed that relief given in the traditional way ultimately degraded and pauperized the recipient. They wanted to get the federal government out of giving relief and into providing jobs for the unemployed."[3]

While there can be little doubt that the New Deal's approach to relief was, from the outset, profoundly influenced by these attitudes, they do not entirely explain the trajectory of policy from 1933 through 1935. Why would the administration embark on an ambitious public employment experiment in the fall of 1933 (CWA), abruptly terminate it a few months later, when it barely had reached its quota, return to an expanded "dole" in the spring of 1934 and then jettison the FERA grant program entirely in favor of a federal work relief policy (the WPA) the next year? The New Deal was legendary for its abrupt and bewildering shifts in relief policy. Yet all these policies—including that of the early FERA described in the previous chapter—were justified in term of replacing "the dole" with work. It would appear that the values of New Deal officials did not, inevitably, produce a specific set of relief policies.

At the heart of the problem was that while nearly everyone associated with the relief program would have liked to replace relief with work, real employment, as opposed to "make-work," which simply kept recipients occupied, was enormously expensive. This reality, after all, had been the downfall of many of the early-depression work relief experiments.[4] For this reason, powerful officials within the New Deal, particularly in the Treasury Department and the Bureau of the Budget, opposed public employment because it would undermine Roosevelt's commitment to balance the federal budget. The fiscal constraints were compounded by the problems implementing a work policy in the context of the existing relief system. Would projects look more like public works—expensive, capital-intensive projects that were politically popular but employed relatively few relief recipients—or traditional work relief, which employed more but appeared to be of marginal public value ("leaf-raking")? Finally, while work relief was portrayed as an alternative to the direct dole, the policy tended to generate enormous demands for more relief because it reduced the stigma of applying for all forms of governmental aid. This was one of the lessons of the employment experiments of the early depression, particularly New York City's influential work program.[5] In short, while Roosevelt certainly valued work, he also feared that work relief programs would become an expensive "habit."

In order to understand how the supporters of public employment overcame these obstacles, it is necessary to look more closely at the work relief experiments of 1933 and 1934, their impact on the existing federal grant program (FERA) and their relationship to the emerging debate within the New Deal over fiscal policy. The Civil Works Administration, initially billed as a short-term employment program that would reduce the need for relief, produced a big expansion of the federal "dole" in early 1934. At the same time, CWA generated strong support for federal public employment among unemployed workers, in Congress and within the New Deal. It also engendered strong opposition to work relief among fiscal conservatives within the administration, Congress and elite financial circles. Initially, the CWA's price tag strengthened the hand of opponents of public employment, who argued that it would cause Roosevelt to renege on his campaign pledge to balance the federal budget. But the strength of the constituencies for work relief, which were at the heart of the New Deal coalition, eventually prevailed. The specter of a permanent federal dole, combined with politically destructive conflicts with the states over the administration of relief, caused Roosevelt to side with "spenders" like Hopkins barely six months after he had discontinued civil works. The CWA had, in Hopkins words, "let loose great forces, both economical and spiritual," which produced the dramatic policy shift of 1935.[6]

The dramatic story of the creation of the Civil Works Administration in the fall of 1933 has often been told, but the radical nature of the program is still not widely appreciated.[7] Between November 1, when the program was announced, and December 15, roughly 3.5 million unemployed workers were placed on work projects under the direction of federal officials. By the middle of January 4 million men and women were receiving paychecks from the federal government. If we add the roughly 2 million recipients who were on the FERA caseload at this time, federal funds were probably assisting nearly 6 million workers and farmers in January 1934, perhaps the highest number at any point in the Great Depression. These numbers tell only part of the story, for CWA was a dramatic break with means-tested relief in a number of ways. Workers' earnings were not linked to family income (the "budgetary deficiency" principle, which governed relief), and they were no longer subjected to investigation by social workers; thus, CWA pulled recipients out of the existing public welfare framework. The improved status of the CWA recipients was enhanced by the quality of their employment. While many projects were inherited from the old relief program, a central focus of civil works was to move beyond "make-work" to well-planned projects of permanent value. This was accompanied by an important shift in administrative personnel and philosophy. As Bonnie Fox Schwartz has shown, engineers, efficiency experts, accountants and personnel managers moved into key positions in Hopkins' new organization—a significant shift from the social work orientation of the FERA.[8]

Above all, CWA was an exhilarating experience for millions of unemployed workers in the fifth winter of the Great Depression, and their response to the program appears to have deeply moved New Deal officials. Hopkins' defense of CWA at a fundraising dinner in the spring of 1934 reflected these feelings:

When we started Civil Works we said we were going to put four million men to work. How many do you suppose applied for those four million jobs? About ten million. Now I don't say there were ten million people out of work, but ten million people walked up to a window and stood in line, many of them all night, asking for a job that paid them somewhere between seven and eighteen dollars a week.[9]

Lorena Hickok, the Associated Press correspondent whose confidential reports strongly influenced Hopkins during this period, described the reaction of workers in Michigan on receiving their first cash wages under CWA: "They took [them] with wide grins and made beelines for the grocery stores, not to shovel grocery orders across the counter but to go where they pleased and buy what they pleased." Frank Walker, the head of the National Emergency Council, who was sent into the field by Roosevelt to check on the reports of graft and inefficiency that bedeviled CWA, was astonished to find former business associates doing manual labor on projects in Montana, "wearing their regular business suits as they worked because they couldn't afford overalls." Although Walker found the experience disturbing, he reported that his old friends were enormously enthusiastic about the program. One pulled some silver coins out of his pocket, exclaiming, "Do you know, Frank, this is the first money I've had in my pockets in a year and a half? Up to now I've had nothing but tickets that you exchange for groceries." The program generated enthusiasm (and no doubt a great deal of political support for the New Deal) not only because it paid cash wages but because it appeared to be a bold move by federal officials to address the crisis of the unemployed. A Washington state relief official wrote to Hopkins that the impact of the program on workers' morale was "all out of proportion to the actual financial benefit received. Everywhere among the rank and file of folk one sense[s] a feeling of sincere respect and confidence in Harry Hopkins and the President and belief in their fairness."[10]

The strong support for civil works within the New Deal's core constituency was, however, a mixed blessing because the program proved to be enormously expensive, quickly overrunning its budget. The initial $400 million, drawn from public works funds, was designed to finance CWA until mid-February, when it would be supplemented by a new congressional appropriation linked to the next fiscal year's budget. This estimate represented, at best, wishful thinking for a program employing 4 million recipients.[11] Administrative costs were high; weekly payrolls exceeded original estimates; and the program's workmen's compensation provisions appeared to create a permanent drain on the treasury.[12] In early January Hopkins told Roosevelt that CWA would run out of funds sooner than expected. According to one account, Roosevelt "blew up" and demanded that Hopkins begin phasing out the program immediately. On January 18 Hopkins ordered weekly wages cut (through a reduction in hours worked) and hinted that the program would be terminated at the beginning of March. The cutback, coming at a time when the program had just reached its promised quota, generated a storm of protest and a movement in Congress to continue CWA through the spring of 1934.[13] These pressures helped the New Deal secure a new emergency relief appropriation of $950 million, but the CWA was phased out in March and April. Although many projects were transferred to the FERA's expanded "work division," the means test was revived, and recipients once again received aid from local welfare agencies.[14]

The brief, mercurial history of CWA once led historians to view the program as a noble, but haphazard, experiment plagued by inefficiency and political conflict. More recently, the program's historical reputation has been enhanced by several monographs that stress CWA's break with traditional relief policies and its significant improvement over the "make-work" that characterized early-depression work relief.[15] Relatively little attention has been paid to the relationship between the CWA and the grant program the FERA continued to administer, but this is crucial to understanding the abrupt shifts in New Deal relief policy. It will be recalled that early FERA policy had been to reduce the national relief caseload and the federal spending role (while improving standards for those remaining on relief). While we do not know precisely what Hopkins told Roosevelt at the late October meeting that launched CWA, it is likely that the employment program was justified as implementing these policy goals. In particular, civil works, through a quick injection of PWA funds into the economy, would stimulate employment, reducing the need for relief. Furthermore, civil work would serve as a transmission belt to employment in Harold Ickes' public works program, whose slowly moving projects would presumably be employing more relief labor in the spring. Immediately after the meeting with Roosevelt on November 2, Hopkins telegrammed state governors, urging them to submit projects immediately so that "the greatest possible flow of dollars shall proceed into local channels of trade and business that recovery may be forwarded and relief eliminated." An in-depth analysis of CWA by a *New York Times* reporter called the program "a dramatic adventure resting on the certainty that the civil works payroll will stimulate business by going immediately into purchases and on the belief that the CWA will take up the slack of unemployment until the NRA and the PWA programs get into their full stride."[16]

The assumption that CWA would help stimulate recovery was certainly plausible, yet it presumed that $400 million was a large enough stimulus to significantly reduce the need for relief. The problem was not only the inadequacy of the appropriation but the fact that the existing relief system was assisting only a fraction of the unemployed. What if unemployed workers not on relief applied for it because this was seen as a way of qualifying for public employment? This policy paradox had confronted some of the more enlightened work relief experiments of the early depression years. Thus, the New York City work relief program, implemented during the winter of 1930–1931, had generated a rush to the relief rolls that nearly bankrupted the city's emergency committee. This development could be avoided by forcing workers to perform menial tasks in exchange for low relief payments (the traditional "work test"), but a central goal of CWA was to upgrade such "leaf-raking" projects. The tendency of work programs to become magnets for the unemployed was one reason that many social workers were skeptical of their value. Thus, Russell Kurtz, one of the *Survey's* relief columnists, suggested that CWA might produce the unintended consequence of the expansion of direct relief:

But what of the needy unemployed who register for one of these jobs, only to be rejected? Will this not be the last straw needed to break their spirits, sending them into the home relief load to take the places of those just transferred out to Civil Works? If the history of local work registration in the last four years is any guide, such an event is likely to occur on a rather large scale.[17]

Kurtz's analysis was prophetic. Indeed, by the time his *Survey* piece was published, mass applications by the unemployed were generating enormous pressures not only on CWA but on the FERA grant program. Hopkins' estimate that 10 million workers applied for CWA jobs was not only a testament to the enthusiasm generated by public employment but also its disruptive effect on existing relief arrangements. According to press reports, 1,500 workers appeared at the offices of the U.S. Employment Service in New York City on November 27, the first day applications were accepted. In Chicago 70,000 people jammed into field houses and armories during the first week of the program. "Registration for CWA jobs at the time I left Illinois to run about six times the number of jobs available," Howard Hunter reported to Hopkins from Illinois. "I am inclined to think we are going to have to give them an additional allotment of money and not cut it off suddenly, because I think we might have some tough riots in certain sections of the state."[18] In Alabama, according to FERA field representative Edith Foster, farmers and agricultural workers "crowded into the county seat" seeking work on CWA. Pierce Williams reported from the West Coast that the pressure on local U.S. Employment Service and CWA offices from applicants was "exceedingly heavy and in some counties has almost reached the point of violent outbreaks."[19]

Of course, the civil works program could employ only a portion of these applicants, and many turned to the relief system for assistance. Reports to the FERA in December indicate that relief caseloads had failed to decline as much as predicted due to the influx of disappointed CWA applicants. Howard Hunter, FERA field representative in the Midwest, reported a "startling" increase in the Michigan relief caseload, which he linked directly to the impact of CWA: "Entirely too many relief cases come on expecting to get on Civil Works and are now staying on relief." St. Louis reported that many "ineligible" persons had applied for relief in order to get CWA jobs.[20] The tendency for CWA applicants to apply for relief continued through the winter. Washington State reported an initial decline in the state relief caseload as a result of transfers to CWA but predicted that the number of recipients on the rolls in January would reach the level of the previous fall. In response to a query from the FERA regarding erratic caseload changes in Illinois, a statistician from the state relief commission pointed to the impact of CWA.[21]

Many recipients who had stayed off relief during the early depression years, Hopkins later recalled, applied when the work program was announced, "fearing that they would lose out if they did not take the final step." But CWA also appears to have produced a significant change in attitude toward applying for governmental assistance, breaking down the barriers erected by the stigma of the "dole." Edith Foster reported from Louisiana that large numbers of agricultural workers who had failed to secure CWA jobs had gone to the relief offices "not knowing exactly what they wanted to ask for, but wishing to share in what the government was providing." The attitude of many disappointed CWA applicants was summed up by Pierce Williams, the FERA field representative on the West Coast: "The government having failed to provide me with a job, it is now up to the government to take care of my family." Williams was so concerned about the disruptive impact of CWA that he called for the termination of the program as quickly as possible. There was, he noted, an "ineradicable conviction in the relief applicant's mind that some obscure connection exists between being on federal relief and later obtaining a federal job."[22]

In fact, the connection was not so obscure. Two million cases were transferred from the relief rolls to the new work program. Despite the innovations in work relief under CWA, many FERA projects—and the recipients they employed—were integrated into civil works in the rush to implement the new employment policy. While CWA dispensed with the means test and much of the public welfare bureaucracy associated it, the core of the civil works administrative apparatus was the FERA and its state Emergency Relief Administrations (which were transformed into CWA units by administrative fiat). While unemployed workers not on relief were to apply for CWA jobs through the U.S. Employment Service (USES), thus avoiding the existing relief system, the USES. may well have appeared like a "welfare" agency, broadly defined. In New York City, USES offices were established at local welfare agencies after the initial surge of applications in late November. According to Edith Foster, tenant farmers and sharecroppers in Alabama flocked to county seats to apply for civil works and, when not assigned to projects, "have gone to the relief offices, which are located in many instances in the same building." In Louisiana, according to the historian of the state's civil works program, "CWA orders were written on [Emergency Relief Administration] stationery and the ERA gave directions to its workers on CWA stationery. The newspapers often reported CWA projects as ERA programs and vice-versa."[23]

Thus, the tendency to conflate CWA and relief was not confined to recipients. Local officials continued to employ relief recipients in December, when quotas were supposed to be filled by non-relief workers through the USES. "The country as a whole did not understand CWA," reported Joanna Colcord in the *Survey*, "and continued to view it as a relief measure." Colcord noted widespread resistance to the concept that workers should be hired irrespective of need: local officials "with their ears close to the ground . . . rebelled at staffing their projects with persons whose need of relief had not been demonstrated." This trend led to an order from CWA headquarters in mid-December forbidding the transfer of relief recipients to civil works.[24] The blurring of the distinction between relief and civil works may also have encouraged the liberalization of local relief policies. In early January the FERA circulated a directive urging relief agencies to tighten up on investigative procedures: "There has been a tendency, since the launching of the Civil Works program, because many people were under the impression that the way to get a job was to get on the relief rolls, for relief officials in some parts of the country to make only superficial investigations before relief was given."[25]

The abrupt cuts in CWA wages and employment, implemented in mid-January, placed further pressures on the relief system. Hopkins' January 18 order reduced the number of hours CWA workers could be employed to a maximum of twenty-four per week. This effectively reduced average weekly earnings to $11.32. Workers with large families then applied for relief to supplement inadequate earnings.[26] The January wage reductions generated a storm of protest and a movement in Congress to extend the program through the summer of 1934, creating great uncertainty about future relief policy. Under these circumstances it was only natural that many workers would apply for relief to position themselves for a future work program. As one relief official reported from Rhode Island, "Many borderline families applied for relief feeling that they were not benefited by the CWA program, with the hope that they might be included in the next [work] relief program."[27]

The demobilization of CWA in March and April produced still more protest and a flood of applications for relief. The *Survey* reported in May that "informal reports from many districts indicate that practically all CWA workers who were assigned [in the fall] from the relief rolls have made application to be reinstated on relief; and that a high proportion of those assigned through the [national employment service] without a 'means test' have applied for relief since being laid off." The FERA field representative from the Midwest noted a "stampede to the relief rolls" from former CWA workers in Wisconsin, which had the highest caseload increase in the region.[28] In New York City, where most CWA recipients were transferred to the FERA work program, the relief caseload rose to over 300,000 during the spring of 1934. Attempts to cut the work relief in April and July were met by mass protests. FERA field representative

Arch Mandel, noting that New York was the "biggest show" in the country, wrote Hopkins that "the city administration does not have control of the [caseload]."[29] In Minneapolis the transition from CWA to work relief caused a major riot, as unemployed workers attacked city hall with bottles, stones and "lumps of coal." ("Looks like a mistake in judgment on the part of our people up [in Minneapolis]," Hopkins told a New York relief official. "They closed down [CWA] entirely for two weeks and were very sure that they could get away with it.") A report from St. Louis suggested that the "CWA seems to have fostered a trend toward group action which is evidenced by complaints and demands from the *groups* affected rather than from individuals."[30] Other cities were calmer because most of the CWA caseload was transferred directly to the FERA work program. In Philadelphia the CWA was shut down for one week and reopened as a work program, with most former employees rehired. "Until those ineligible are eliminated," Arch Mandel wrote to Aubrey Williams, "the program is a continuation of CWA." In other states, the FERA avoided disorder by increasing the work program quota. Ohio officials requested (and received) an additional allotment for April, noting that "every effort had been made to stop discontent but need additional funds to meet present crisis satisfactorily."[31]

Once again, federal policies and the rhetoric of New Deal officials tended to break down the theoretical distinction between public unemployment and relief. Although CWA was demobilized, and its caseload was transferred back to local welfare agencies, the new FERA grant program was portrayed as radically different from traditional relief. A CWA-style work program would be implemented to assist the urban unemployed; a "rural rehabilitation" policy for farmers would focus on self-help and in-kind aid (with assistance to include seed and feed for livestock); a third group, called "stranded populations" (recipients in regions marked by chronic poverty) would receive retraining and even resettlement to "subsistence homesteads" constructed in conjunction with other federal agencies.[32] The sense that the new program would reduce the need for relief by targeting different segments of the national caseload with work and self-help permeated the administration's rhetoric during the spring of 1934. Roosevelt suggested that the post-CWA program was designed to eliminate the dole, which he called "repugnant to American ideals of self-reliance." The *New York Times* predicted that the 1934 program would be a continuation of civil works, "but on a much smaller scale."[33] Aubrey Williams, in a lengthy *Times* article, argued that "[h]istorically, relief has made little effort to right the system which has caused the distress of those it sought to relieve." Williams portrayed the new policy as an effort to "pull [recipients] back into the shelter of the economic roof."

In practice, the so-called second FERA of 1934 fell far short of these goals. Former CWA workers were returned to the relief rolls, where they were once again subjected to the income tests, investigations by social workers and the ubiquitous food order. Despite the rhetorical commitment to work for the urban unemployed, the number of recipients on work projects during the summer of 1934 averaged around 2 million, half the level of CWA at its peak.[34] Thus, demobilization of CWA has correctly been viewed by historians as a concession to conservative budget balancers. Social workers on the front lines of the relief system certainly viewed the new policy as a "Right About Face," in Joanna Colcord's words.[35]

On the other hand, it would be an error to see the "second FERA" simply as a retreat to relief as administered before the CWA.[36] For all its drawbacks, the new work program resembled public employment far more than the "make-work" of the early FERA period. The quality of projects, many of them inherited from CWA, improved considerably. According to one account, the local work relief programs of the pre-CWA period were "largely abandoned" when civil works were established.[37] Although federal officials did not directly control or approve local projects, as during the CWA period, the FERA's "work division" retained considerable influence over state and local work relief through earmarked grants and "practice sheets," which served as guidelines. An FERA directive in late July urged local officials to submit all projects to the state work division planning departments, where the FERA had considerable influence, for approval. So-called white-collar projects, many of them initiated under CWA, were expanded after being cleared with FERA headquarters in Washington.[38] Thus, Joanna Colcord, although considering the New Deal's decision to dismantle CWA a turn to the "right," called the new relief program "more a constructive extension of the [CWA] experience, and not so complete a reversion to earlier methods."[39]

For those lucky enough to be assigned to work projects, the improvement over traditional relief was considerable. Workers were generally paid in cash, and their "wages" were considerably higher than relief standards for those on "direct relief." Although FERA directives required that former CWA workers be investigated by relief officials, they also encouraged a less rigid application of the means test for those on work projects. The agency required states to pay the "prevailing rate for the occupation and the locality in which work is done." While in theory the number of hours worked was to be reduced so that weekly payments would conform to individual relief budgets, determined by income tests, in practice the need for labor continuity on projects inherited from the CWA made such an approach difficult to implement.[40] Other aspects of FERA policy encouraged higher payments to recipients on work relief. Federal officials opposed state "work for relief" policies that simply required work in return for the average general relief benefit. The agency encouraged states to allow payments "to provide for car fare and the extra amounts of food and clothing needed by persons employed on projects."[41] Higher wages and the liberalization of the means test were particularly pronounced for workers on professional and other "non-manual" projects, financed by earmarked federal grants. The FERA directed that wages could be no lower than $2.50 per day and were to be determined by "county wage rate committees consulting with appropriate organizations of professional groups."[42]

The liberalization of relief policy was experienced primarily by those on the work program (approximately 40% of the caseload). The majority of workers and farmers remained on direct relief, where they continued to receive grocery orders, were subjected to income tests, and were supervised by social workers. For these recipients, the dole continued to be, in Hopkins' words, a "miserable business." Yet the policy changes encouraged by the CWA and the FERA work program appears to have reduced the stigma of relief for all classes of recipients. The means test was administered by the same agencies employing the same social workers for both classes of recipients: the "needs" of a family of four probably did not vary that much as one moved from work to direct relief. Furthermore, higher average standards created by the work program increased the number of workers who would qualify under the means test. Perhaps most importantly, being on relief was now seen as a way of getting work.[43]

A good example of the policy changes initiated by the work program that reduced the stigma of relief for all recipients was the trend toward relief payments in cash. The requirement that recipients present a "standard food order"—essentially a list of commodities approved by the local relief administration—was considered to be one of the most degrading aspects of being "on the dole." Prior to the CWA only a few cities provided any relief in the form of cash, and these were holdovers from the pre-depression years. Indeed, the relief crisis of the Hoover years had seen a trend away from cash payments in favor of the distribution of commodities. The early FERA, although clearly sympathetic to cash relief, did not make this official policy, and the New Deal even appeared to encourage the use of commodities by creating the Federal Surplus Relief Corporation. Social workers had strongly opposed the mass distribution of commodities and increasingly advocated relief payments in the form of cash but made little headway until the massive influx of CWA workers in 1934. Then in the summer and fall of that year, cities such as San Francisco, New York and Detroit began to provide cash payments for significant numbers of direct relief recipients. At the same time, those states that continued to pay work relief wages "in kind" became the target of mass protest movements. By the beginning of 1935, over 60 percent of all recipients were paying cash for their food, rather than presenting a standard order that identified the shopper as "on the dole."[44]

The trend toward cash relief suggests that the liberalization of relief policy, although consistent with FERA objectives, owed much to the actions of local relief officials, social workers and the demands of unemployed workers themselves. The CWA and its aftermath produced an upsurge in grassroots protests of the unemployed directed at the relief system and the growth of formal organizations of recipients and social workers. The mass reaction to the demobilization of CWA and the implementation of the new federal work relief program created the conditions for the expansion of formal protest organizations of the unemployed. The work program proved to be fertile ground for organizers: recipients congregated on work projects, were able to build alliances with the emerging union movement and often appeared to have the support of federal officials.[45] At the same time, a strong "rank-and-file movement" developed within social workers that challenged the sometimes cozy relationship between established organizations in the field, such as the American Association of Social Workers, and relief administrators.[46]

The relationship between protest and relief was complex. On one hand, protest organizations tended to demand the expansion of work relief and an end to the direct "dole." A report from the Midwest in the spring of 1934, for example, emphasized "demands for more hours of work—grumbling over wage scales—protests against limitation of employment on the basis of relief need." The New Jersey relief program was "in an uproar" during the spring of 1934 over efforts to pay work relief recipients in grocery orders.[47] Recipients employed by the work division viewed themselves as workers demanding prevailing wages, compensation for accidents on the job and an end to the means test. The CWA, as James J. Lawrence has noted, fostered "the idea that the unemployed were workers subject to organization on a labor union model." There was also a tendency for those on the better-organized relief projects—which the FERA was encouraging—to view public employment as a "government job." A report from New York City suggested that a large number of clients on well-organized, "white-collar" projects "no longer think of themselves as relief workers, but rather as permanent administrative employees."[48]

Yet despite widespread opposition to the "dole" within organizations of the unemployed, the protests no doubt encouraged more liberal relief policies for all recipients. The Chicago Workers Committee on Unemployment demanded cash relief for the entire caseload and the "abolition of the dictatorship by caseworkers in the giving of relief." A strike in Milwaukee by recipients on work relief projects led not only to the granting of workmen's compensation to FERA employees but to a cash relief plan for direct relief recipients.[49] In response to a request to explain the big caseload increases in big cities in the state, an Ohio relief official stressed that "more agitation was experienced in these counties and this resulted in former CWA cases returning to the relief rolls more rapidly than [in] other Ohio counties." (The official also noted that many applicants believed that relief recipients would be given preference for a new CWA-style program.) The leader of the Unemployed Council in Flint, Michigan, whose 300 members had successfully resisted a relief cut in November 1934, told an FERA investigator that his organization "was looking realistically on relief as a program to stay [and thus] was fighting for more and better relief."[50] Most importantly, the FERA was forced to respond to the post-CWA protests with increases in federal aid. Consider, for example, the case of Ohio, where the level of federal spending increased dramatically during the spring of 1934, undermining Hopkins' efforts to force the state to bear a larger share of the relief burden. Much of this was a direct result of grant increases in response to the mass mobilization against cuts in work relief, as the following conversation between Hopkins and the head of the Ohio ERA, F.E. Henderson, suggests:

Hopkins: How are things going out there generally?

Henderson: Things are just fine.

Hopkins: Is that million dollars going to do the trick?

Henderson: I think so. There is only one county where we are having trouble with communists. This is the only case we have had and we really expected we would have a lot.[51]

The situation in Ohio reflected a nationwide trend. The overall impact of the liberalization of relief policy in 1934 was a significant expansion of the federal relief program. The national caseload, which had declined to under 3.5 million recipients during the early months of the grant program, increased to over 4 million in April of 1934. The FERA made an effort to reduce the caseload during the summer, but local resistance to relief cuts, coupled with a new drought in the Midwest, undermined this policy. By the fall of 1934 the national caseload approached 5 million, approximately the level when the FERA was created.[52] The caseload increase, coupled with higher payments to those on the work program, produced a massive increase in relief expenditures, which rose from approximately $65,000 in October 1933 (the month prior to CWA), to $157,000 in October 1934. Furthermore, the federal share of total expenditures also rose, increasing to nearly 75 percent under the second FERA. The combined impact of these trends was to produce an enormous increase in the federal relief bill. Prior to the CWA, federal spending had averaged approximately $45 million per month (a level that Hopkins had considered unacceptably high); by October of 1934, the federal agency was spending at a rate exceeding $120 million.[53]

The expansion of relief—coupled with the increasingly "demanding attitude" of many recipients—made the FERA a magnet for political attacks. As the 1934 Congressional elections approached, Howard Hunter warned Hopkins that campaigns in the Midwest would be "unusually violent" due, in part, to the "widespread feeling of concern over the continuance of the enormously high relief caseload. . . . The relief administrations are being accused, where definite accusations are made, of extravagance and high administrative costs and of extending relief to a large number of people who do not need it."[54] The attacks on relief came from both political parties. Democrats linked complaints about the high relief caseload to populist attacks on federal "meddling" in state affairs and the role of social workers in relief administration. Meanwhile, Republicans, facing unprecedented losses in the off-year congressional elections, began to blame their woes on the "relief vote." This boiled down to the claim that the federal relief program—particularly the work relief component—was creating a vast Democratic political machine (a charge that would become a staple of GOP rhetoric during the WPA period). When the FERA announced state grants totaling over $135 million on October 30, the Republican National Committee charged that "Santa Claus was around again today and again he is playing New Deal politics with the money of all its people." After the election Idaho senator William Borah, suggesting that the misuse of relief funds constituted the "greatest political scandal of modern times," called for a congressional investigation of the federal program.[55]

The growth of the national relief program also produced predictable fears in elite circles about the impact of mass relief-giving on the national character. Newton Baker complained in an *Atlantic Monthly* article entitled "The Decay of Self-Reliance" that various forms of federal aid, although responding to real needs, were now received "in a bad spirit." Americans, he warned, now "look upon the state as a source of well-being." Similarly, the *New York Times* warned that the victims of the depression "not only seek special relief but approach [their] problems with the premise that it is the duty of the state to provide relief."[56] The *Survey* noted a "growing protest on the part of conservatives, loosed by the elections, the Chest campaigns and Senator Borah's charges of waste and inefficiency, mounted to a crescendo during the last week of 1934. From trade associations, business leaders and others came 'warnings' that federal relief must be curtailed."

New Deal officials defended the relief program, stressing the unprecedented duration of the depression and its impact on the savings of

unemployed workers. Yet they were also concerned that the high national caseload reflected the growing tendency for workers to view relief
as a right. A confidential memo in the FERA files on caseload trends
emphasized that a higher percentage of the unemployed had exhausted
their savings and qualified for aid, but it also stressed "the changed
attitude on the part of the unemployed in many areas toward applying
for relief. The attitude of applying for a job rather than for charity has
been built up—an attitude undoubtedly strengthened by the Civil Works
program."[57] A similar view was emphasized by observers whom Hopkins sent into the field in late 1934 to report on the local relief situation.[58]
Wayne Parrish, a journalist who had covered relief policy, reported from
New York that "the psychology of relief has gone through the whole
population in the past year": "Relief is regarded as permanent by both
clients and relief workers. Clients are assuming that the government has
a responsibility to provide. The stigma of relief has almost disappeared
except among white collar groups."[59] A report from Indianapolis stressed
that the unemployed "get panicky more easily and apply for relief sooner
than they used to." An FERA staff member, writing on conditions in
Pennsylvania, suggested that an increasing number of clients in the national program viewed relief "as a regular and accepted way of life."[60]

These reports coincided with a good deal of rhetoric by administration
officials concerning the dangers of a permanent federal relief system. "It
is unthinkable that this relief scheme would be carried out beyond the
emergency," Hopkins told the *Survey* in September. To a *New York Times*
reporter he pledged that "Americans will not stand for a dole and we
are going to put them to work on great public projects and pay them
decent wages."[61] Speaking to Jewish philanthropists in November, Hopkins defended relief recipients but expressed alarm at the expansion of
the federal relief program: "I want to warn you as solemnly as I can that
the danger of attaching public outdoor relief to our American political
system is very real."[62]

Hopkins' sharp criticisms of relief—particularly his increasingly frequent use of the term "dole"—alarmed social workers and have convinced some historians that the decision to abandon the federal relief
program in late 1934 reflected traditional attitudes about the "pauperizing" effects of public assistance.[63] Yet Hopkins' rhetoric, although perhaps excessive, was consistent with the position he had taken since the
creation of the FERA. He had always argued that relief for unemployed
workers was bad public policy, that work was preferable to welfare and
that the emergency relief program would end as quickly as possible.[64]
Rather than view the New Deal's late-1934 criticisms of "the dole" as a
concession to elite attacks on the relief system, it is more useful to see
this rhetoric as part of a broader struggle over the direction of the New
Deal's recovery program. Hopkins and other "spenders" within the ad-

ministration relied heavily on traditional ideas about relief to justify an
expanded public employment program. Their rhetoric put fiscal conservatives within the administration and in the business community on the
defensive: by opposing a new CWA-style program, the conservatives
were, in effect, arguing for a permanent federal "dole." Ironically, Hopkins used the expansion of the federal grant program, which his own
work relief experiments had encouraged, to make his case.

To understand the increasingly strident anti-dole rhetoric of the New
Deal—and the decision to jettison the grant program in favor of federal
public employment—it is necessary to evaluate developments in relief
policy in the context of the debate within the administration over so-
called emergency expenditures. The early conflicts among Roosevelt's
advisers over federal spending have been obscured by the fact that a
full-blown debate over fiscal policy, leading to the triumph of Keynesian
theories of deficit spending in liberal circles, did not begin in earnest
until late 1936.[65] But the origins of this debate can be found in the ten-
sions within the administration produced by Hopkins' work relief experiments and the maneuvering over the administration's early budget
recommendations to Congress. The central issues were the high cost of
work relief and the speed with which the New Deal should eliminate
the deficit it had inherited from the Hoover administration.

The story of Roosevelt's "fiscal conservatism" has often been told.[66]
During the 1932 election he accepted, and helped popularize, the idea
that a balanced federal budget was crucial to economic recovery. He had
denounced Hoover for running a deficit and had made balancing the
federal budget an important policy goal during the famous first 100 days.
The Economy Act of March 1933 slashed veterans' payments by $400
million and the pay of federal employees by $100 million. Yet Roosevelt
also supported increased expenditures for relief and public works, precisely spending programs that had produced the budget deficit in the
first place. The FERA appropriation of $500 million and the millions
earmarked for Harold Ickes' Public Works Administration more than
offset the savings under the Economy Act. In a sense, the administration
sought to implement two contradictory approaches to recovery—encouraging the revival of business confidence by reducing the budget deficit and stimulating the economy through public spending initiatives
("pump-priming"). The rather obvious contradiction was initially resolved by distinguishing between a "regular" and an "emergency"
budget. The former would be balanced through measures like the Economy Act, fulfilling Roosevelt's campaign pledge; the latter would produce a temporary deficit, which could be blamed on the failure of the
Hoover administration to stimulate recovery.[67]

The so-called double-budgeting strategy was designed by the director of the Bureau of the Budget, Lewis Douglas, and had obvious political appeal. Yet Douglas was the leading advocate of fiscal austerity within the administration: while his accounting device was used to justify an initial increase in expenditures, it also focused attention on the size of the emergency budget, serving as a lightning rod for those who wished to control it. The initial policies of the FERA—the efforts to reduce the relief caseload and the federal spending role—were consistent with Douglas' approach. So was Harold Ickes' snails-pace implementation of the public works program. But Hopkins' use of PWA funds to finance the CWA alarmed Douglas and other fiscal conservatives. When the cost of civil works exploded, and the program developed a strong political base, the balanced-budget strategy appeared to be in danger. Perhaps even more disturbing was the growing popularity of proto-"Keynesian" theories stressing the need to stimulate consumer demand through deficit spending. In late December 1933 Keynes, encouraged by Felix Frankfurter, sent a well-publicized "Open Letter" to Roosevelt challenging the economics of the New Deal's recovery program and calling for "a great campaign of public works" and a "great drive [for] "unemployment relief and other social services."[68] The Keynes letter coincided with growing concern among influential New Dealers about the administration's recovery strategy. Brain-truster Rexford Tugwell believed that the policies of the National Recovery Administration, the centerpiece of the recovery program, were producing higher prices, which retarded the revival of consumer demand. Hopkins and Aubrey Williams began meeting with a small group of liberals attracted to Tugwell's arguments in the fall of 1933. Against these emerging "spenders" were arrayed influential fiscal conservatives like Douglas, Treasury secretary Henry Morgenthau and Russell Leffingwell, a partner in the J.P. Morgan Company and an influence on Roosevelt's inner circle of economic advisers.[69]

The conflict within the administration did not primarily take the form of a principled debate over economic theory (this would come later in the depression) but involved maneuvering over the size of the emergency budget and contours of the federal relief program. The role of work relief was central. According to a *New York Times* analysis, Roosevelt, when confronted with the explosion of CWA costs, had hoped to phase out the program in mid-February. But Hopkins' announcement of wage cuts in mid-January sparked grassroots protests and a movement in Congress to extend the program through the summer (a development the editors of the *Times* considered "ominous").[70] In late January Lewis Douglas launched a concerted attack on public employment. In two memos to Roosevelt, he warned that the work relief experiments threatened to destroy the balanced budget and create a permanent dole under the guise of "make-work." These arguments were echoed by Roosevelt, who told the National Emergency Council that civil works needed to be curtailed before it "becomes a habit with this country."[71]

The abrupt end of CWA in March of 1934 is generally viewed as a victory for budget balancers like Douglas. Hopkins is often depicted as the loyal servant, dismantling a program he strongly supported and publicly justifying a return to direct relief.[72] In fact, the situation was a good deal more complex than this. First, there is no evidence that Hopkins had ever entertained the thought that CWA would be continued beyond the spring. As William Bremer has pointed out, the FERA administrator had warned relief officials in early December that "it is humanly impossible for anybody to inject any chance of permanence in this thing [CWA]." At that time Hopkins envisioned a slow phase-out of the program beginning in mid-March and ending in May.[73] Second, by abruptly discontinuing the CWA in March, Hopkins not only stimulated grassroots protest in support for work relief but also provided continuity between CWA and the new FERA work program. By transferring numerous projects (and workers) directly to the FERA, he saved funds for work relief and transformed the old grant program into a policy that more closely resembled public employment.[74]

The effect of Hopkins actions' and the protests they encouraged was to keep emergency spending high. The budget for the 1935 fiscal year, which began in July 1934, was generally perceived to be the first that bore the stamp of the New Deal. The budget cycle actually began with a "supplemental request" for relief submitted to Congress in February. Initially, the administration had expected to limit this to $600 million ($350 million for phasing out CWA and $250 million to continue the FERA into fiscal year 1935). Responding to the pressures to continue work relief, the administration requested and received a $950 million stopgap appropriation.[75] Then in June, following the great increase in relief costs in the spring, Roosevelt asked for a $1.3 billion "recovery chest," to be allocated either to the FERA or to public works, and for broad powers to draw on "unobligated balances" of the PWA and RFC. The final appropriation for the fiscal year beginning in July, which included an additional $525 million for drought relief added by Congress, officially totaled $1.7 billion. If funds remaining from the February appropriation and potential transfers from the RFC were included, the emergency budget, according to a *New York Times* analysis, now exceeded $3.7 billion.[76] Far more of these funds were now available for Hopkins' work relief experiments, as opposed to the more conservatively administered public works program of Harold Ickes. With the FERA spending at a rate of over $100 million per month, the president was forced to "dip into discretionary funds" to finance relief beginning October 1934.[77]

Thus, the retreat from CWA was not as clear-cut a victory for budget-balancers like Douglas as is often supposed. In late May, John Maynard Keynes, who had called for a dramatic increase in public works spending the previous year, made his case personally to Roosevelt. As numerous historical accounts have noted, the encounter was a something of a disaster: Roosevelt was put off by the overly technical presentation of the great economist, and Keynes left the meeting questioning the president's economic literacy.[78] The story of Keynes' visit is often told to underline the fact that deficit spending as a mechanism for stimulating economic recovery—a central tenet of liberal theory in the midcentury "New Deal order"—was not accepted as administration policy until much later in the depression. But one should also be careful not to minimize the impact of Keynes' ideas within the New Deal circles. His equations may not have moved Roosevelt, but they appear to have created a general sense that there were rational economic arguments for higher emergency expenditures, which were usually justified on strictly "humanitarian" grounds. As Walter Lippmann noted in late 1934, the fiscal conservatives were not the only "realists" in the administration, and "[the spenders] are not so tenderhearted as they often make themselves out to be."[79]

A more powerful argument for increased spending for public employment was that continued reliance on direct relief threatened to create a permanent national dole. Lippman noted that "the case of the humanitarians (Hopkins et al.) is usually presented as one of profound concern with the misery and demoralization of a mere dole" and "against resigning ourselves to the dole as a more or less permanent feature of American life." The *New York Times'* Arthur Krock, who closely followed the debates within the administration over emergency spending, made a similar point in a column in April 1934. Krock noted that the broad spending powers requested by Roosevelt for the 1935 fiscal year reflected continued divisions within the New Deal over work relief. Fiscal conservatives, arguing that recovery might be retarded by continued budget deficits, urged the administration to reduce spending for public employment and focus on direct relief. Those who supported "pump-priming" expenditures—Krock called them the "left wing of the New Deal"— stressed the fact that the dole was "character wrecking and humiliating" and warned of the dangers of a permanent federal relief program.[80] The great expansion of the relief caseload and federal spending in 1934 provided the evidence to justify these warnings.

The appeal of the arguments put forward by spenders like Hopkins and Aubrey Williams was enhanced by the New Deal's experience administering the grant program. The FERA, viewed as a temporary agency whose purpose was to strengthen state and local relief administration, was increasingly being held responsible for the entire relief burden. As the level of federal financing had jumped to nearly 75 percent in the spring of 1934, the agency was under enormous pressure to provide even more. The trajectory of the relief program in Ohio was not atypical. Prior to the demobilization of the CWA, the FERA's statistician J.R. Blough estimated that Ohio might be able to pay two-thirds of its relief bill for the coming fiscal year if expenditures did not exceed $3 million per month. By June 1, following the influx of CWA workers, the Statistical Division had doubled its monthly needs estimate (to $6 million) and noted that state and local units had only $1.5 million aggregate for the rest of the year. Meanwhile, the state legislature had defeated, for the third time, a proposal to expand the state sales tax to finance relief. As a result, federal funds financed nearly all the relief bill during the summer and fall of 1934. After a great deal of pressure from the FERA and a series of bruising legislative battles, the state passed a broad-based sales tax in the fall. However, the new levy financed only one-quarter of the state's relief bill (which now exceeded $10 million monthly), and Hopkins' organization had become enormously unpopular among both mainstream Democrats and Republicans.[81]

A similar expansion of the federal relief role, accompanied by a politically debilitating battle between state and federal officials, occurred in Pennsylvania. In the spring of 1934, Gifford Pinchot, the Republican governor who had played a central role in the movement for federal relief, demanded that the FERA accept the entire burden of financing relief, whose cost had doubled with the demobilization of CWA. Arguing that constitutional restrictions prohibited further state appropriations, Pinchot, in a letter to Roosevelt, suggested that "the proper method [of financing relief] is to borrow funds to be repaid in more prosperous times. This the federal government can do. Pennsylvania cannot." FERA officials, on the other hand, saw Pennsylvania as a test case. Noting that two-thirds of all state contributions to relief came from a small group of industrialized states, a memorandum to Hopkins argued that "if one of these states is relieved of the necessity of continuing to contribute a large percentage of its unemployment relief costs, it will be difficult to maintain large contributions from the others."[82] Using a threat to withhold federal grants as a club, the FERA was able to force a special session of the state legislature in September. But the effort to fashion "bipartisan" legislation drew the FERA into byzantine conflicts between Democratic Party leaders, mainstream Republicans and Pinchot's "Progressive" faction. Even Roosevelt got involved with a personal demand that the state assume its fair share of the relief burden. After Hopkins threatened to withhold federal funds for the state's October relief bill, the state legislature voted $20 million for unemployment relief.[83]

As the Ohio and Pennsylvania examples show, threats to withhold federal aid were often effective in forcing state relief appropriations, but these successes came at a significant political cost. FERA officials found themselves at odds with state politicians, often key leaders of the Dem-

ocratic Party.[84] In New Jersey FERA demands for state relief appropriation coincided with a movement led by business elites—and opposed
by labor—to pass a sales tax to resolve the state's fiscal crisis. While the
FERA denied that it was endorsing any particular tax program, federal
relief officials appeared to be supporting a tax opposed by a key constituency of the Democratic Party. The political fallout from state tax
battles, particularly those over the sales tax, put federal officials on the
defensive. "Let me state definitely that the FERA has never endorsed one
method of raising relief funds as against another," assistant administrator Corrington Gill told the *Survey*. "I am particularly anxious to avoid
the impression that the FERA is bringing pressure on states to adopt
certain specific revenue measures, for example the sales tax."[85]

Similar conflicts emerged over the FERA's efforts to promote professional administration and sound standards of relief. There is a good deal
of evidence that the grant program played a major role in modernizing
state administrative capacity, laying the basis for the expanded role of
state agencies in welfare policy in the late 1930s. But in the process, state
emergency relief administrations came to be viewed as virtual extensions
of the federal welfare bureaucracy ("parallel government," in William R.
Brock's phrase). Furthermore, these reforms came at a significant political
cost for the New Deal.[86] Once again, there are appears to be a persistent
pattern of conflict with state-level Democrats. In Louisiana and Georgia
conflict with Democratic leaders over "standards of relief administration" led to federal takeovers of state relief machinery. The FERA began
administering the work relief program directly in Massachusetts (federal
aid ceased to be used for direct relief) after it was discovered that the
state was encouraging cities and towns to use relief funds to lower property taxes. The FERA "federalized" the administration of relief in
Oklahoma after populist Democrat William Murray announced that he
would not apply for federal aid unless he was allowed to ignore FERA
rules and regulations. A similar development occurred in Ohio, where
Democratic governor Martin Davey spent a good deal of his 1934 gu-
bernatorial campaign denouncing the FERA and the social workers associated with it. Relief in Ohio was "federalized" on evidence that Davey
had attempted to solicit contributions from relief officials.[87]

Attacks on social workers and the FERA "bureaucracy" were encouraged by the emphasis on work relief. Pierce Williams wrote to Hopkins
in February of 1934 that the CWA had greatly increased political pressure on state relief administrations. "The politicians did not especially
mind turning relief over to a group of citizens, for they felt there was
nothing but grief in that job," he noted. "However it drove the politicians
wild to find themselves without anything to say about who was to get
a job on public work [CWA]."[88] Williams' comments were prophetic, for
during the next year he was to be at the center of the most celebrated

conflict between "New Deal politicians and social workers." In the spring of 1934 Williams and several other FERA officials were indicted in California on charges of fraudulent administration of the CWA program. The true source of the indictments, however, was state Democratic boss William Gibbs McAdoo. McAdoo, who had handed a decisive bloc of Democrats to Roosevelt at the 1932 convention, was enraged that Williams and the Republican state relief administrator, Ray Branion, would not allow him to use the work relief program as a source of patronage.[89] A similar political controversy over work relief erupted in New York City in the spring of 1935. In May the Board of Alderman, dominated by Democrats linked to the Tammany Hall political machine, launched an investigation of the work relief program (which the president of the Board attacked as being dominated by "a small group of professional social service workers").[90] Public hearings, which the *Survey* characterized as a "Roman Holiday," settled upon ridiculing relief projects for unemployed "white-collar" workers. The investigation revealed that relief funds had been used to finance a study of poultry consumption (dubbed a "chicken survey") and for the collection of clocks displayed at a "temple of time" exhibit at New York University. The denouement of the hearings was the revelation by one relief worker that he had been teaching recipients to make "boon doggles." The term, he explained, had originated in "pioneer days" to refer to a wide range of marginally useful "gadgets" whose primary function was to keep idle youth occupied ("boondoggle" quickly replaced "leaf raking" as the label used to disparage work relief).[91]

Populist attacks on the role of professionals in the relief bureaucracy thinly masked a desire on the part of local and state politicians to use the work program for patronage. They also reflected the fact that the FERA was being drawn into the intense class and social conflicts that characterized the American polity in 1934. Historians have frequently emphasized the role of protest movements—the Townsend movement for a radical old age pension program, the mass following of populist demagogues like Huey Long and the "radio priest" Charles E. Coughlin and the surge of unionization that culminated in "general strikes" in a number of industrial centers—as influencing New Deal policy and encouraging a "turn to the left" in late 1934.[92] The explosion of protest directed at the relief system was a key part of this phenomenon. We have seen how the demobilization of CWA produced sustained protests in many urban centers and the creation of formal organizations of recipients that sought to bargain over relief policy. State ERAs in Minnesota, Wisconsin and New Jersey experienced sustained and often violent protests, primarily directed at the failure of the work program to pay prevailing wage rates on work projects.[93]

The impact of protest on New Deal relief policy was to encourage both the transition to work relief and the abandonment of the federal grant program. First, unemployed workers generally demanded the expansion of work relief, a demand that strengthened the position of Hopkins and Aubrey Williams within the administration. Although organizations of unemployed workers often complained of "slave wages" under the FERA work program, the mass protests in response to the demobilization were generally viewed as expressing support for public employment and opposition to the direct dole. A June 1934 conference of workers in Minneapolis, for example, demanded direct employment by the government "at trade union hours and wages," while an organization that included both relief and public works (PWA) employees demanded that those laid off by the CWA demobilization be placed on jobs "without investigation [by social workers.]"[94]

One finds, therefore, a great deal of sympathy for work protests in the documents in the FERA files. When the New Jersey work relief program exploded in violent protest over attempts by the state to pay recipients in standard grocery orders, the FERA sided with the workers in demanding that the state "work for relief" program be ended. A relief official in Ohio met the leader of Ohio's League of Unemployed in July of 1934 "at the insistence" of a member of the FERA work division. He reported to Aubrey Williams that "considerable progress was made in establishing rapport between himself (and possibly the league) and the federal emergency relief administration."[95] While such efforts were no doubt designed to reduce conflict by co-opting the protest leadership, they also served to signal protest organizations that their demands were supported by key elements of the New Deal relief bureaucracy. Indeed, the correlation between the demands of protest movements and New Deal relief policy was so great that some of Hopkins' critics suspected him of deliberately encouraging protest by threatening dramatic and unnecessary cuts in the work program.[96]

Second, relief protests exacerbated a central problem faced by the grant program—the tendency for the FERA to be held responsible for the actions of local and state relief administrators not under its control. Howard Hunter, the field representative in the Midwest, urged Hopkins to adopt an official policy toward organizations of the unemployed because local officials got into "some serious jams" that reflected back on the FERA. In one particularly embarrassing case, workers protesting cuts in work relief in Wichita, Kansas, were jailed in a building they had constructed under the CWA. Two FERA officials sent to the scene wrote Hopkins that they were working with local officials to free the jailed workers in an effort to "[save] our mutual faces."[97]

The growth of the unemployed workers' movement in 1934 dovetailed with a strike wave among industrial workers, which created other complications for the federal grant program. In a number of states, striking workers appear to have swelled the relief rolls. Howard Myers reported to Hopkins from the Midwest that "[i]f strike conditions get serious in the steel mills or coal mines, we may have to throw some extra money into these states." Reports to the FERA showed that efforts to reduce the caseload in the "federalized" Massachusetts work relief program were undermined by unrest in the textile industry. During the San Francisco general strike in July FERA officials closely monitored the relief caseload in the city.[98]

Yet the central problem for the New Deal was not the caseload increases caused by strikes per se but the perception that the relief program was abetting the emerging union movement by giving aid to striking workers. Official FERA policy allowed aid to strikers if they qualified under the means test. Thus, according to a 1933 directive, the agency took no position "on the merits of strikes."[99] This policy might have been a reasonable compromise had it not been for the strike wave of 1934 and, in particular, the effort by the American Federation of Labor to organize southern textile workers. Leaders of the organizing drive, calling for a strike in early September, had publicly suggested that workers could apply for relief. In response, Henry I. Harriman of the U.S. Chamber of Commerce protested that federal relief policy encouraged "strikes and industrial unrest," while the more verbose Illinois Association of Manufactures claimed that strike relief was "an invitation to the representatives of organized minorities to engage in wholesale and perhaps universal promotion of industrial warfare." The attacks from organized business interests were predictable, but the political implications of the strike, which threatened to fracture the party's base in the "solid" Democratic South, alarmed Roosevelt. When Aubrey Williams suggested to Hopkins that an expert on labor relations monitor the strike, the FERA administrator replied:

He wants me to watch that like a hawk, personally. . . . If you get a field person who puts some heat on some relief officer who is not in sympathy with our policy you will get a fight in our organization in some relief office, and I don't want that to happen.

Hopkins later publicly warned union leaders that they should not count on strike relief: "If they think we are going to underwrite their strike they are mistaken and they will find out soon enough." In the end, the FERA refused to enforce the official policy on strike relief, and the organizing drive collapsed.[100]

Hopkins' comments to Williams underline the difficulties of administering a program that was widely viewed as federal (and that was financed primarily by federal funds) but was nominally under state and local administrative control. A similar problem was encountered by the FERA's "production for use" program, a highly publicized component of the 1934 work relief policy. Production for use, or "self-help," as it was often called, began in the early 1930s a grassroots movement among the unemployed to produce items for use and exchange. Particularly popular on the urban West Coast, where it took the form of a politicized protest movement, self-help was seen as a way of avoiding the demoralizing features of the "dole"—a kind of voluntarist work relief policy.[101] The FERA seized on the concept in 1934 as a relatively inexpensive way to provide work relief and utilize surplus commodities being generated by the New Deal's agricultural programs. The agency approved earmarked grants for local cooperatives, while a new federal "Division of Self-Help Cooperatives" issued a ream of bulletins outlining procedures to be used in relief workshops.[102] But the program quickly aroused a great deal of local opposition. Manufacturers attacked the program as "government in business," while labor unions argued that the policy undercut wages. Henry I. Harriman of the Chamber of Commerce reported to Hopkins in early September that he had received a "flood of protest" from manufacturers concerning the program. When the FERA hinted that surplus cattle hides might be turned over to federally funded workshops to produce shoes for the unemployed, the outcry reached a crescendo."[103]

To further complicate matters, a radical version of production for use became the centerpiece of the novelist Upton Sinclair's challenge to the Democratic Party in California. Sinclair, a socialist turned Democrat, proposed that the state take over idle factories to hire the unemployed and establish land colonies for impoverished farmers. Although Harry Hopkins was sympathetic to the End Poverty in California (EPIC) movement, Roosevelt wanted to distance the New Deal from Sinclair and his challenge to the Democratic Party establishment. Furthermore, victory for Sinclair would have created a serious dilemma for the FERA: would the federal agency be required to finance his radical version of self-help? Sinclair's campaign strategy included an effort to suggest New Deal support for the goals of EPIC based on FERA financing of self-help units.[104] Further complicating the politics of self-help was the fact that relief officials in Ohio had embarked on a modest experiment that appeared to resemble the EPIC plan. The state relief administration had purchased a number of idle factories and was employing relief recipients to produce garments, blankets, chinaware and furniture. Although the "Ohio Relief Production Units" was not an official FERA program, it was widely viewed as a response to FERA directives. Yet from Hopkins' viewpoint, the takeover of idle factories by the state went well beyond the production of clothing and shoes in makeshift FERA workshops. Hopkins warned Aubrey Williams to keep the Ohio experiment at arms' length: "This thing [production for use] is a political issue and the Republicans are using it all over the country. This gets into big stuff politically and I have to hold the bag."[105]

The difficulties of administering the relief program in the context of the social upheavals of 1934 provided strong support for eliminating grants in favor of a federally administered work relief program. Under such an approach, federal officials would not be left "holding the bag" as a result of the policies of state ERAs, nor would they be drawn into state legislative battles over taxes and spending.[106] A dramatic shift in relief policy was also encouraged by the administration's decision to propose a national social insurance program, a process that began with the creation of the Committee on Economic Security (CES) in June of 1934 and produced the Social Security Act the following year. The various political and social forces that produced "Social Security" have been frequently described—and debated—by historians.[107] It is important to emphasize here that the context for the creation of the CES in the spring of 1934 was profound dissatisfaction with the existing federal relief program. Thus, the committee was portrayed as planning a "permanent program" that would replace the "emergency" relief policy. "I am getting the conviction that the situation has to be handled on some other basis than a relief basis," Hopkins told reporters soon after the creation of the CES. A Washington state relief official visiting the capital in June 1934 reported that even FERA field representative Pierce Williams, a conservative holdover from the Hoover relief committees, had come to support social insurance:

Pierce believes that the whole casework and relief approach has proved its inadequacy. Something more far-reaching must come—probably social insurance and employment programs. Strong federal council to be set up soon to consider, along lines of social insurance. Feeling of insecurity growing in capital, as well as [among] unemployed.[108]

The CES also encouraged the transition to federal work relief; indeed, planners in the committee appear to have believed that public employment would be part of the "permanent program." By late summer a "technical committee on public employment and relief" had produced a report that outlined various options for a work relief program to replace the FERA. The planning for what became the WPA was quickly taken out of the hands of the CES—signaling that the public employment would not achieve a permanent status in federal policy—but work relief and the "security program" continued to be portrayed as a two-pronged attack on the existing "dole."[109]

It not clear precisely when Hopkins decided to press Roosevelt for the elimination of the FERA in favor of federal work relief, the policy first articulated by Aubrey Williams in his October 1933 memo. In his comments to the press at the time of the creation of the CES, Hopkins stressed long-term alternatives to relief such as unemployment insurance ("the British system has worked very well"), a floating public works appropriation, and "industrial decentralization."[110] In July Hopkins toured Europe to observe social insurance and public works programs (while Aubrey Williams ran the FERA). On July 25 he wrote to the president that "the more I see of this show over here the more convinced I am that we have got to adopt a plan of our own that is particularly suited to our economic situation," noting widespread "opposition to a scheme of insurance which gives a man a cash benefit over a long period of time without doing any work for the benefit." On his return on August 23 the FERA administrator renewed his criticisms of the relief program and hinted that the unemployed would be "put to work on great public projects."[111] Publicly, he called for an expansion of work relief during the coming winter under the aegis of the FERA. Privately, he was urging Roosevelt to jettison the grant program entirely. On the weekend of September 1, according to Harold Ickes in his "secret diary," Hopkins met with Roosevelt to urge an end to relief and the creation of a new federal public employment program:

He urged upon the President a public works program beginning next year involving the expenditure of $5 billion a year for five years. He thinks the relief administration ought to be abolished next year. He doesn't believe in unemployment insurance. He wants the public works program to take up any slack in employment and there is much to be said for his plan. He thinks the relief situation is going to be very serious next winter.[112]

Over the same weekend, Lewis Douglas, the most vocal opponent of work relief within the administration, resigned as budget director.

On October 1, Roosevelt convened a meeting with Hopkins, Ickes and Secretary of the Treasury Morgenthau. According to Morgenthau's notes, Roosevelt opened the meeting by announcing that at a specific date all relief cases should be returned to the states, and the federal government would initiate a public employment program for the unemployed. He suggested that the program would cost $5 billion the first year, declining to $3 billion by the third year: "The idea is that this would sufficiently prime the pump to the point where industry could relieve the Government of further burden."[113] But opposition to the new policy within the administration remained strong. The following week, Joseph Kennedy, then chairman of the Securities and Exchange Commission, and Undersecretary of the Treasury Coolidge raised objections to an expensive new work program, expressing, in Harold Ickes' words, "the confident belief that we were on the very edge of a business revival." This prognosis, which Ickes noted had been made by critics of bold government action

since 1929, did little to move the president. More effective was Morgenthau's demand that Hopkins and Ickes produce a detailed plan for the
program, listing projects and employment estimates. This pointed to serious practical difficulties of creating a program that would assist all
needy "employables" on the relief rolls and not be a rerun of CWA. It
also threatened to create friction between Ickes and Hopkins over the
administration of the program.[114]

During November and early December, press leaks and trial balloons
dominated press coverage of the emerging relief policy, as jockeying
within the administration continued. Comments by Hopkins and Roosevelt, reviving rhetorical attacks on "the dole" not heard since the Hoover years, indicated that a decision to withdraw from relief had been
made. But the contours of the new policy were not clear.[115] Would it
resemble work relief under the FERA, the public employment approach
of CWA or Ickes' public works program? What would be the cost and
the impact on the deficit?[116] Just before Thanksgiving, Secretary of Commerce Daniel Roper, a pro-business Democrat from South Carolina, assured business leaders that the administration was making, in the words
of the New York Times, "a determined effort to facilitate business recovery
by fostering confidence in the federal government's ability to handle its
relief program in a conservative manner." The following day, the Times
reported that Hopkins was about to present to Roosevelt an ambitious
work program based on "production for use" with a price tag approaching $9 billion.[117] While there is very little evidence that the FERA ad-
ministrator seriously believed such a proposal would be acceptable to
the president (the FERA was retreating from its own self-help program
in the face of attacks from business and labor), the trial balloon produced
an extreme reaction from the right wing of the business community. In
mid-December leaders of the National Association of Manufacturers "descended" on a national conference of leading business organizations
(dubbed a Joint Business Conference for Economic Recovery) and demanded a frontal attack on the emerging work relief program. The conference produced a statement that, while generally adopting a
conciliatory tone, suggested that the New Deal should abandon work
relief and continue the grant program. This, in turn, provided an opening
for Hopkins and congressional supporters of public employment, who
sharply attacked the business leaders for advocating the "dole."[118]

The anti-dole rhetoric with which the administration justified the shift
to work relief also profoundly influenced the emerging Social Security
program. The administration rejected proposals to continue federal aid
for general relief through a federal Department of Public Welfare, pre-
ferring instead to provide matching grants to state "categorical" programs (primarily Old Age Assistance and mothers' pensions). Roosevelt
also sided with the more conservative proposals for state-administered

unemployment compensation and called for a "contributory" old age pension plan, rejecting more liberal schemes for financing from general revenues. Historians have seen these "conservative" features of the 1935 law as concessions to elite corporate interests or, alternatively, as responses to the political realities of passing and maintaining congressional support for social insurance.[119] But they were also shaped by the administration's strong aversion to anything that appeared to have the characteristics of relief. "We must not allow this type of insurance to become a dole through the mingling of insurance and relief," Roosevelt told a National Conference on Economic Security in November. "It is not charity. It must be financed by contributions not taxes." The FERA's Josephine Brown, who was part of an insider lobbying effort to create a permanent federal department of public welfare, made this clear to Walter West of the American Association of Social Workers. She stressed the need to emphasize the "administrative gains which need to be consolidated," not the relief aspects of the proposal: "if [a federal welfare department] is to be accepted by Mr. Roosevelt as part of his program it must be put up not as a continuation of direct relief, which the FERA is dropping but a welfare program. . . . In other words, this is not a program of relief to the unemployable as a regrettable substitute for wages but a welfare program for the disabled and handicapped."[120]

Thus, opposition to the "dole" became the justification for the administration's decision to set aside, temporarily, the goal of a balanced budget and embrace public employment. The argument, in perhaps its most extreme form, appeared in Roosevelt's speech to Congress on January 4, 1935, when he made the famous pledge that "the federal government must and shall quit this business of relief":

The lessons of history, confirmed by the immediate evidence before me, show conclusively that continued dependence on relief induces a spiritual and moral disintegration fundamentally destructive to the national fiber. To dole out relief in this way is to administer a narcotic, a subtle destroyer of the human spirit. It is inimical to the dictates of sound policy. It is a violation of the traditions of America. Work must be found for able-bodied but destitute workers. . . . I am not willing that the vitality of our people be further sapped by the giving of cash, of market baskets, of a few hours of weekly work cutting grass, raking leaves or picking up papers in the public parks.[121]

Roosevelt's rhetoric dismayed social workers, who believed that the administration was caving in, in Russell Kurtz's words, to "the growing pressure, now coming from the middle classes rather than the possessors of large wealth, that the 'dole' must go."[122] Similarly, some historians have depicted the program as an effort to force unemployed workers into the labor market. But whatever one may think of the descision to end the FERA grant program, the WPA was also a victory for liberals who had fought for public employment since the demobilization of CWA. These included not only Aubrey Williams, who had considered federal public employment a "hallucination of grandeur" when he had first proposed the policy in October 1933, and Hopkins, who had waged a skillful, yearlong battle within the administration, but the congressional defenders of the CWA, social workers who had opposed the demobilization of CWA and the grassroots movement of unemployed relief recipients, most of whom supported work relief rather than public "charity." As Anthony Badger has argued, the 1935 program "was not a conservative contraction of the government's welfare commitment; rather it represented a progressive expansion of that commitment, an expansion long sought by professional social workers. . . . It was also what the unemployed themselves wanted."[123] This reality has been obscured by the sharp criticisms of the FERA's decision to dismantle the grant program by these same forces; by the New Deal's own rhetoric, which appeared to be a concession to its conservative critics; and by the chaos that followed the end of the FERA in 1936.[124]

NOTES

1. A note on terminology: The terms *public employment* and *work relief* are used interchangeably throughout this chapter to describe the New Deal's various work experiments (CWA, the FERA's work program and the WPA). There are, however, important distinctions between the two policies that should be noted. Work relief generally referred to the employment of relief recipients at "wages" geared to welfare benefits, as determined by the means test. Thus, workers, despite being employed and generally receiving higher benefits, remained within the existing relief framework. Public employment programs utilized relief labor but paid hourly wages and pulled workers out of the public welfare system. Workers were not subjected to income testing and investigation by social workers. By these standards, the CWA was a public employment program, the FERA's 1934 work program was not and the WPA was a hybrid, paying standard monthly "security wage" but requiring an initial income test. Bonnie Fox Schwartz has argued that by these measures—and the predominance of efficiency experts rather than welfare officials in the civil works bureaucracy—the CWA was the only true public employment program of the New Deal. In my view, CWA was the closest to public employment but never entirely broke the connection with relief. Both the second FERA's work program and especially the WPA paid significantly higher wages than traditional work relief and involved a less rigid application of the means test. Thus, I argue that all these programs were much closer to public employment than work relief prior to CWA. Bonnie Fox Schwartz, *The Civil Works Administration: The Business of Emergency Employment in the New Deal* (Princeton, NJ: Princeton University Press, 1984).

2. Harry Hopkins, *Spending to Save* (New York: W.W. Norton, 1936), 124.

3. Kenneth Davis, *Franklin D. Roosevelt: The New Deal Years, 1933–1937* (New

York: Random House, 1986), 306; George McJimsey, *Harry Hopkins, Ally of the Poor and Defender of Democracy* (Cambridge, MA: Harvard University Press, 1987), 76; Robert S. McElvaine, *The Great Depression* (New York: Times Books, 1993), 254; Roger Biles, *A New Deal for the American People* (De Kalb: University of Illinois Press, 1991), 104; Anthony Badger, *The New Deal* (New York: Hill and Wang, 1989), 197, 200–201. For an influential analysis that sees the origins of the New Deal's work relief philosophy as rooted in the social work reform tradition see William W. Bremer, "Along the American Way: The New Deal's Work Relief Programs for the Unemployed," *The Journal of American History* 62 (December 1975): 636–637. Bonnie Fox Schwartz, on the other hand, sees work relief as a rejection of social work principles. Schwartz, *The Civil Works Administration*, 221–225.

4. Russell Kurtz, "Relief from Relief," *Survey* (December 1933): 404. On the problems faced by early depression work relief experiments see Joanna Colcord, William Koplovitz and Russell Kurtz, *Emergency Work Relief* (New York: Russell Sage Foundation, 1932), 248–249.

5. Kurtz, "Relief from Relief." On the various forms of work relief see Colcord, Koplovitz and Kurtz, *Emergency Work Relief*, 225–228.

6. Hopkins, *Spending to Save*, 124.

7. Until the late 1970s, the CWA had not been the subject of a monographic study. Then Forrest Walker's *The Civil Works Administration: An Experiment in Federal Work Relief, 1933–1934* (New York: Garland Publishing Company, 1979) and Schwartz's *The Civil Works Administration* filled this important gap. As a result, recent studies of the New Deal (Badger, *The New Deal* and Biles, *A New Deal for the American People*) have stressed the significance of the CWA. Yet the program's role in transforming the Roosevelt administration's welfare policy is still not widely appreciated.

8. Schwartz, *The Civil Works Administration*, 52–71.

9. Transcript of speech to Millbank Memorial Fund, April 16, 1934, FERA-OSF, Box 17, File: Hopkins, H.L. Speeches.

10. Richard Lowitt and Maurice Beardsley, eds., *One Third of a Nation: Lorena Hickok Reports on the Great Depression* (Urbana: University of Illinois Press, 1981), 117; Sherwood, *Roosevelt and Hopkins* (New York Bantam Book, 1950), 66; Clarence King to Harry Hopkins, March 12, 1934, FERA, Box 306, File: Washington Field Reports.

11. Like so much about the decision-making process that produced CWA, the financing of the program is poorly documented and has been influenced by anecdotal accounts. Robert Sherwood, for example, reports Roosevelt, at the meeting that decided to launch the program, as musing, "Let's see. . . . Four million people—that means roughly four hundred million dollars." Yet it is hard to imagine that Hopkins believed $400 million would be sufficient to finance the employment for nearly three months. According to George McJimsey, Hopkins initially proposed spending $600 million, with FERA funds supplementing the PWA transfer. Sherwood, *Roosevelt and Hopkins*, 63; McJimsy, *Harry Hopkins*, 59. For Harold Ickes' account of CWA financing see *The Secret Diary of Harold Ickes, the First Thousand Days* (New York: Simon and Schuster, 1953), 116–117, 119.

12. Schwartz, *The Civil Works Administration*, 213, 219; Hopkins to the Presi-

dent: Budget Estimates, December 29, 1933, FDR Library, OF444, File: FERA, September–December 1933.

13. McJimsey, *Harry Hopkins*, 59, 62.

14. Memo on CWA Wages, January 18, 1934, FERA, Box 12, File: Forms—January 1933; Russell Kurtz, "An End to Civil Works," *Survey* (February, 1934): 36.

15. Forrest Walker has systematically reviewed the letters received at CWA headquarters in Washington and found that only a small percentage expressed complaints about local political interference in the program. Bonnie Fox Schwartz has portrayed the CWA as the New Deal's only true public employment program. Walker, *The Civil Works Administration*; Schwartz, *The Civil Works Administration*, 259.

16. Schwartz, *The Civil Works Administration*, 48–49; *New York Times*, November 19, 1933, VIII, 1; Arthur Burns and Edward A. Williams, *Federal Work, Security and Relief Programs* (New York: Da Capo Press, 1971), 29.

17. Kurtz, "Relief from Relief," 404.

18. New York: *New York Times*, November 28, 1933, 26; Howard Hunter to Hopkins, December 4, 1933, in Harry Hopkins Papers (Group 24 at FDR Library), General Correspondence, 1933–1940, Container 20, File: Howard Hunter; Schwartz, *The Civil Works Administration*, 43.

19. Edith Foster, Field Report from Alabama, December 4–6, 1933, Box 3, File: Alabama Field Reports; Pierce Williams to Harry Hopkins, December 13, 1933, Box 26, File: California Field Reports, both in FERA Files.

20. Michigan: Howard Hunter to Hopkins, December 29, 1933, FERA, Box 37, File: Michigan Field Reports. St. Louis: "Relief and Economic Background in St. Louis, Missouri," undated memo, FERA-OSF, Box 11, File: Surveys.

21. Washington, Michigan, Illinois: Robert J. Myers to Corrington Gill, April 12, 1934, Box 76, File: Illinois, January–May 1934.

22. Hopkins, *Spending to Save*, 116; Edith Foster, Report from Louisiana, December 7–10, 1933, FERA Box 114, File: Field Reports; Pierce Williams to Harry Hopkins, December 13, 1933, FERA, Box 26, File: California Field Reports. Williams' argument for the termination of CWA was contained in a memo dated February 6, 1934, FERA-OSF, Box 10, File: Field Representatives Reports.

23. Edith Foster, Report from Alabama, December 4–6, 1933, Box 3, File: Alabama Field Reports; Virgil L. Mitchell, *The Civil Works Administration in Louisiana: A Study in New Deal Relief, 1933–1934* (Lafayette: University of Southwest Louisiana Press, 1976), 26.

24. Joanna Colcord, "Right About Face," *Survey* 70, no. 4 (April 1934): 11; Doris Carothers, *Chronology of the Federal Emergency Relief Administration*, WPA Research Monograph no. 6 (1937), 38.

25. Memo re Investigation of Relief Applicants, January 3, 1934, FERA, Box 12, File: Forms—January 1934.

26. Carothers, *FERA Chronology*, 41; Burns and Williams, *Federal Work, Relief and Security Programs*, 34.

27. *New York Times*, January 23, 1934, 1, 2; Kurtz, "An End to Civil Works," 36; BJ Loucks to Corrington Gill, June 16, 1934, FERA, Box 265, File: June–December 1934.

28. *Survey* 70, no. 5 (May 1934): 169; Howard Hunter to Hopkins, April 1, 1934, FERA-OSF, Box 10, File: Field Reps. Reports.

29. Mandel to Hopkins, June 20, 1934 FERA-OSF, Box 27, File: Memorandum M. See also reports in Box 196, Files: January–July 1934; *New York Times*, April 1, 1934, 3; May 6, 1934, 8.

30. Minneapolis: Transcript of Hopkins Telephone Conversation with Daniels, April 7, 1934, FERA Box 196, File: New York: January–April 1934; "Relief and Economic Background in St. Louis, Missouri," undated report, FERA-OSF, Box 11, File: Surveys.

31. Arch Mandel to Aubrey Williams, April 9, 1934, in FERA, Box 250, File: Pennsylvania Field Reports; F.D. Henderson to Hopkins, April 5, 1934, FERA, Box 222, File: Ohio, January–June.

32. *New York Times*, April 1, 1934, 12; Colcord, "Right About Face," 111.

33. *New York Times*, March 1, 1934, 1, 14.

34. In March Hopkins announced that the work program caseload for the spring and summer would average between 1.5 and 2 million workers (*New York Times*, March 30, 1934, 2). Pressure from local officials and former CWA recipients forced the administration to finance a slightly higher work program caseload, and the total national caseload, averaged in excess of 4 million. According to Russell Kurtz, writing in the *Survey*, FERA officials were generally disappointed with the work program that followed the CWA. See Russell Kurtz, "Work—And More of It," *Survey* 70, no. 9 (September 1934): 275.

35. William Hodson, "The Social Worker and the New Deal," *Proceedings of the National Conference on Social Work* [hereafter NCSW] (Chicago: University of Chicago Press, 1934), 6–7; Mary Van Cleeck, "Our Illusions Regarding Government," NCSW, 1934, 477–480; Colcord, "Right-About Face," 111. Mary Van Kleeck "electrified" the same conference with a Marxist critique of New Deal policy, arguing that the demobilization of CWA was a clear retreat in the face of attacks from elite business interests.

36. Thus, I am not convinced by Bonnie Fox Schwartz's argument that the work program was "really a return to the FERA work division, which had existed prior to CWA." A significant retreat from CWA it was, but this view seems excessively dismal. Schwartz, *The Civil Works Administration*, 239.

37. Arthur Burns, "The Federal Emergency Relief Administration," in Clarence E. Ridley and Orin F. Noltin, eds., *The Municipal Yearbook, 1937* (Chicago: International City Managers Association, 1937), 395; Edward A. Williams, *Federal Aid for Relief* (New York: Columbia University Press, 1939), 109–110; Corrington Gill, *Wasted Manpower* (New York: W.W. Norton, 1939), 170.

38. "Practice Sheets," memo from Jacob Baker, March 21, 1934, and "Outline of Suggested Projects for Work Division," March 20, 1934, both in FERA, Box 12, File: Forms—March 1934; Jacob Baker, "Opening Statement to Conference on Demolition," March 23, 1934, FERA-OSF, Box 7, File: Conferences; memo to Directors of Local Work Divisions, July 25, 1934, FERA, Box 13, File: Forms—July 1934. The latter memo emphasizes the difference between the role of the work division under the second FERA and the CWA program. See also "The Emergency Work Relief Program of the FERA," April 1, 1934–July 1, 1935, Federal Emergency Relief Administration Publications, vol. 4, 10–18; and Schwartz, *The Civil Works Administration*, 240–243. Regarding federal approval of white-collar

projects see Hopkins memo on White Collar Projects, April 20, 1934, FERA-OSF, Box 13, File: Forms—April 1934.

39. Colcord, "Right About Face," 111. Similarly, the *New York Times*, in early March, suggested that "civil works will be continued much as at present but on a smaller scale and not so named," *New York Times*, March 1, 1934, 14.

40. According to the FERA directive of March 6, work program "wages shall be at the prevailing rate for the occupation and the locality in which the work is done, and in no case will the pay be less than will yield thirty cents per hour, provided, however, that hours shall be limited so that the maximum weekly earnings shall not in any case exceed the amount necessary to meet budgetary requirements." Prevailing rates were to be determined by a committee appointed by the local relief administrator, which was to include representatives of business, labor and the ERA. "Work Program-Statement of Policy," FERA-OSF, Box 12, File: Forms, March 1934.

41. In Los Angeles the higher cost of work relief was explained by higher "retail costs for work relief against wholesale costs to the Department of Charities." In addition, the monthly allowance included $1.50 for clothes and $2.00 for "carfare." Report of Los Angeles County—Supplementary Report, July 30–October 5, 1934, FERA Box 25, File: California Field Reports; Josephine C. Brown, *Public Relief 1929–1939* (New York: Henry Holt and Co., 1940), 195; *New York Times*, September 3, 1934, 1. On the FERA policy see Pierce Williams to Harry Hopkins, February 6, 1934, FERA-OSF, Box 10, File: Field Representatives Reports.

42. Memo on professional and nonmanual work projects, July 2, 1934, File: Forms (July 1934); telegram from Jacob Baker on drought relief, June 4, 1934, File: Forms (June), both in FERA-OSF, Box 13. The original rural relief program, announced in March of 1934, explicitly called for cash payments only in "exceptional cases." "Rural Program: Statement of Policy," March 20, 1934, FERA-OSF, File: Forms (March).

43. "Review of Economic Conditions," November 20, 1934, FERA, Jacob Baker Files, File: Working Papers and Plans for New Work Program; Wayne Parrish to Hopkins, November 11, 1934, in Roosevelt Library, Official File 444, File: FERA, November–December 1934.

44. Federal Works Agency, *Final Statistical Report of the FERA*, 21; Joanna Colcord, *Cash Relief* (New York: Russell Sage Foundation, 1936), 32–43; "Cash Relief and Relief in Kind," *Monthly Report of the Federal Emergency Relief Administration*, January 1935, 16–23.

45. James J. Lorence, *Organizing the Unemployed: Community and Union Activities in the Industrial Heartland* (Albany: State University of New York Press, 1996), 90–96; Jacob Fisher, *The Response of Social Work to the Great Depression* (Cambridge, MA: Schenkman, 1980), 108–110. The argument here would appear to contradict Roy Rosenzweig's analysis of the relationship between New Deal policy and protest. Rosenzweig found a decline in support for the Unemployed Leagues, organized by radical followers of the socialist A.J. Muste primarily in Ohio and Indiana, during 1934—a decline that he suggested was caused by the liberalization of relief policy under the New Deal. The argument here is that policy liberalizations following CWA produced an expansion of protest. In the case of Ohio, it would appear that protest organizations, which focused on work relief projects, replaced and absorbed those organized by the followers of Muste. See

Roy Rosenzweig, "Radicals and the Jobless: The Musteites and the Unemployed Leagues. 1932–1936," *Labor History* 6, no. 1 (Winter 1975): 63, 72.

46. Fisher, *The Response of Social Work*, 119–121; John Earl Hines, "The Rank and File Movement in Social Work," *Labor History* 6, no. 1 (Winter 1975): 82–83.

47. "Brief Summary of Conditions in Hunters Group," FERA, Box 229, File: Ohio Field Reports; William Nunn to Jacob Baker, June 25, 1934, FERA, Box 183, File: June–September 1934.

48. Lorence, *Organizing the Unemployed*, 82; John Gambs to Jacob Baker, February 27, 1935, FERA, Jacob Baker Files, Box 4, File—Labor Relations—WD.

49. Memo on Milwaukee, August 30–31, 1934, FERA-OSF, Box 4, File: Labor Relations, July–December 1934; telegram from Harold L. Hall (Chicago Workers Committee to Hopkins), March 14, 1935, FERA, Box 77, File Illinois: February–March 1935.

50. Ohio: W.B. Hooper to Corrington Gill, June 21, 1934, FERA Files, Box 222, File: June–September 1934. Michigan: Lorence, *Organizing the Unemployed*, 93.

51. Hopkins telephone conversation with Henderson, April 10, 1934, FERA, Box 222, File: Ohio, January–May 1934. See also Hopkins to H.E. Braught in the same file. The FERA responded to strikes on work relief projects in Michigan by granting the state an additional $250,000 for the month of July. See Howard Hunter to Aubrey Williams, June 26, 1934, Box 137, File: Field Reports, Michigan.

52. Federal Works Agency, *Final Statistical Report*.

53. Much of the increase in federal relief spending can be explained by the cost of the new "work program." Monthly expenditures for work relief, which had averaged $23 million under the grant program of 1933, averaged $64 million after CWA. Yet the actual number of recipients on work relief was not significantly higher in the spring and summer of 1934 than during the same period the previous year. Most of the increase in work relief expenditures is explained by benefit levels to recipients on work projects. Furthermore, federal funds were now used to pay for professional and supervisory personnel attached to projects but not on relief. Finally, the federal government began to incur obligations for the purchase of materials and equipment. Throughout 1934, nonrelief expenditures accounted for approximately 20 percent of total work relief spending. In short, increased federal expenditures for work relief under the "second FERA" reflected the cost of moving beyond "make-work."

Spending for direct relief was also considerably above that for the previous year. For example, data collected by the FERA shows that average monthly obligations for direct relief were approximately 50 percent higher during the summer of 1934 than during the same period in 1933. Most of the increase was produced by the higher caseload resulting from the influx of workers as CWA was terminated. Furthermore, the caseload failed to decline during the summer of 1933 and began to rise again in the fall. The other important factor leading to an increase in direct relief expenditures during 1934 was higher allowances paid to recipients. Indeed, benefit levels for those not employed on work relief appear to have increased by 50 percent between April and December of 1934.

54. Howard Hunter to Hopkins, August 16, 1934, FERA-OSF, Box 10, File: Field Representatives' Reports.

55. *New York Times*, October 31, 1934, 1; November 10, 1934, 1; November 20, 1934, 1. Republicans appear to have genuinely believed that the "relief vote" was

responsible for their political woes. As Clyde P. Weed has suggested, this may
have been a way of avoiding the reality of the emerging political realignment.
But attacking political interference in relief was also a way of criticizing the New
Deal without opposing popular work relief initiatives in principle. See Clyde P.
Weed, *The Nemesis of Reform: The Republican Party during the New Deal* (New York:
Columbia University Press, 1994), 47, 73.

56. *Survey* 70, no. 1 (January 1935): 23; Howard Hunter to Hopkins, August
16, 1934, in FERA-OSF, Box 10, File: Field Representatives Reports; *New York
Times*, November 22, 1934, 2.

57. "Review of Economic Conditions," November 20, 1934, FERA, Jacob
Baker Files, File: Working Papers and Plans for New Work Program.

58. Hopkins to Wilfred Reynolds, October 22, 1934, FERA, Box 77, File: Illinois, November–December 1934. A lengthy summary of the reports was trans-
mitted to Roosevelt in March 1935. See "Summary of Relief Reports to the
President," March 8, 1935, Roosevelt Library, Official File 444, File: FERA,
March—May 1935.

59. Wayne Parrish to Hopkins, November 11, 1934 in Roosevelt Library, Official File 444, File: FERA, November–December 1934.

60. David Maynard, Report from Indianapolis, November 17, 1934; Bruce Mc-
Clure, Report from Pennsylvania, in Roosevelt Library, Official File 444, File:
FERA, November–December 1934. See also McElvaine, *The Great Depression*, 178–
179.

61. Hopkins to the President, July 25, 1934, OF 444, File: FERA, July–August
1934; *Survey* 70 (September 1934): 277; *New York Times*, August 16, 1934, 2.

62. *New York Times*, November 12, 1934, 5. See also August 16, 1934, 2; November 24, 1934, 13; *Survey* 70, no. 9 (September 1934): 277.

63. William R. Brock, *Welfare, Democracy and the New Deal* (Cambridge: Cambridge University Press, 1986), 262–265.

64. In late March of 1934, for example, he told reporters that the relief rolls
were made up of "the finest people in America" but added that the "federal
government [should not] be encouraged to stay in the relief picture forever. We
have done nothing and will do nothing to encourage the setup of a permanent
relief machinery of this kind." Similarly, Aubrey Williams suggested that "[t]here
is not a person from the top to the bottom of the Federal Emergency Relief
Administration who would not like to work himself out of a job," adding that
the "bread of charity is bitter bread, and no man likes to grind his wheat to make
it."*New York Times*, April 1, 1934, IX, 1.

65. Alan Brinkley, *The End of Reform* (New York: Alfred Knopf, 1995), 83–85,
94–104; Dean May, *From New Deal to New Economics* (New York: Garland, 1981),
chs. 6–7.

66. Perhaps the best account of depression-era budget debates can be found
in May, *From New Deal to New Economics*, 31–36. See also *New York Times*, January
6, 1932, VIII, 1.

67. *New York Times*, June 6, 1933, 27; May, *From New Deal to New Economics*,
35–36.

68. Davis, *FDR: The New Deal Years*, 302–305; Jordan A. Schwarz, *The New
Dealers* (New York: Random House, 1994), 134–135; Robert Skidelsky, *John Maynard Keynes: A Biography*, vol. 2 (New York: Viking Penguin, 1994), 491–494.

69. McJimsey, *Harry Hopkins*, 74. See also Williams, "The New Deal—A Dead Battery," 74, in Aubrey Williams Papers, FDR Library, Box 44, File: same as title; John Salmond, *Southern Rebel: The Life and Times of Aubrey Williams* (Chapel Hill: University of North Carolina Press, 1983), 69. On Roosevelt's economic advisers see Schwarz, *The New Dealers*, 101.

70. *New York Times*, January 28, 1934, IV, 4. On the protests against the CWA cuts see *New York Times*, January 23, 1934, 1, 2: Kurtz, "An End to Civil Works," 36.

71. Schwartz, *The Civil Works Administration*, 219–220; Lester G. Seligman and Elmer E. Cornwell, eds., *New Deal Mosaic* (Eugene: University of Oregon Press, 1965), 76.

72. Badger, *The New Deal*, 200; Biles, *A New Deal for the American People*, 103–104.

73. William Bremer, *Depression Winters: Social Workers and the New Deal* (Philadelphia: Temple University Press, 1984), 136; "Hopkins Statement at Staff Conference, "December 1933, in Hopkins Papers, Group 29, Container 49 Folder: Staff Conferences, November–December 1933.

74. On the early FERA termination see *New York Times*, March 6, 1934, 13. In an undated memo to the president (probably in late March or early April 1934), Hopkins estimated that he had saved $100 million by terminating CWA on March 31 instead of April 30. Hopkins to the President, "Funds Required by the Federal Emergency Relief Administration, April 1, 1934, through June 30, 1934," Roosevelt Library, Official File 444, File: FERA, April–June 1934.

75. *New York Times*, December 14, 1934, 7.

76. The evolution of the "emergency budget" for fiscal year (FY) 1935 is based on *New York Times* reports, particularly April 16, 1934, 1; April 17, 1934, 34; May 15, 1934, 38; May 16, 1934, 1; June 5, 1934, 10; June 16, 1934, 1; June 19, 1934, 18. See also *New York Times*, September 1, 1934, 2.

77. *New York Times*, August 26, 1934, 12; September 1, 1934, 2; Kurtz, "Work—And More of It." For a detailed discussion of the financing of the second FERA and the methods of allocation from the various congressional appropriations see Arthur Burns, "Federal Financing of Emergency Relief," *Monthly Report of the F.E.R.A*, February 1936, 10–16; Burns, "Federal Emergency Relief Grants to the States."

78. Davis, *FDR: The New Deal Years*, 319–321; Schwarz, *The New Dealers*, 135.

79. Walter Lippmann, "Inflation and the Dole," *Delaware Journal-Evening News*, December 26, 1934, News Clip in Jacob Baker Files, Files: Committee on Economic Security. For an analysis that stresses the influence of Keynes on the debate between spenders and fiscal conservatives see *New York Times*, January 6, 1935, VIII, 1. See also Skidelsky, *John Maynard Keynes*, 494, 508.

80. *New York Times*, April 17, 1934, 20.

81. The story of relief financing in Ohio may be followed in FERA, Files, Box 222. See especially J.R. Blough, "Ohio Relief Financing," February 9, 1934, File: February—May. 1934; Ohio Relief Estimate June 1, 1934, File: June–September 1934. See also Ohio Need Estimate, February 9, 1935, Box 221, File: Ohio Official—February, March 1935; David Maurer, "Public Relief Programs and Politics in Ohio" (Ph.D. diss., Ohio State University, 1962), 129.

82. For relief estimates in Pennsylvania see estimates in Box 250, File: Penn-

sylvania Official. See especially needs estimates on June 1, 1934, and October 1, 1934. For Pinchot's demands on the FERA see material in Box 248, File: Pennsylvania, June–July 1934, especially Pinchot to FDR, June 10, 1934; "Memorandum on Governor Pinchot's Letter of June 10," June 27, 1934.

83. See memoranda and correspondence in FERA, Box 248, File: Pennsylvania, August–September 1934, especially "Plan for Financing Emergency Relief in Pennsylvania . . . ," August 27, 1934; E.T. Leech to Fred W. Perkins, August 30, 1934; Landsdale to Hopkins, September 17, 1934; Aubrey Williams to Biddle, September 28, 1934. In Illinois, where the monthly post-CWA relief bill had nearly doubled over the previous year, the state legislature had not passed legislation for relief since a 1932 bond issue. Hopkins warned that no funds would be available after November unless the FERA received "definite assurance" that the state would provide "a substantial and proper proportion of the relief funds which will be required within the state." After more prodding and threats, the state passed legislation that would provide $3 million for relief in 1935 but then refused to appropriate the funds after April. At this point, yet another crisis ensued as the FERA threatened to withhold federal aid entirely. See material in FERA, Box 78, Files November–April 1934, especially Hopkins to Horner, November 6, 1934, and Howard Hunter to Hopkins, April 27, 1934.

84. Conflicts between FERA and the states have been emphasized in James T. Pattterson's *The New Deal and the States: Federalism in Transition* (Westport, CT: Greenwood Press, 1981), ch. 3; Brock, *Welfare, Democracy and the New Deal*, ch. 6.

85. Corrington Gill, "Collecting the Relief Billions," *Survey* (October 1934): 311.

86. Brock, *Welfare, Democracy and the New Deal*, 173–174; Patterson, *The New Deal and the States*, 73.

87. Williams, *Federal Aid for Relief*, 177–178; Brock, *Welfare, Democracy and the New Deal*, 253–256; Maurer, "Public Relief Programs and Politics in Ohio," 129–136.

88. Williams to Hopkins, February 6, 1934, FERA-OSF, Box 10, File: Field Representatives Reports.

89. Bonnie Fox Schwartz, "Social Workers and New Deal Politicians in Conflict: California's Branion-Williams Case, 1933–1934," *Pacific Historical Review* 43, no. 1 (February 1973). California was not the only place where the civil works program produced political conflict. In Tacoma, Washington, the local Democratic Party attacked the CWA organization as a "big farce" because it was administered by a Republican not loyal to the New Deal. See *Ryan's Weekly*, February 24, 1934, news clip in Warrren Magnuson Papers, Box 1, Folder 18, University of Washington Library-Pacific Northwest Collection.

90. *New York Times*, April 1, 1935, 1. On the political motivations for the attacks see *New York Times*, April 16, 1935, 20.

91. *New York Times*, April 3, 1935, 1; April 4, 1935, 1; *Survey* 71, no. 5 (May 1935): 150.

92. See, for example, Biles, *A New Deal for the American People*, 119–127; McElvaine, *The Great Depression*, 249. Edwin Amenta, however, has forcefully argued against the conventional wisdom which sees the social policy legislation of the "second New Deal" as a response to protest. Amenta, *Bold Relief: Institu-*

tional Politics and the Origins of American Social Policy (Princeton NJ: Princeton University Press, 1998), 108–117.

93. An excellent source that captures the upsurge of protest during the spring and summer of 1934 is the files of the head of the FERA work division, Jacob Baker. See particularly files marked "Labor Relations" in Box 4, FERA Files.

94. Memos dated July 14 and 16, 1934, in Jacob Baker Files, Box 4, File: July–December 1934.

95. On New Jersey see William Nunn to Jacob Baker, June 25, 1934, FERA, Box 183, File: June–September 1934. Regarding the Ohio meeting see C.C. Stillman to Aubrey Williams, July 16, 1934, FERA, Box 222, File: Ohio Field Reports.

96. Concerning the CWA cuts see Arthur Krock in *New York Times*, January 28, 1934, IV, 1. Krock noted that some "cynics" saw the January 1934 CWA wage reductions as a "charade" by the New Deal to provoke protest. But Krock saw Roosevelt's policy as based on the "firm conviction" that the budget should be balanced. See also Russell Kurtz, "An End to Civil Works," 36. On the impact of CWA protest on relief policy see *New York Times*, January 28, 1934, IV, 4.

97. Howard Hunter to Harry Hopkins, August 16, 1934, Box 10, File: Field Reps. Reports. Hopkins received numerous requests to adopt an official policy on organizations of the unemployed, but the FERA administrator refused to promulgate a specific set of guidelines. See FERA, Box 195, File: New York, October–December 1935; T.J. Edmunds to Hopkins, May 17, 1934, FERA—Jacob Baker Files, Box 4, File: Labor Relations, January–June 1934. See also in the same files transcripts and memos on the arrest of protesters in Oklahoma City on charges of "seditious conspiracy."

98. Howard Hunter to Hopkins, April 6, 1934, Old Subject File, Box 10, File: Field Reps. reports. Re the impact of the San Francisco general strike on the FERA caseload see documents in FERA, Box 22, File: California, July 1934.

99. Doris Carothers, *Chronology of the Federal Emergency Relief Administration*, WPA Research Monograph no. 6 (Washington, DC: Government Printing Office, 1937), 22; *New York Times*, August 2, 1934, 31; August 30, 1934, 5; James Myers, "Relief to Strikers' Families," *Survey* 70, no. 10 (October 1934): 307–308.

100. Transcript of Telephone Conversation between Hopkins and Aubrey Williams, August 30, 1934, FERA—Jacob Baker Files, Box 4, File: Labor Relations, July–December 1934; McJimsey, *Harry Hopkins*, 73–74.

101. The most detailed history of self-help in the early 1930s is Clark Kerr, "Productive Enterprises of the Unemployed, 1931–1938" (Ph.D. diss., University of California, 1939). See also Clark Kerr and Paul S. Taylor, "Whither Self-Help?," *Survey Graphic* 23 (July 1934): 399.

The relationship between self-help and protest was complex and highly controversial in the 1930s. Since the movement often advocated public financing of low-level productive activities (and even government seizure of idle factories), it was generally viewed as radical and socialist by the business community. Elements of the Left, on the other hand, often argued that production for use co-opted workers, giving them a stake in the administration of relief and, in the words of Leonard Leader, taking them "off the soap boxes." Even Upton Sinclair argued that "if the real conservatives of this hour only understood, they would not try to thwart your EPIC program." Conversely, a number of observers in the 1930s argued that political action—in the form of protest or electoral politics—

tended to undermine the grassroots cooperative movement. See Kerr, "Productive Enterprises of the Unemployed," 338–339; Leonard Leader, "Los Angeles and the Great Depression" (Ph.D. diss., UCLA, 1972), 120, 145; James Hannah, "Urban Reaction to the Great Depression, 1929–1933" (Ph.D. diss., University of California, 1963), 128–129.

102. Kerr, 777–788. For an example of FERA practice sheets see "Specifications for Mattress, Double Bed," July 5–6, 1934, in FERA-OSF File: Forms July 1933; "Cooperative Self-Help," Monthly Bulletin for Cooperatives of the Unemployed, FERA Publications, vol. 4, in FERA Files.

103. Harriman to Hopkins, FERA-OSF, Box 17, File: Goods, T–U. For other complaints about production for use see Box 14, File: Forms October 1934; New York Times, December 8, 1934, 11; Poppendieck, Breadlines Knee Deep in Wheat: Food Assistance and the Great Depression (New Brunswick, NJ: Rutgers University Press, 1986), 163–169.

104. Kerr, Productive Enterprises of the Unemployed, 463–464.

105. Hopkins Telephone Conversation with Aubrey Williams, August 30, 1934, FERA, Jacob Baker Files, Box 4, File: Labor Relations—July, December 1934. For an excellent discussion of the Ohio Relief Production Units (ORPU) see Maurer, "Public Relief Programs and Politics in Ohio," 91–94; see also Joanna Colcord, "Ohio Produces for Ohioans," Survey 70, no. 12 (December 1934): 371–373.

106. For a discussion that stresses the problems encountered by the grant approach to relief as a key influence on the decision to create a federally administered work program see Burns and Williams, Federal Work, Relief and Security Programs, 55–56. See also New York Times, May 5, 1935, IV, 8, which stressed the fact that a federal public employment program would eliminate the battles over state relief financing.

107. See, for example, Edward G. Berkowitz and Kim McQuaid, Creating the Welfare State: The Political Economy of Twentieth Century Reform (New York: Praeger, 1980); Jill S. Quadagno, "Welfare Capitalism and the Social Security Act of 1935," American Sociological Review 35 (October 1984); Theda Skocpol with G. John Ikenberry, "The Road to Social Security," in Skocpol, Social Policy in the United States (Princeton, NJ: Princeton University Press, 1995), J. Craig Jenkins and Barbara A. Brents, "Social Protest, Hegemonic Competition and Social Reform: A Political Struggle Interpretation of the Origins of the American Welfare State," American Sociological Review 54 (1989): 891–909; and a critique by Edwin Amenta and Sunita Parikh, "Capitalists Did Not Want the Social Security Act: A Critique of the Capitalist Dominance Thesis," American Sociological Review 56 (1991): 124–129. For Amenta's recent contribution to this debate see Amenta, Bold Relief, ch. 3.

108. New York Times, June 26, 1934, 1, 3; John Hall to Charles F. Ernst, July 28, 1934, Ernst Papers, Box 1, File 7.

109. On the linkage between the economic security program and relief see Survey 70, no. 9 (September 1934): 277. The "Preliminary Report of the Staff of the Committee on Economic Security," prepared by Edwin E. Witte in September 1934, placed the "permanent policy" squarely within the context of the need to reform the existing relief program: "emergency relief is essentially poor relief with most of the demoralizing effects the latter term implies. . . . It is a stop-gap not a solution" (35). CES Box 6, File: Preliminary Report. An appendix of this

report, prepared by the FERA's Emerson Ross, discussed a range of options for public employment. For the CES committee on public employment see the material in FERA—Jacob Baker Files, File: Economic Security. See also "Security Employment—Part of a Program for National Economic Security," November 21, 1934, unsigned memo in Aubrey Williams Files, Box 27, File 2, at the FDR Library,

110. *New York Times*, June 26, 1934, 1, 3. The *Survey* editorialized that Hopkins comments on relief's not being the American way "recalls the old story of the man who couldn't be put in jail—but there he was." The editors, writing in July, noted Hopkins' policy proposals but did not mention a new federal work relief program. *Survey* 70, no. 7 (July 1934): 222.

111. Hopkins to the President, July 25, 1934, FDR Library, OF444, File: FERA July–August 1934; *Survey*, 70 (September 1934): 277; McJimsey, *Harry Hopkins*, 70.

112. Ickes, *The Secret Diary of Harold Ickes*, 194.

113. Bell notes on meeting on relief policy, October 1, 1934, Morgenthau Diaries, Book 2, 84. For Harold Ickes' account of the meeting see Ickes, *The Secret Diary*, 200–201.

114. Ickes, *The Secret Diary*, 203, 206; Morgenthau Diary, Book 2, 82, 101–102, 111–112

115. *New York Times*, November 12, 1934, 5; Ickes, *The Secret Diary*, 216–217, 223–224.

116. On November 23, for example, Hopkins told the U.S. Conference of Mayors that "the present method of relief must be supplanted in the near future" but admitted that he did not know what the new method would be. *New York Times*, November 23, 1934 13. Although Morgenthau pressed Ickes and Hopkins for more details on projects and employment, Roosevelt studiously avoided serious discussion of the specifics of implementation. See Ickes, *The Secret Diary*, 239–240.

117. *New York Times*, November 28, 1934, 1; November 29, 1934, 1; December 2, 1934, 1 and IV, 1; December 3, 1934, 1; Morgenthau Diaries, Book 2, 246; Ickes, *The Secret Diary*, 239–240.

118. The first draft of the business conference statement had apprarently actually used the term "dole" to refer to the policy it supported. *New York Times*, December 20, 1934, 1, 19; December 21, 1934, 1, 4. For an analysis of the controversy over the business conference statement see Arthur Krock's column in *The New York Times*, December 23, 1934, IV, 1. One of the few historians who has taken the business critique of the New Deal seriously is Gary Dean Best in *Pride, Prejudice, and Politics: Roosevelt versus Recovery, 1933–1938* (New York: Praeger, 1991).

119. The debate over the influences shaping the Social Security Act has been part of a broader and more theoretical controversy regarding the influence of "corporate liberal" capitalists on American social policy and, even more broadly, the relationship between the state and modern capitalism. The debate tends to assume that some pressure external to the New Deal (politics or corporate interest groups) encouraged the Roosevelt administration to adopt a more conservative social insurance program. I argue that the administration's antidole ideology, which played a crucial role in shaping Social Security, was clear from

the beginning of the New Deal and was magnified by the experience of administering the grant program. This point is suggested in Skocpol, *Social Policy in the United States*, 159. For the classic argument that elites shaped Social Security see G. William Domhoff, *The Higher Circles* (New York: Random House, 1971), 207–218. See also Jill Quadagno, *The Transformation of Old Age Security: Class and Politics in the American Welfare State* (Chicago: University of Chicago Press, 1988); Theda Skocpol and Edwin Amenta, "Did Capitalists Shape Social Security?," *American Sociological Review* 50 (August 1985): 572–575.

120. President Roosevelt's Remarks to the National Conference on Economic Security," November 14, 1934, Box 49, File: President Roosevelt; Josephine Brown to Walter West, December 3, 1934, Working Papers of the Committee on Economic Security, File: Correspondence—December 1934, both in CES Files.

121. Franklin D. Roosevelt, "Annual Message to the Congress," January 4, 1935, in Samuel L. Rosenman, ed., *The Public Papers and Addresses of Franklin D. Roosevelt*, vol. 4 (New York: Random House, 1938), 19–20.

122. Russell Kurtz, "No More Federal Relief," *Survey* 71, no. 2 (February 1935): 36–37.

123. Badger, *The New Deal*, 202. Even Russell Kurtz, who sharply attacked the administration's decision to end the grant program, called the work relief policy "a long step away from the evils of direct mass relief." Kurtz, "No More Federal Relief," 35.

124. Liberal social workers, particularly the "rank and file movement" in the profession, and organizations of the unemployed spent most of 1935 attacking the administrations' relief program, not only the decision to end the FERA but limitations placed on the WPA employment and wages. By the end of 1936, reality had set in, and the Left was actively defending the WPA against its critics. See Fischer, Statement by Workers Alliance, November 26, 1935, in FERA—Jacob Baker Files, Box 4, File: Labor Relations, November–December 1935.

Chapter 6

Ending the Dole as We Knew It

Of all the ironies and myths that surround the history of American social policy, perhaps the most intriguing is the current view that the New Deal sought to create an "entitlement" to welfare. Liberal critics of recent changes in federal policy have argued that the 1996 welfare reforms abandon the "safety net" created by the Roosevelt administration in 1935. Conservatives, on the other hand, suggest that the new federal policy ends a failed liberal experiment in social reform, which presumably began during the New Deal era. Both these arguments appear to have in common the assumption that a national welfare program was New Deal policy.

Yet, as we have seen, the central goal of New Deal relief policy in 1935 was not to create a welfare entitlement but to replace the existing national "dole" with public employment and social insurance.[1] The Federal Emergency Relief Administration (FERA), which was assisting over 5 million unemployed workers and impoverished farmers, was dismantled. A work program was created to provide jobs for all "employables" on the relief rolls. Federal grants for small state categorical programs (mainly Old Age Assistance and Aid to Dependent Children) were included in the Social Security Act to help states assist the remaining "residual" relief caseload.[2] These measures, in conjunction with the unemployment compensation and the old age pension program, were portrayed as a dramatic break with relief as it had been administered during the early depression years. The administration's calculations appeared to show that means-tested general relief would be relegated to an insignificant feature of the emerging American "welfare state." With $4.5 billion allocated to the WPA and millions more to finance the Social

Security Act, the 1935 program remains the most ambitious effort to reform welfare in American history.

In the end, the 1935 program did not significantly reduce the role of relief in income assistance policy. While there can be no doubt that for millions of unemployed, the elderly, and single-parent families, the program of 1935 represented a significant advance over conditions that had prevailed under the earlier relief system, it never came close to eliminating the need for means-tested relief. State relief caseloads included large numbers of "employable" workers who were not absorbed by the WPA, the federal relief role remained large through grants to the expanding categorical programs and the resulting state "welfare" programs were subjected to the same kinds of political and ideological attacks as the FERA grant program.[3] In the postwar years, the inadequacies and vulnerabilities of general relief were transferred to the Aid to Dependent Children (ADC) program, whose caseload exploded in the 1960s. In the process, "welfare" replaced "the dole" as a symbol of failed social policy.

The failure of the 1935 program to eliminate the existing "dole" no doubt accounts for much of the confusion surrounding the New Deal's social welfare agenda. Yet historians, who are certainly aware of the Roosevelt administration's hostility to relief, may have unwittingly contributed to the mythology of a New Deal welfare entitlement. Seeking to explain the unique American welfare state—with its heavy reliance on state-administered welfare—they have focused on the legislation of 1935, particularly the Social Security Act. The act, it has been argued, "institutionalized" a "two-tiered" welfare system: one set of popular programs (old age insurance and unemployment compensation) for the working and middle classes and another group of "welfare" policies targeted to the poor, which are marked by the inadequacies and vulnerabilities of traditional relief. Some accounts have faulted the decision to "quit this business of relief," suggesting that the end of the federal grant program produced a retreat to pre-FERA relief standards. Others have suggested that the Social Security Act, reflecting reform traditions inherited from the Progressive era, unnecessarily embedded sharp distinctions between welfare and social insurance in social policy. Another line of criticism focuses on the implementation of the law, arguing that the Social Security Board "denigrated" public assistance in order to promote social insurance policies.[4] Underlying these complaints is the assumption that the low status of "welfare" in American policy can be traced, in part, to flawed policy decisions and reform traditions embodied in the legislation of 1935.

A central argument of this study is that the role and status of public assistance have far less to do with the Social Security Act than is generally assumed.[5] The act certainly did not create means-tested relief, which was already assisting 5 million workers when legislation was presented to Congress in the spring of 1935. The chief weakness of the 1935 reform program was that the New Deal failed to secure adequate funding for federal public employment (the WPA).[6] Given the size of the relief caseload in 1935, a large—and politically unpopular—public welfare program was inevitable in the absence of a full employment policy. Responding to this reality, federal officials and state-level reformers aggressively promoted the modernization of state welfare programs, essentially transforming the emergency relief organizations into permanent public welfare departments. This process institutionalized state-administered relief, creating the present policy patchwork that so many historians have decried. But the primary goal of the modernizers in the late 1930s was the destruction of local "poor law" relief through administrative reform, not the elimination of poverty through an expanded dole. The persistence of welfare cannot be explained by emphasizing flawed liberal reforms, as both critics of the Left and Right would have it. Rather, "welfare" was produced by uncontrolled and unplanned expansion of relief during the early years of the Great Depression (and before), political opposition to financing public employment and state-level administrative modernization.

To understand the persistence of means-tested welfare, we need to look more closely at the implementation and financing of what became known as the Works Progress Administration (initially referred to as the "work program"). The WPA was the most ambitious and effective public employment program in American history.[7] Drawing on the experience of the CWA and FERA Work Program, it provided jobs for millions of workers who would otherwise have been on general relief. Its roads and bridges, airports and recreation facilities, art projects and public records collections remain monuments to the New Deal's vitality and its faith in experimentation by the state. The WPA should be distinguished from the more punitive "work for relief" programs (policies now frequently called "workfare"), which states attempted to implement and which the New Deal opposed. Historians should not be misled by the New Deal's high-minded and somewhat offensive attacks on "the dole" that were used to sell the program. This was not a policy imposed on the unemployed but arose, in part, from grassroots demands for public employment and against direct relief. The long waiting lists for the limited number of WPA slots and the mass opposition to cuts in the program are clear evidence of its essentially progressive nature.[8]

The central problem was that the WPA did not, in fact, eliminate the dole because the program's caseload was well below the level necessary to assist all "employable" workers who qualified for relief. Historical accounts have often emphasized aggregate work program unemployment (the total number of workers employed during the six years of the

program's existence) in describing the policy, but this measure is misleading. Average monthly employment is a far better measure of the
program's adequacy, in terms of both its impact on the unemployed and
its role in reducing the need for relief. The average monthly WPA caseload from 1936 through 1941 was approximately 2 million workers.
Other federal agencies employed an average of 521,000 from work program funds. To this we might add the expanded caseload of the Civilian
Conservation Corps and the National Youth Administration. Still, the
total number of recipients assisted by the work program, however it is
defined, rarely exceeded 3 million and was generally much lower.[9] When
the FERA was dismantled in 1935, the average monthly relief caseload
financed by federal funds was approximately 5 million. Thus, if we measure the impact of the WPA program strictly in terms of its impact on the
relief caseload, the New Deal's decision to "quit this business of relief"
produced a cut of approximately 50 percent.

Of course, such a calculation produces a one-dimensional analysis: it
ignores the declines in the level of unemployment in 1936 and 1937, the
higher "wages" paid WPA workers and the expanding categorical programs financed under the Social Security Act, which absorbed many former relief recipients. Still, the comparison between the WPA and FERA
caseloads is an important policy measure. The administration had portrayed the employment program as an effort to eliminate the "dole,"
with all its presumed negative consequences for unemployed workers
and the national character.[10] The relatively small WPA caseload meant
that means-tested general relief remained the safety net for large numbers of unemployed workers. It also impacted the caseloads of state categorical programs, which, despite the administration's claims, were not
entirely composed of "unemployables."

The story of the financing of the WPA has not been carefully examined
by historians of the New Deal era. Initially, the work program appeared
to be lavishly funded, particularly when compared to the earlier appropriations. The administration requested $4.8 billion to finance the new
program during the fiscal year beginning July 1. To phase out the general
relief program (FERA), $800 million would be used. The remaining $4
billion would employ 3.5 million former relief recipients at the security
wage of $50 per month, leaving nearly $2 billion for materials and administrative personnel. At this level of funding, there was a reasonable
expectation that the "dole" could be virtually eliminated for employable
needy workers. In January of 1935 the FERA caseload stood at 5 million
and could be expected to decline during the summer months.[11] Thus, the
work program was budgeted to absorb at least 70 percent of the national
caseload. By the end of 1934, states and localities were already financing
30 percent of the national bill for relief, so it could be assumed that the
"residual" relief burden could be absorbed without a big increase in state

relief expenditures. Furthermore, the states would soon receive matching federal grants for categorical relief programs (Old Age Assistance [OAA] and ADC), many of whose recipients had worked their way onto the FERA caseload. (Studies conducted by the FERA suggested that a very large percentage of the "residual" caseload thrown back on state relief consisted of "unemployables" who would be assisted by categorical relief.) If the FERA had simply expanded the caseload of its work program, which was already employing over 2 million, and transferred these recipients to the WPA, the transition to the new policy might have been accomplished without a major relief crisis.[12]

Instead, the transition from relief to public employment encountered political and administrative obstacles, producing "heartbreaking delays" that threatened to destroy the entire program. First, the appropriation bill was delayed in Congress by opposition to the proposed security wage. Liberals allying with organized labor favored reduced hours to produce a higher wage rate. They were joined by fiscal conservatives who, in the words of Arthur Krock, "hoped to make the [employment] bill as obnoxious as possible and then bring back the dole." The administration, which strongly opposed higher wage rates, expended a good deal of political capital—and time—resisting the demands of this rather odd congressional coalition. When the work relief appropriation finally passed in the late spring, Congress could not resist influencing the allocation process. As a result, large sums were earmarked to specific employment categories and federal agencies, a development that undermined a smooth transition from the existing FERA work program. In the meantime, a struggle arose between the FERA's Harry Hopkins and Harold Ickes of the Public Works Administration over control of the program (and the New Deal's approach to work relief itself). Roosevelt responded with an elaborate and unwieldy administrative plan that divided responsibility between the two men. The compromise produced long delays in approving projects and encouraged agencies not directly linked to the existing FERA work program to submit proposals.[13]

By mid-September of 1935, well into the fiscal year, only 800,000 workers were employed by the new program, and barely $1 billion of the original $4.8 billion appropriation remained. Allocations to existing federal agencies (made in response to congressional pressure) and the need to finance the FERA through the fall had absorbed most of the funds. To make matters worse, the FERA, faced with a shortage of funds, had begun to dismantle its own work program before transferring projects to the WPA. With state relief caseloads higher than ever, there was widespread speculation that the administration would have to bring back the dole, suffering a major policy setback with ominous consequences for the 1936 elections. (Roosevelt, according to one *New York Times* analysis, had "staked his reelection" on the WPA's success.)[14] At this point Roo-

sevelt handed the remaining funds to Hopkins, who rapidly expanded
the program's caseload by transferring recipients from the FERA work
program. By the end of November, approximately 2 million workers
were employed by the WPA, and New Deal officials were promising
that the program would reach quota by the beginning of the winter. At
a press conference on December 23, Roosevelt announced that the program had reached the targeted caseload, declaring the new policy "99
7/8%" successful. In fact, implementation had been delayed six months,
and the administration had retreated significantly from its original promise to assist all employables on the national relief caseload. At the beginning of 1936, WPA employed under 3 million workers, requiring the
administration to pad its estimates with the caseloads of the Civilian
Conservation Corps and other agencies that did not necessarily employ
workers from the general relief rolls. While sticking to the claim that the
policy had achieved its goal, Roosevelt suggested that states should
never have assumed that the WPA would aid all employables, only a
"substantial portion" of those on relief.[15]

Clearly, the administration had retreated from its promise to assist all
employable cases on the federal relief rolls. There was pervasive evidence that the end of the FERA had left the states with an enormous
general relief burden.[16] Protests from local officials, social workers and
organizations of the unemployed poured into Hopkins' office. The
AASW and the American Public Welfare Association (APWA), along
with most prominent social work leaders, called for a new federal grant
program for general relief. During the coming months they supported
their campaign with numerous studies on the devastating impact of the
return to state and local relief; these reports were buttressed by research
monographs produced by the WPA's Division of Research and Statistics.
Even federal officials like Aubrey Williams, although maintaining that
the work program had achieved its quota, admitted to the AASW that
it was "incontrovertibly true" that the WPA was not meeting the entire
need.[17]

Yet in spite of overwhelming evidence that large numbers of employables remained on the state relief rolls, the administration submitted substantially reduced budget requests to Congress for the WPA. In the
spring of 1936, Roosevelt asked for $1.5 billion, a sum that would have
produced large work program cuts had Congress not passed a supplemental appropriation later in the fiscal year. The administration's 1937
emergency request, another $1.5 billion, was accompanied by a promise
to bring the federal budget into balance during the coming fiscal year.
The federal funding cuts produced a steady decline in the WPA caseload:
by the end of the summer of 1937 the number of workers on WPA projects had been reduced to below 1.5 million. It appears that once the
FERA was dismantled, eliminating the "dole" for unemployed workers

was no longer a central New Deal policy goal. Perhaps the most detailed study of the WPA during these years has suggested that after 1935, New Deal officials never evaluated federal public employment in the context of the overall relief situation:

> The size of appropriation requests for the works program after 1935 . . . [was] never determined in the light of fully worked-out estimates and an orderly posing of alternatives. The WPA developed careful records of the man-year cost of giving a person a work relief job at various kinds of tasks in different states. But no standards of employability were formulated, and at any one time the WPA had no certain information about the number of employables on public relief rolls eligible for work relief.[18]

Why did the administration fail to secure adequate funding for the WPA after 1935? This question has not been systematically evaluated by historians. Some have noted the opposition to public employment within the New Deal coalition, particularly among southern Democrats concerned about the impact of WPA wage rates on low wage (primarily African-American) workers. The period after 1935, after all, saw the rise of a "conservative coalition" opposing the extension of the New Deal.[19] Other accounts of New Deal policy have emphasized the president's own fiscal conservatism, particularly his 1937 pledge to balance the federal budget.[20] While there is no doubt some truth to both these explanations, more emphasis needs to be placed on two other factors: the broad-based political opposition to deficit spending and the problems of implementing a public employment program attached to the existing welfare system.

The politics of the balanced budget were paramount. As the 1936 elections approached, the conventional wisdom held that Roosevelt was "extremely vulnerable to attacks on his spending program." Morgenthau predicted that the Republicans would focus on the New Deal spending, just as Roosevelt had attacked Hoover in 1932. ("But the Republicans have ten times as much material as you did three years ago," Morgenthau told the president.) Roosevelt's problem was compounded by two other developments in early 1936: Congress finally agreed—over the president's veto—to finance early payment of the World War I veterans' "bonus," and the Supreme Court invalidated the Agricultural Adjustment Act (and its processing taxes). These actions added nearly $2 billion to federal expenditures, creating the biggest peacetime deficit in history during the year of a presidential campaign. Under these circumstances, there was little support in Congress for an expansion of the WPA. Key committees were controlled by conservatives who called for big cuts in emergency expenditures. While the southerners among them may well have been concerned about the impact of the work program on labor and race relations, they tended to focus on fiscal issues. This reflected the broad-based appeal of the balanced budget. The columnist Arthur Krock believed that most Democrats would "look first at the [emergency spending] totals, hoping they will be low enough for campaign purposes yet not too low to make trouble for them among the municipalities and relief beneficiaries in their districts."[21]

Krock's comment reflected the fundamental political reality of public employment in 1936. Cuts in the existing WPA quota produced strong opposition from the Democratic Party's core political base, but this did not translate into spending increases sufficient to eliminate the state-level dole for unemployed workers. State and local officials aggressively lobbied against cuts in the work program, but their emergency spending proposals, reflecting political realities, tended to maintain the status quo. The militant Left—represented by organizations of the unemployed, labor unions and activists in the social work community—rallied around Representative Vito Marcantonio's bill for a $6 billion combined relief and public works program, but the measure, perhaps useful as a grassroots organizing device, did little to increase congressional support for the WPA. Indeed, New Deal officials like Aubrey Williams believed that such calls for a return to federal general relief only played into the hands of the "forces of reaction." Williams charged that social work critics of the administration's relief policy had been cited "again and again by those who favor a lower [WPA] appropriation, return of relief to the states and abandonment of the work program."[22]

After floating several trial balloons, the Roosevelt administration decided to limit its request for the work program to $1.5 billion, a big reduction from the previous year and not enough to maintain the existing WPA quota without a large supplemental appropriation before the fiscal year ended. Krock believed that the decision to keep the request below $2 billion had helped turn the "political tide" in favor of Roosevelt in the spring of 1936.[23]

The New Deal's 1936 emergency appropriation request was a major setback for public employment. Only Hopkins' considerable political and administrative skills, honed during the FERA-CWA budget battles, kept the program at a reasonable employment level as the fiscal year progressed. The WPA administrator encouraged protest by announcing large cuts in the work program quota while the administration or Congress was considering emergency appropriations. Hopkins also worked to maintain good relations with Morgenthau, who came to support the WPA as less costly than traditional public works and feared that abrupt cutbacks in the program would produce pressure for higher emergency expenditures.[24] The strong grassroots response to CCC cutbacks during the spring of 1936 was typical. The proposed caseload reductions, part of the administration's initial response to demands for reduced emergency spending, produced unexpectedly strong protests in farm-state congressional districts where the Corps was active in flood control. It appears to have set a pattern. Approaching congressional consideration of emergency spending requests would be accompanied by the announcement of large program cuts by Hopkins' office. The resulting outcry from mayors, governors, and organizations of the unemployed would send Morgenthau scurrying to reallocate funds from other agencies and create momentum to fund the WPA at existing levels.[25]

This tactic was particularly effective in late 1936. Hopkins had kept the WPA caseload high prior to the 1936 election, but this nearly exhausted the appropriation passed the previous spring. In December WPA announced a large cut in state quotas, which produced the predictable response from the grass roots and a supplemental appropriation of $750,000 from Congress. Hopkins "would wait until the last minute before letting [Budget Director] Bell and me know they were overspending," Morgenthau complained in his diary. " 'Then they would appeal to our emotions by reminding us of the plight of the jobless.'"[26]

Such tactics helped sustain the WPA but did little to generate congressional support for an increase in emergency expenditures. Indeed, Hopkins' maneuvering may help explain why Roosevelt in early 1937 decided, rather recklessly, to pledge a balanced budget. The request for a large supplemental appropriation in December 1936, coming on the heels of campaign promises that the federal budget would soon be balanced, was a great embarrassment for the New Deal.[27] Morgenthau, using highly optimistic revenue estimates for the coming year, convinced Roosevelt that a balanced budget could be achieved by 1939. Meanwhile, Congress added language to the 1937 emergency appropriation—once again limited to $1.5 billion—that appeared to prohibit another request for supplemental funds and launched an investigation of the administration's entire relief program. By September of 1937 the monthly WPA quota was below 1.5 million, and the end of federal work relief appeared at hand.[28]

The 1938 recession revived the WPA and, for a brief moment, appeared to generate significant political support for a permanent full employment policy. The economic collapse, which began in the fall of 1937, coincided with big cuts in the WPA caseload. Recession and work relief cuts produced yet another of the seemingly endless crises of state and local general relief, generating new demands for federal action. Furthermore, the recession appeared to vindicate the arguments of "spenders" within the administration, who argued that the economic downturn was a product of efforts to balance the budget, which reduced consumer demand. Hopkins quickly shifted gears, spearheading a successful campaign to convince Roosevelt to abandon the balanced budget and adopt deficit spending as administration policy. It was, as a number of recent studies have shown, a historic moment that heralded the ascendancy of Keynesian economic ideas in the liberal "New Deal order."[29] The im-

mediate beneficiary of this shift was the WPA. During the winter of
1937–1938 Hopkins had again kept the program above quota in response
to rising state relief caseloads. This had produced new threats of spring
budget cuts, more protests and another supplemental appropriation.
Then in June of 1938, Congress appropriated sufficient funds to finance
a WPA caseload of over 3 million. It stayed at approximately this level
until renewed political attacks, this time focusing on "communist influence" in white-collar projects, and the economic expansion generated by
World War II produced the end of depression-era public employment.[30]

Yet despite the triumph of the spenders in 1938, the revival of the
WPA did not significantly reduce the importance of the state-financed
dole. As Alan Brinkley has noted, the 1938 spending program was a
good deal more modest than it was later portrayed by supporters of the
"Keynesian revolution" in fiscal policy. An analysis of emergency appropriations buttresses this argument. In 1938 Congress initially appropriated $1.4 billion for the WPA and approximately $296 million for
"other agencies." Later in the fiscal year there were two supplemental
appropriations totaling $825 million, for a grand total of approximately
$2.5 billion in fiscal year 1939. The emergency appropriation that
launched the WPA in 1935, by comparison, was $4.5 billion. As a result,
the expansion of the work program quota in 1938 barely kept pace with
unemployment, which rose to nearly 11 million during the recession.[31]
According to one estimate, state general relief averaged approximately
1.8 million cases during the year, higher than the averages for 1936 and
1937. Coupled with the growth of categorical relief (particularly Old Age
Assistance) funded under the Social Security Act, the high general relief
caseload during the recession played a key role in institutionalizing state-
level public welfare.[32] In retrospect, the New Deal's 1938 spending program was designed to promote recovery, not eliminate direct relief for
unemployed workers.[33] That goal had been abandoned at the end of
1935, a victim of fiscal politics.

The broad-based political opposition to adequate financing of work
relief was compounded by major policy obstacles to implementing public
employment as an alternative to the dole. The 1935 battles over wage
rates, the allocation of the congressional appropriation and the administration of the work policy reflected fundamental contradictions in the
philosophy and the political base of support for the work relief. The goal
of placing relief recipients on "public work," the central rationale of administration policy, conflicted with the origins of public employment as
a countercyclical, "pump-priming" measure and its political constituency
among mayors, rural legislators and members of Congress. The latter
saw the "work program" as a policy promoting local infrastructure development (and the political patronage that went with it).[34] Yet, projects
that satisfied this powerful constituency did not necessarily employ the

workers in sufficient quantities—or with the proper skills—to reduce the relief rolls. To further complicate matters, Hopkins' administration of the FERA had often brought him into direct conflict with precisely the politicians who supported these "capital-intensive" projects. To overcome these obstacles, Hopkins appears to have been willing to disguise his role behind a complex administrative structure, breaking the continuity between the FERA work program and the WPA. But this maneuvering undermined the central goal of the new policy: eliminating the dole for unemployed workers.[35] The WPA, as has frequently been noted, was a "hybrid," combining public works and work relief. But such a compromise undermined the program's effectiveness as an anti-dole measure.

Conflicts over the nature of public employment were linked to another central policy dilemma: how should workers for public employment be recruited? The WPA, like the other New Deal work relief experiments, never completely severed the connection between public employment and relief. The initial work program caseload quota was filled with workers from the federal relief rolls. After 1935, employment was restricted to those "in need." While states evolved a variety of administrative mechanisms for determining eligibility, the most common was a means test administered by local or state welfare agency. Once on the WPA, workers were pulled off the traditional relief framework, but initially, one virtually had to qualify for general relief in order to be accepted by the federal work program.[36]

This produced a dynamic familiar from the FERA/CWA period: workers would apply for general relief in order to be eligible for WPA, or, conversely, those rejected by the federal work program had a tendency to remain on state-level relief.[37] The problem was particularly acute during the early months of the transition to the WPA. Federal officials, fearing another rush to relief similar to what had occurred under the CWA, initially restricted eligibility for federal work relief to those on the FERA rolls before May 1935. But the delay in implementing the new federal program made this policy untenable. A number of states reported caseload increases in August and September, even as the WPA began taking workers off the relief rolls. The initial impact of the WPA on New York City, for example, was to increase the caseload of the Emergency Relief Bureau, as applications for "home relief" rose by more than 50 percent. According to one account, "persons who had previously shunned home relief as demoralizing were encouraged to apply because they hoped to qualify for the federal work program." The Washington state representative of the National Emergency Council reported that the Department of Public Welfare was "subjected to terrific pressure" by people who wanted to get on relief to be eligible for WPA.[38] Precisely the opposite pattern can be observed in 1936 and 1937: efforts by the administration to cut the WPA generated increased pressure on state and local general relief caseloads.[39] Finally, when the recession of 1938 struck, the WPA responded by taking workers off the expanding general relief programs, creating yet another incentive to apply for relief.

The experience of the WPA and the New Deal's other work experiments should give pause to liberals who advocate public employment as an alternative to "welfare." An inadequately financed work relief program attached to the existing relief system can easily produce demands for more relief. Effective work programs break down the stigma of applying for relief, and the "dole" is seen as the avenue for landing a "government job." This development could be avoided by making work relief resemble the traditional, degrading "work test" or, conversely, financing a program that would assist virtually all the unemployed. But the former policy is precisely what enlightened public employment has sought to replace, and the political obstacles to financing the latter have been, to say the least, formidable. This central policy dilemma—which undermined all the New Deal's work relief experiments—may help explain why public employment has not been at the center of efforts to eliminate poverty since the 1930s.

This is not to suggest that a more generous public employment policy might not have replaced the "dole" in the late 1930s. Had the FERA work program been expanded to 3.5 million in July 1935 as originally planned, and had this employment level been maintained by the WPA through the 1938 recession, the residual relief burden left to the states would have been small. "The government has to face the question as to whether it is going permanently into what is known as the 'great public works program,' " Hopkins declared at a meeting with Roosevelt and Morgenthau in July 1935. "Anything short of ten billion dollars will not do the trick of putting people to work. This four billion eight does something but does not begin to get home." If the New Deal had been willing to fight for such a program and embrace a "Keynesian" rationale in 1936, the course of American social welfare history might have been different. Perhaps, as Anthony Badger has suggested, "the New Deal compromised too much in anticipation of opposition."[40] Yet Aubrey Williams' analysis of the level of support for expanded public employment and relief, presented in an address to the American Association of Social Workers, would appear to reflect the real political possibilities in 1936. While admitting that the conventional wisdom among political elites and the press about the need to balance the federal budget did not necessarily reflect "public opinion," he argued that "the vast, controlling majority of our population either actively oppose or are passively indifferent to appropriating the necessary increase in funding to bring about the state of affairs you are advocating." Political and ideological resistance to financing public employment was, and is, so strong that even the relatively modest program implemented after 1935 has come to seem quite revolutionary. Americans have been drawn to rhetoric that promises to replace welfare with work but have consistently opposed allocating the funds to implement such a policy.[41]

The inadequate funding of the WPA, coupled with the expansion of the categorical programs financed under the Social Security Act, led inexorably to the institutionalization of state-administered "welfare." The impact of the 1935 shift in administration policy was, in a sense, a revival of the public welfare movement of the 1920s—a movement that had been short-circuited by the relief crisis of the depression.[42] This crucial policy development has been obscured by the fact that the initial devolution of general relief to the states in late 1935 produced a major relief crisis. Historians, relying on the accounts of social workers who opposed New Deal policy during this period, have occasionally created the impression that the end of the federal grant program produced a retreat to pre-FERA relief standards—a regression to traditional "poor law relief." Thus, the end of the federal grant program is seen as part of the process by which "welfare" was relegated to its low status in American social policy.[43]

This view, although one-sided, captures a fundamental reality of social policy in late 1935: in state after state WPA quotas appeared to be below levels promised when the work program was originally announced, leaving states with a large general relief burden. The impact of the WPA on relief in New York City showed how large the "residual" caseload could be. In early 1935, the caseload financed by the FERA averaged approximately 265,000; the following year, with the WPA quota nearly filled, the city was left with a caseload averaging approximately 210,000. According to an occupational survey of these cases, 75 percent were able-bodied and employable.[44] In Illinois, the "residual" caseload, initially calculated to be 65,000, approached 150,000 by January of 1935, and an additional 30,000 on WPA projects required supplementary aid. State officials pleaded with the FERA for continued federal grants, but eventually the state was forced to assume the added burden. The stage was set for annual relief funding crises, which were a feature of political life in Illinois through the end of the depression.[45] Many states attempted to end general relief entirely, arguing that "employables" were the responsibility of the federal government. In Washington State, the WPA quota left the state with approximately 30,000 general relief cases; state relief director Charles Ernst responded by ordering draconian cuts in the program during the spring of 1936 and spent the next three years trying to eliminate state-funded general relief altogether.[46] The situation was even more desperate in rural states. A widely publicized study of recipients dropped from the relief rolls in Macon, Georgia, found that none were "provided with adequate care by another welfare agency." Former recipients reported that they had begged, received irregular "donations" from neighbors and friends, and salvaged food from local markets.[47]

The Macon study was reported in the *Survey* under the title "1932— When Relief Stops—1936," an explicit reference to the relief crisis that produced the first federal welfare program. The author, Ewan Clague, was suggesting that, with the decision to return direct relief to the states, social policy was reverting to a pre-FERA level: "this represents a retreat from a standard of relief which, during the past two years has been reasonably well maintained. . . . Is this the first step toward a return to the 'good old days' of chaos and confusion in relief?" "Have we lived through the agonizing years of depression to produce nothing better than this?," asked Dorothy Kahn, the director of the Philadelphia relief program in a review of relief policy in early 1937. The question was a direct response to *Survey* columnist Gertrude Springer's contention that general relief since the advent of the WPA was being "carried on under the traditional practices of old-line poor officers or the methods of private charities."[48]

The perception of a retreat to "poor law relief" was encouraged, in part, by political attacks on social work professionals and the welfare bureaucracy that seemed to pervade the politics of relief in the late 1930s. Illinois retained its "emergency" relief machinery but resisted proposals to create a permanent Department of Public Welfare. In the process, legislators passed punitive residency requirements that seemed as much an attack on the social work reformers as on the unemployed themselves. "Those who wish to 'return relief to the states' may well take notice and warning of the reactionary state poor-law amendments and the refined cruelties of local relief administration [in Illinois]," commented Edith Abbott in the *Social Service Review*. In New Jersey, where the state emergency relief administration had been abolished in 1935, the city of Camden briefly employed the former city chauffeur to run the local relief program.[49] Pennsylvania integrated the emergency general relief program into permanent public welfare departments at the state and local level, but political machines retained considerable influence over local relief policy. This appears to have led to the firing of Philadelphia's relief director Dorothy Kahn, one of the leading voices of reformist social work, who had resisted political appointments in Philadelphia. Local poor relief administrators in Michigan launched a successful referendum campaign to repeal legislation creating a uniform, centralized public welfare system. Perhaps the most bizarre and vindictive attack on a state relief program inherited from the FERA period occurred in Ohio. Legislation passed in January of 1938 required that applicants file "poverty affidavits"; that the names of those on the relief rolls be published monthly "in a newspaper of general circulation"; and that relief be distributed only in kind, with recipients required to pick up food orders in person. William Haber, the former director of the Michigan Emergency Relief Administration, suggested in the *Survey* that "these harsh and inhuman provisions were deliberately required to destroy many of the social workers' tenets."[50]

Yet Haber, one of the most influential voices in the expanding field of public welfare administration, rejected the notion that such attacks were evidence of a retreat to the poor laws. While admitting that "many state [welfare] administrators succumbed to local political machines and to patronage control over personnel," he argued that the conflict between politicians and social workers reflected the expansion of administrative capacity and the modernization of welfare policy:

The basic factor in the conflict arises from the fact that social work was once an obscure profession. In the last decade it has taken its place in the sun. It now appears a major activity of government. The social worker's field of operations is largely in the public welfare area. The problem is now a mass and not an individual problem. The nation appears committed to a program of providing protection for low income groups. . . . It now has become the concern of the entire community; of all who pay taxes, of all who are interested in public finance, in governmental policies, yes, in politics. Social work has become a mass problem. It has drawn the attention of that expert in public relations—the politician. The vast sums involved, the large numbers who are employed in administration-these factors alone are sufficient to attract the politically minded.[51]

Even those who believed that the status of general relief had declined to the level of the poor laws were ambivalent about developments in the late 1930s. Gertrude Springer, the *Survey*'s columnist on relief since the Hoover years and a persistent critic of the New Deal policy after 1935, admitted that with the expansion of general relief in late 1937, the total number of recipients aided by state and federal funds probably equaled that of the peak FERA period. Similarly, Wilfred Reynolds, in a highly critical 1937 review of relief policies in Illinois, concluded, "There are today approximately the same number of families and individuals receiving assistance in Illinois in the forms of direct relief grants and WPA wages as were given relief in 1933. While the employment and payroll indexes show a substantial improvement over 1933, there has been no decrease in the public assistance rolls." One year later, the *Survey*'s Washington correspondent estimated that 6.9 million households nationally were receiving relief or emergency work, well above the levels that had prevailed under the FERA even if we include the categorical programs.[52]

These estimates suggest that, after an initial decline, the national relief caseload—including those on the WPA—exceeded the levels that had prevailed under the earlier grant program. If we measure post-FERA relief policy in terms of spending, then the notion of a "retreat to the poor laws" is even more problematic. For the last six months of 1938, for example, total expenditures for all forms of relief—general, categorical and work relief—totaled approximately $1.9 billion. Total spending for the same period in 1935, the last six months of the FERA grant program, was approximately $1.3 billion.[53]

These numbers support Haber's contention that the political attacks on social work were the product of the expansion of relief, which was rapidly becoming a permanent function of state government. The end of the FERA did not produce a wholesale retreat to the poor laws because the forces that produced the growth of relief—mass unemployment, fear of social disorder encouraged by protests, the lobbying of reformist coalitions led by social workers and the increasing influence of welfare bureaucracies on social policy—did not disappear after 1935. Furthermore, most of these influences had been felt on the state and local levels, even during the period of federal relief.

Although most organized protest activities after 1935 focused on the defense of the WPA, resistance to wholesale cuts in general relief remained a factor in state policy making. The *Survey*'s Gertrude Springer noted that the WPA had "drawn off the protesting element and left a relatively inarticulate group [on state relief programs] who take it as it comes." But this did not mean that state and local governments could simply dismantle the general relief machinery built up under the FERA. During the relief crisis of 1938, the *Survey* reported that clients and social workers in Chicago were becoming more sophisticated in framing their demands: "Clients in picket lines allege that only about half the sales tax in the state treasury [is] actually being used for relief purposes and there is now in that fund about eighty million dollars." In New York City, pressure from relief clients was reported to be "constant but orderly."[54] Even in states where public officials were successful in cutting relief, implementing the policy could be politically hazardous. When the state legislature in New Jersey adjourned without appropriating funds for relief in the spring of 1936, the Workers' Alliance occupied the state legislature, meeting in mock sessions and passing resolutions. In Washington, where the state relief director Charles Ernst refused a request for supplementary aid to Seattle in the early months of the recession, city officials reported that the corridors of the building housing the Welfare Department had been "in a bedlam": "Committee after committee is waiting upon us, demanding that we take some action before the conditions reach such a crisis as to force a showdown." Ernst was eventually able to implement draconian cuts in the state general relief program, but the policy helped create strong opposition to the relief director—and to his mentor, Governor Homer Martin—within the increasingly powerful liberal wing of the state Democratic Party.[55]

An even more important influence on state policy after 1935 was the expansion of categorical relief financed by federal grants under the Social Security Act. This development was primarily the product of the growth of Old Age Assistance (OAA) caused by state-level political pressure and massive applications by the elderly to the new OAA programs. We have been conditioned to think of the Social Security Act as a response to these pressures, particularly to the Townsend Movement, which exploded on the national scene in 1934. In fact, the Act may have done more to stimulate grassroots protest than mollify it.[56] A variety of state-level protest and lobbying organizations sprouted after 1935 in conjunction with the implementation of the Act. Officials administering OAA were besieged with demands for "noncontributory" pensions to be distributed as a matter of right.[57] The Washington State Department of Public welfare, for example, was "bombarded" with applications from the elderly who believed that the state's new OAA law "provided for a standard pension to be given to all people 65 years old and over, irrespective of need." Grassroots organizations not only pressured states to liberalize legislation but organized the elderly to apply for aid. In Massachusetts the leadership of the Senior Citizens and Associated of America not only was a powerful interest group in the corridors of the state house but also "tutored [the elderly] in exploiting the state welfare department's procedures for appealing local agency decisions."[58] Between 1935 and 1939 the national OAA caseload, as estimated by the Social Security Board (SSB), rose from a monthly average of 300,000 to nearly 2 million. By the latter it exceeded the combined state general relief caseloads.[59]

The growth of Aid to Dependent Children, the program that would evolve into what is now called "welfare," was more modest and not caused by an organized grassroots protest movement. The national caseload nearly tripled between 1935 and 1939, as federal funds initially reimbursed states for one-third of the cost of aiding children formerly assisted by "Mothers' Pension" programs.[60] While the Social Security Act has frequently been criticized for institutionalizing the chief weaknesses of mothers' aid, the federal law was, in fact, more liberal with regard to eligibility than most state legislation. It did not restrict aid to children whose mothers were widowed or deserted and allowed assistance to "any one of a comprehensive list of relatives." Furthermore, the federal law did not include a "suitable home" requirement, a key policy that had limited eligibility under the older state programs. As the critics of the law have noted, states were not required to broaden eligibility, and many resisted federal guidelines (Illinois initially refused to participate in the federal program at all), but the lure of federal grants encouraged reform. Federal officials, working with the increasingly influential American Public Welfare Association, promoted language that eliminated the recourse to moral judgment and defined the suitable home as "meeting the standards of care and health, fixed by the laws of this state." By 1939 half the states had incorporated the proposed language in their statutes; only three retained the language requiring a moral judgment.[61] States used federal funds to clear waiting lists, which were a normal feature of the older programs, and to assist single-parent families that had worked their way onto the general relief caseload.

The expansion of ADC suggests that critics of the categorical provisions of the Social Security Act have focused too much congressional resistance on strong federal controls and not enough on the mechanisms by which the law promoted reform. While it is certainly true that states could apply for aid without modifying restrictive mothers' aid policies, such an approach often proved untenable. Washington State initially administered ADC and mothers' pensions separately but eventually adopted federal standards for all recipients. In Massachusetts the lure of federal funds initially served to liberalize state policies without modifying existing legislation. The ADC caseload in the state doubled from 1935 to 1938, an increase that Martha Derthick has attributed to "a relaxed interpretation of the [state's traditional] fit-parent clause" by welfare officials. The change was not primarily a response to federal demands but to the opportunity to share the cost of assisting single-parent households, many of which had worked their way onto the locally financed general relief caseload. Then on January 1, 1937, the state issued new rules that stipulated that single women with "illegitimate" children qualified for relief under ADC.[62]

The impact of the new categorical programs on state relief—and the fact that by the end of the 1930s their caseloads generally exceeded those of the general relief programs—might suggest that the Social Security Act was a key factor in institutionalizing "welfare." This, after all, has been a central theme of recent histories of the evolution of the American welfare state. But the initial impetus for the creation of permanent state welfare departments was the need to deal with the large residual caseload left by the WPA and to respond to the administrative vacuum created by the end of the FERA. By 1935 state "Emergency Relief Administrations," although nominally temporary, had come to play a dominant role in welfare policy: they were, in a sense, the administrative forerunners of the state public welfare departments. It is also important to emphasize that the low WPA caseload had an impact on categorical relief. Blanche Coll's recent monograph on income assistance policy, for example, notes that the WPA cuts beginning in 1936 produced an "avalanche of applications for [OAA]" from older workers who had originally been transferred from the FERA work program. Coll also notes that "thousands of women . . . most of them with dependent children, were dropped from WPA projects at the same time as older persons" and "had to line up at the local welfare office," (presumably for ADC).[63]

The large "residual" state general relief caseloads and the new federally financed categorical programs provided the impetus for a revival of the public welfare movement, which had, in a sense, been interrupted by the relief crisis of the early depression years. In state after state there emerged powerful elite reform coalitions energized by the end of the FERA and the prospect of applying for categorical grants under the Social Security program. These coalitions included reformers aligned with state social work conferences, academics in the growing field of public welfare administration and "enlightened" business leaders who had participated in the various state emergency committees.[64] In state after state during the late 1930s, governors and legislators created commissions of "experts" to revise state welfare legislation. The activities of state-level reformers were encouraged and publicized by the American Public Welfare Association, whose influence in the field of social work had grown considerably during the period of federal relief. The APWA had played a key role in coordinating state emergency relief efforts during the Hoover years; with the end of the federal grant program in 1935, it resumed this role as a national clearinghouse for public welfare activities. The association produced model state welfare laws, conducted studies of state and local reforms, and publicized these efforts in its monthly bulletin, the *Public Welfare News*. According to Josephine Brown, the APWA played a key role in recruiting personnel for state agencies, filling a gap that the SSB, "for reasons of strategy and expediency could not do."[65]

Brown was referring to the fact that Congress had restricted the powers of the Board to influence personnel selection and relief standards in the states receiving federal grants. Yet we should be careful not to minimize the role of the SSB's "Division of Public Assistance" in the expansion of relief and modernization of administrative capacity after 1935. In fact, the federal welfare role did not end with the dismantling of the FERA because, as I have argued, the weakening of federal standards during the legislative process was not the end of the story. Brian Balogh has shown that the SSB "moved cautiously to achieve through administration of the law what had been lost when the law was written." Frank Bane, the executive director of the federal board and former director of the APWA, was "constantly on the road, negotiating with governors and pushing the Board's view of social security." The SSB provided "technical assistance to states," in Bane's words, "little task forces" to help develop legislation," and occasionally "intervened in the actual personnel selection process." The Board even withheld grants in three cases where state policy appeared to violate federal standards, but its influence on state policy was exerted primarily through "persuasion" and the connections between Board members, the APWA, and the expanding public welfare bureaucracies.[66] It may well have been that the small but popular categorical programs were better vehicles for encouraging reform than general relief or the politically charged work programs of the late FERA period. A report on the status of professional education and social work, published in the *Social Service Review* in 1938, noted that "the outlook [for administrative modernization] has been greatly improved with the substitution of the Social Security Board, with its permanent public program, succeeding the old hand to mouth uncertainty of the FERA."[67]

This analysis of the role of the SSB in liberalizing state welfare policy and in modernizing relief administration would appear to contradict an influential interpretation of the implementation of the Social Security Act, which argues that the Board was in fact hostile to public assistance. A number of historians have argued that the SSB denigrated public assistance in order to strengthen the social insurance provisions of the Social Security Act (old age pensions and unemployment insurance). Federal officials are thus accused of "insuring inequality," in Jerry Cates' influential formulation, and laying the foundation for the "two-tiered" welfare system. Cates has shown that the SSB often opposed the liberalization of state relief programs for the elderly (OAA) in order to build support for the contributory old age pension program slated to begin in the early 1940s. Fearing that OAA would preempt the pension program, the Board resisted radical state old age pension schemes and opposed efforts by some states to liberalize eligibility for OAA. Furthermore, the directors supported regressive 1939 federal legislation tightening eligibility for OAA by "tak[ing] into account" income from relatives.[68]

There is ample evidence that the SSB feared that the expansion of OAA would undermine the federal pension program and strongly opposed popular proposals, particularly those advocated by the grassroots Townsend Movement, to create a welfare-style entitlement for the elderly. Yet it is a rather long leap from these findings to the conclusion that the Board was responsible for the low status of means-tested public assistance. There is little evidence that a significantly more liberal or popular welfare policy would have emerged in the absence of the SSB's pressure. Some states might have liberalized the means test, ignored the income of relatives and otherwise broadened eligibility. Yet it is highly unlikely that a popular entitlement would have been created by the state OAA programs of the 1930s. Most states simply could not afford more liberal public assistance policies, which were financed by general revenues. In 1939 the *Survey* reported that although state legislatures were "flooded with bills calling for increased old age assistance allowances" and some broadened eligibility, "few put up any cash of their own." These fiscal constraints forced some previously liberal states, such as Washington and Utah, to restrict eligibility to " 'financial assistance to those in need rather than a 'pension' granted as a matter of right."[69] Furthermore, the Board was willing to finance a significant expansion of OAA to smooth the transition to the federal insurance program. According to Brian Balogh, the Board "sought to dampen enthusiasm for more radical pension plans by getting benefits in the hands of the elderly as quickly as possible." In the process, the SSB speeded the transition to the federal program. Federal officials did not resist liberalization of state OAA programs to denigrate public assistance but to replace it with a universalist national social insurance policy.[70] While the board may be faulted for promoting the myth of "contributions" to the old age pension plan, thus making "welfare" seem less virtuous, the overall policy would appear to be precisely the kind of approach that critics of the "two-tiered" welfare state would advocate.

Furthermore, the critics of the SSB would appear to conflate Old Age Assistance and Aid to Dependent Children. Yet it was the latter program that became the second "tier" of the modern American welfare state. The effect of the 1935 law and its administration by the SSB was to liberalize state Mothers' Pension programs.[71] Indeed, one might argue that by encouraging *liberalization* of ADC, the 1935 law "sowed the seeds of welfare" by breaking down the distinction between the mothers' aid, a "pension" for a small group of deserving widows, and relief. The distinction was further eroded by the welfare explosion of the 1960s, the increase in single-parent families and the rise in women's labor force participation. As a result, ADC assumed the characteristics of the 1930s "dole"—an unpopular income subsidy for low-wage workers. But this development is properly located in the post-war years, not in the 1935 legislation.

For better or for worse, the overall impact of the SSB's policies was to encourage a national movement for state welfare reform in the late 1930s. "It is apparent that we are just on the threshold of an extensive public welfare development in the year 1937," wrote Marietta Stevenson, assistant director of the APWA. When Stevenson wrote, eighteen states had established new departments of public welfare, five more had made substantial changes in welfare programs, and nearly every state had established commissions to review the status of existing relief machinery. Reviewing the work of these commissions, the *Survey*'s Martha Chickering reported that despite the great diversity of approaches to state-level reform, "a chorus of practically unanimous opinion" was heard on key issues: the need for relief was a chronic, not a temporary, problem; emergency organizations should become or be absorbed by permanent state welfare organizations; and local agencies should continue to play a key role in dispensing relief. "The impressive thing in all these reports," she observed, "is their departure from the deterrent spirit of the old poor law." APWA director Fred Kohler was more circumspect. Describing the intense political resistance to reform in states such as Ohio and Pennsylvania, he used the term "crabwise" to characterize the progress of public welfare in 1937: "politically-minded governors and legislators ... insisted on retaining outmoded, separate bureaus for administration and spoilsmen personnel procedures, all because the faithful must keep their jobs in existing bureaus or be taken care of in new programs unprotected by the merit system." But Kohler also recognized that there had been significant "progress, most encouraging in that the states have made a start toward meeting their obligations and responsibilities."[72]

The fact that Stevenson and Kohler, both officials in the APWA, could produce such different evaluations of developments in 1937 suggests the complexities and ambiguities of state-level administrative modernization. Not only did reform encounter a great deal of resistance from entrenched political cultures, but it produced the enormous variations for which the American social policy is infamous. Reviewing the work of the state commissions, Chickering noted that when "one considers the wide variety of local conditions . . . it would be natural to expect that, if ten reports were made in ten different states, then most of the [key questions about welfare reform] would be given ten different answers." The proliferation of federal work and relief programs after 1935 only added to the "categorical confusion."

A 1938 review of state welfare administration by the Social Security Board captures some of the complexity. Thirty-eight states appropriated some funds for general relief, but only thirty provided for state supervision of local relief administration. Nine states, on the other hand, administered general relief directly. All states were in the process of creating agencies to receive categorical relief under the Social Security Act, but in only twenty-four were categorical and general relief programs integrated at the state level. In some states, general relief was administered locally, while in others there were separate, state-level agencies for the two forms of relief.[73] Diversity in administrative structure was accompanied by the enormous policy variations for which the American public welfare system has become infamous. Nineteen states administered relief in cash and in kind, ten provided cash only, and twenty gave aid only in kind (food orders, used clothing, direct payments to landlords). Thirty-two states supplemented WPA wages with relief, and thirty-four supplemented categorical programs with general relief. General relief standards reported by the SSB in December 1939 ranged from a high of $30.89 per case in California to an abysmal $2.91 in Mississippi. The most generous state in OAA benefits paid $32.97 per month, while the least generous was Arkansas, where the elderly poor received $6.01. Average ADC monthly allowances ranged from $61.07 in Massachusetts to $8.10 in, again, Arkansas.[74]

Despite these variations it is possible to make some key generalizations about the course of administrative expansion in the late 1930s. In southern and western states with relatively undeveloped local welfare organizations, state-level administrative modernization proceeded rapidly. Of the seventeen states that established new welfare departments in 1937, all but two were west of the Mississippi and south of the Mason-Dixon line. One historian of the "New South" has called the growth of public welfare in that region during the late 1930s a "welfare revolution." As the FERA's Josephine Brown noted in her classic study of public relief, "the southern and western states [with] less local autonomy, almost no township jurisdiction and fewer traditions regarding relief to the poor" were able to make the transition to centralized administration more smoothly.[75] Resistance to reform was stronger in the states of the and eastern Midwest. Here, in Brown's words, the "Elizabethan poor law had taken deep root in the townships and the towns were accustomed to care for their own and make their own rules." Political conflict between local poor boards and state-level reformers was exacerbated by urban-rural divisions, which focused on the financing of relief in the larger cities.[76] Yet opposition to reform did not produce a wholesale return to the poor laws, as fiscal realities forced most states to centralized welfare administration. Conversely, successful administrative modernization in the South and West did not necessarily produce more adequate relief. Relief standards, as now, tended to be closely correlated with levels of economic development.[77] Thus, we have the apparent contradiction of the state welfare systems providing the most adequate relief also showing the most resistance to administrative reform. But this was precisely Haber's point: the conflicts over relief reflected, in part, the big increases in spending and caseloads, which were greatest in the states of the Northeast and Midwest.

Perhaps the most important generalization one can make about state-level reform in the late 1930s involves the new public image associated with "welfare." Increasingly, state departments focused on the provision of public assistance rather than the broad range of services envisioned by the public welfare reform movement. In the process, "welfare" came to assume the negative connotations associated with the "dole." Early surveys of public opinion showed chronic hostility to the institutionalization of state-level relief. A Gallup poll during the recession of 1938 revealed that 70 percent of those polled agreed that "people on relief in your community are getting as much as they should."[78] The expansion of general relief during the recession, coupled with the growth of the categorical aid and the increase in the WPA quota, created the appearance of a chronic problem that was not being solved by the proliferation of government programs. One *Survey* columnist even romanticized the early depression years, when "interest was keen and there was an immediate response to stories of human suffering. But as 'emergency' followed 'emergency' the public gradually acquired immunity." Explaining the proliferation of punitive state "work for relief"—precursors to more recent "workfare" policies—the WPA's Corrington Gill stressed a "growing sentiment against the dole."[79] The continued hostility to relief, now focused on state public welfare, may help explain one of the central paradoxes one encounters in evaluating policy in the late 1930s—the rapid success of the public welfare reform movement coupled with the widespread perception of a retreat to "poor law relief" among the reformers themselves.

One way to illustrate these generalizations is to look briefly at the experiences of two states, Washington and New Jersey, which responded to the end of federal general relief grant program in radically different ways. In Washington, state political leaders and public welfare officials had worked closely with federal officials since the beginning of federal relief under the Reconstruction Finance Corporation. Despite a conflict over Washington's attempt to use relief funds for public works, state and federal officials generally saw eye-to-eye on administrative issues during the FERA period. Charles Ernst, the state's relief director, had been instrumental in reorganizing Seattle's relief program (essentially seizing control from the radical Unemployed Citizens League), by the late 1930s a rising star in the field of public welfare. The expansion of state authority during the early depression was unencumbered by resistance for entrenched local poor law administration. By 1934 the state was administering relief through a district system, essentially bypassing the traditional county poor law administrations.[80]

Preparing for the end of the FERA and the Social Security program, state officials established a new Department of Public Welfare in March of 1935. The agency was designated to administer a small, "residual" general relief program (it was assumed that the WPA would take nearly all "employables" off general relief), the categorical programs financed by matching federal grants and unemployment compensation. The 1935 legislation did not repeal the poor laws, and the counties continued to play an important role in administering general relief and "mothers' aid." But the state financed most of the program and administered the OAA and ADC directly. The ease with which Washington moved toward centralized authority reflected not only the political weakness of county administration but a strong commitment to expanding state authority on the part of public officials. "[The] tendency now is toward a transfer of government from county and city to the state," declared Governor Homer Martin in late 1934. "The state must assume more and more responsibility toward our educational system, our highways, the development of our resources and the care of the aged. The state is the logical centralized unity of government." In late 1936 relief director Ernst initiated a movement to complete the transition to state authority. In September the welfare director, along with representatives of the U.S. Children's Bureau, officials in a number of state agencies and members of the county commissioners' association, met to develop a new welfare code. A subcommittee was appointed, producing a bill that easily passed the legislature. The new law abolished both the poor laws and the 1913 Mothers' Aid law, placing nearly all welfare functions in the hands of a new state Department of Social Security.[81]

New Jersey, on the other hand, had a strong tradition of politicized "poor law" relief administration. Local officials had consistently resisted attempts by reformers to transfer the administration of relief to nonpartisan county welfare boards. When a 1931 Pension Survey Commission, created to design a state OAA program, recommended that county boards be placed in charge of general relief, the legislature balked. "Unwilling to affront the local overseers of the poor," they refused to make the county boards mandatory. The most influential public welfare official in the state, commissioner of institutions and agencies John Ellis, presented a sharp contrast to Washington's Ernst. Although Ellis nominally supported centralized relief administration, he was a cautious reformer who operated "in the old political way . . . advancing a step here and a step there."[82] The primary impetus for centralization was the relief crisis of the early 1930s and the role of state and federal financing after 1932. By the FERA period, the state and federal governments were financing most relief in the state, a fact that weakened local political control. At the beginning of 1934, municipalities were given the option of continuing to administer relief themselves or paying into a central fund, with the state assuming virtually all administrative responsibility. By the beginning of 1936, relief in approximately 400 of 564 municipalities, constituting 90 percent of the state's relief population, had passed to direct state control.[83]

The end of the FERA, however, appeared to produce a wholesale retreat to traditional relief administration. When federal relief grants were withdrawn at the end of 1935, state officials proposed that general relief be administered by county boards under state supervision. But the legislature gridlocked over financing, and the reform program was narrowly defeated. In April of 1936 general relief once again returned to local control under the poor laws. The state Emergency Relief Administration was replaced by a Financial Assistance Commission, which disbursed state aid for relief costs above a fixed percentage of the local property tax rate. This automatic formula ended state influence over relief standards and methods of administration. Like most states, New Jersey quickly applied for federal matching grants for categorical relief under the Social Security Act. But, unlike the Washington case, these programs did not appear to promote uniform, centralized administration but rather "categorical confusion." The OAA program was administered by county welfare boards under state supervision (the approach preferred by reformers). ADC was administered directly by a state Board of Children's Guardians.[84] In many respects, the New Jersey experience conformed to the worst fears of social workers and public welfare officials contemplating the end of federal relief—a return to local poor law administration of general relief and fragmented responsibility for the categorical programs. "The veritable labyrinth of agencies and services makes intelligent understanding of present problems and needs either by the citizenry or their elected representatives virtually impossible," wrote Princeton University's Paul Stafford in his 1941 study of the state's welfare system. "The system literally defies public comprehension."[85]

At first glance it might appear that the policies of Washington and New Jersey were polar opposites. But on closer examination the experiences of the two states contain some important similarities. In neither case can state policy be characterized as a retreat to pre-FERA relief standards. Administratively, Washington's public welfare system had been dramatically transformed by the crisis of the depression and the impact of the categorical programs funded by federal grants. Aggregate relief spending and caseloads in Washington had, by 1938, returned to the levels that had prevailed under the FERA. A similar situation prevailed in New Jersey. While local officials resisted efforts to modernize administration, the state continued to finance approximately 75 percent of all emergency relief. Total state and local spending remained at roughly the level of the FERA period. A *Survey* reporter reviewing the state's general relief program in 1936 found "relatively little change from the [FERA] period" in most cities; only in rural sections and a few smaller industrial communities had "the fear been realized that the abandonment of the [state] ERA program would cause a return to the worst features of traditional poor law administration."[86] Furthermore, in both states general relief was being replaced by categorical aid under the Social Security program. In Washington Charles Ernst consistently allocated funds to the federally reimbursed categories at the expense of general relief. The state relief director was a strong supporter of the ADC program and, although less enthusiastic about OAA, increased funding in response to mass applications and pressure from the elderly lobby. The expansion of categorical aid in New Jersey, where there were less bureaucratic support for the programs and a strong grassroots campaign to defend general relief, was more modest. Yet ADC and OAA were expanding, while the general relief program remained relatively stable, and the categories rested on a far more secure financial and administrative base.[87]

Finally, while the idea of a post-FERA retreat to the poor laws cannot be sustained, the experiences of both Washington and New Jersey show that the emerging public welfare system was unpopular and politically vulnerable. Funding crises were annual affairs in New Jersey, as legislators gridlocked over revenue sources, and the state Board of Control waited until late in the fiscal year before reimbursing municipalities. As late as 1939, local grocers were forced to wait five months before being reimbursed for food orders, while the state legislature debated the relative merits of new taxes or a bond issue. Stafford called relief in the state a "political football" and blamed instability on "the stubborn survival of those same attitudes upon which the old poor-law system had been founded."[88] Yet even the modernizers, under constant fiscal pressure, could adopt draconian policies and justify them using traditional rhetoric. Bruce Blumell has shown how the Washington State Department of Public Welfare, a model social agency by the standards of the late 1930s, consistently underfunded the general relief program, even though it was abundantly clear that large numbers of needy workers were not being accepted by the WPA. Indeed, state relief director Charles Ernst seemed intent on eliminating general relief altogether. In May of 1936 he called on local relief administrators to purge the relief rolls of all but the most needy applicants: "home visitors should increase their drive to put the burden of proof on the able-bodied client that he has made every effort to find employment before we give him relief." Later he told officials that "the main thing . . . is your change of attitude from one in which we are feeling responsible for providing relief, to the new attitude of expecting the client to be responsible for getting a job."[89]

The 1935 shift in national welfare policy did not end the "dole," as New Deal officials had hoped, nor did it result in a retreat to traditional "poor law" relief, as many social workers feared. Rather, modernized public welfare became the safety net for low-wage workers. The emergency relief administrations of the FERA period had been institutionalized as state public welfare departments. The welfare reform movement of the 1920s had succeeded in creating professional public agencies at the state level, but in the process "welfare" was now almost exclusively associated with relief-giving. Initially, the targeted programs financed under the Ssocial Security Act proved more popular than general relief, but they were eventually tainted with the stigma of the "dole." These developments left an unpopular, bureaucratic welfare system vulnerable to periodic assaults from critics of the welfare state and to futile reform efforts by its liberal defenders. This was the central dynamic of welfare policy until Bill Clinton promised to "end welfare as we know it" (and coupled this promise with an important policy breakthrough—time limits).

NOTES

1. Edwin Amenta has described the New Deal's 1935 program as a "work and relief" policy. This is certainly an accurate description of the policy that emerged in the late 1930s. But a national relief program was precisely what administration officials hoped to avoid. Although the social insurance provisions of the Social Security Act initially took a back seat to relief—in the form of federal

grants to state old age assistance programs—for the elderly, this was considered to be a temporary (and not entirely welcome) feature of national policy. Edwin Amenta, *Bold Relief* (Princeton, NJ: Princeton University Press, 1998).

2. Some definitions are in order. As in the previous chapters, *general relief* refers to a form of public welfare in which eligibility is based simply on income, as determined by a local public or private agency administering a means test. This was the primary form of aid to the unemployed prior to 1935. *Categorical* programs, on the other hand, required that the recipient be part of a particular category of the poor (elderly, single-parent, blind). *Social insurance* refers to a European-style welfare program in which eligibility was not determined by income, and the public and private welfare bureaucracies did not play a central role. Social insurance also implies that the programs are financed by "contributions" from employed workers themselves, rather than from general revenues. The term *work program*, rather than WPA, is used here because that was what the program was called by administration officials until late 1935. Again, I also use the terms *public employment* and *work relief* when referring to the WPA.

3. The most comprehensive studies of public employment and its impact on public welfare in the late 1930s remain Josephine Brown, *Public Relief, 1929–1939* (New York: Henry Holt and Co., 1940); Donald S. Howard, *The WPA and Federal Relief Policy* (New York: Russell Sage Foundation, 1943); Marietta Stevenson, *Public Welfare Administration* (New York: Macmillan, 1938); and Arthur E. Burns and Edward A. Williams, *Federal Work, Security and Relief Programs* (New York: Da Capo Press, 1971). The 1930s also produced a number of valuable studies of state public welfare administration. For this chapter I have drawn on Paul Tutt Stafford, *Government and the Needy: A Study of Public Assistance in New Jersey* (Princeton, NJ: Princeton University Press, 1941) and Douglas H. MacNeil, *Seven Years of Unemployment Relief in New Jersey* (Washington, DC: Social Science Research Council, 1938). These are digested in James Leiby, *Charity and Correction in New Jersey: A History of State Welfare Institutions* (New Brunswick, NJ: Rutgers University Press, 1967), chs. 12, 16.

James T. Patterson's seminal *The New Deal and the States: Federalism in Transition* (Westport, CT: Greenwood Press, 1981) contains a chapter on relief after 1935. Valuable local studies of relief in the late 1930s include Barbara Blumberg, *The New Deal and the Unemployed: The View from New York City* (Lewisburg, PA: Bucknell University Press, 1977); Bruce Blumell, "The Development of Public Assistance in the State of Washington during the Great Depression" (Ph.D. diss., University of Washington, 1973) and Blumell, *The Development of Public Assistance in the State of Washington during the Great Depression* (New York: Garland, 1984); David Maurer, "Public Relief Programs and Politics in Ohio" (Ph.D. diss., Ohio State University, 1962); John F. Bauman, "The City, the Depression and Relief: The Philadelphia Experience, 1929–1939" (Ph.D. diss., Rutgers University, 1969).

The most recent efforts to evaluate the impact of the New Deal's 1935 program on public welfare are James T. Patterson, *America's Struggle against Poverty* (Cambridge, MA: Harvard University Press, 1994), ch. 4; William R. Brock, *Welfare, Democracy and the New Deal* (Cambridge: Cambridge University Press, 1988), chs. 7–8.

4. Brock, *Welfare, Democracy and the New Deal*, 6, 345; Linda Gordon, "Social Insurance and Public Assistance: The Influence of Gender in Welfare Thought in

the United States, 1890–1935," *The American Historical Review* (February 1992): 19–21, and Gordon, *Pitied but Not Entitled* (New York: Free Press, 1994), 5–6, chs. 6, 9; Theda Skocpol, *Social Policy in the United States* Princeton, NJ: Princeton University Press, 1995), ch. 6, and Skocpol, *Protecting Soldiers and Mothers* (Cambridge, MA: Harvard University, Press, 1992), 535–536; Cristopher Howard, "Sowing the Seeds of 'Welfare': The Transformation of Mothers' Pensions, 1900–1940," *Journal of Policy History* 4, no. 2 (1992): 188–227; Jerry Cates, *Insuring Inequality* (Ann Arbor: University of Michigan Press, 1983), ch. 6. For recent syntheses of New Deal welfare policy that reflect the ambivalence described here see Robert H. Bremner, "The New Deal and Social Welfare," in Harvard Sitkoff, ed., *Fifty Years Later: The New Deal Evaluated* (Philadelphia: Alfred Knopf, 1985), 76, 85–86; Anthony J. Badger, *The New Deal* (New York: Farrar, Straus, and Giroux, 1989), 242–244; Roger Biles, *A New Deal for the American People* (De Kalb: Northern Illinois University Press, 1991), 112–116.

5. Amenta, *Bold Relief*, 43–44.

6. Badger, *The New Deal*, 244; Skocpol, *Social Policy in the United States*, 214–218; Margaret Weir, *Politics and Jobs: The Boundaries of Employment Policy in the United States* (Princeton, NJ: Princeton University Press, 1992); Margaret Weir and Theda Skocpol, "State Structures and the Possibilities for Keynesian Responses to the Great Depression in Sweden, Britain and the United States," in Peter B. Evans, Dietrich Rueschmeyer and Theda Skocpol, eds., *Bringing the State Back In* (Cambridge: Cambridge University Press, 1985), 137–146.

7. Bonnie Fox Schwartz has argued that the WPA was not a true public employment program, because it required an initial means test of all employees (CWA, by contrast, took half its caseload from non-relief workers applying through the U.S. Employment Service). New Deal officials tended to see the program as a "hybrid," combining features of public works and relief. Bonnie Fox Schwartz, *The Civil Works Administration: The Business of Emergency Employment in the New Deal* (Princeton, NJ: Princeton University Press, 1984); Don D. Lescohier, "The Hybrid WPA," *Survey* 75, no. 6 (June 1939): 167–169.

In addition to the works cited previously (Howard, Brown, Burns and Williams, Blumell and Blumberg), an indispensable source on the WPA is Arthur W. MacMahon, John D. Millett and Gladys Ogden, *The Administration of Federal Work Relief* (Chicago: Social Science Research Council, 1941), 124–126. There is a fairly extensive literature on particular WPA projects, particularly the Arts Projects (see Badger, *The New Deal*, 349–350). Biographies of Hopkins contain the most useful overviews of the origins and implementation of WPA. See Searle F. Charles, *Minister of Relief: Harry Hopkins and the Depression* (Syracuse, NY: Syracuse University Press, 1963); George McJimsey, *Harry Hopkins, Ally of the Poor and Defender of Democracy* (Cambridge, MA: Harvard University Press, 1987). On the origins of federal relief and public employment see also William W. Bremer, "Along the American Way: The New Deal's Work Relief Programs for the Unemployed," *Journal of American History* 62 (1975): 636–652.

8. Margaret C. Bristol, "Personal Reactions of Assignees to WPA in Chicago," *Social Service Review* 12, no. 1 (March 1938): 69–100. Bristol found that workers strongly supported the program and made a distinction between the WPA and "work relief." They did not, however, consider the program to be a "regular job," as New Deal officials sometimes claimed.

9. Howard, *The WPA and Federal Relief Policy*, 531. Federal officials tended to inflate the work program caseload by including employment on the CCC and in other agencies financed by emergency appropriations. Yet the latter did not necessarily employ workers on the national relief caseload. Approximately 97 percent of WPA employment was relief labor. The figure for the CCC was 86 percent and for "other agencies," 55 percent. McMahon et al., *The Administration of Federal Work Relief*, 124–126.

10. Technically, the administration never promised to assist all needy "employables" but only an estimate of those on the FERA rolls. However, the rhetoric certainly implied that the goal of the policy was to eliminate the "dole" for unemployed workers. Furthermore, the employment target set when the program was announced was clearly not met. Franklin D. Roosevelt, "Annual Message to Congress," January 4, 1935, in Samuel L. Rosenman, ed., *The Public Papers and Addresses of Franklin D. Roosevelt*, vol. 4 (New York: Random House, 1938), 19–23; Howard, *The WPA and Federal Relief Policy*, 561–563; Russell Kurtz, "Yourtown," *Survey* 71, no. 11 (November 1935): 323; Brock, *Welfare, Democracy and the New Deal*, 270.

11. *New York Times*, April 8, 1984, 18; Brock, *Welfare, Democracy and the New Deal*, 280.

12. This appeared to be a real possibility in early 1935. A January memo from the FERA work division, while uncertain about the contours of the proposed employment policy, stressed the continuity between work relief under the FERA and the new program. "Preliminary Outline of a Proposed Study of Work Relief for FERA," January 25, 1935, FERA Files—Old Subject File (National Archives), Box 15, File: Forms—January 1935.

13. The story of the WPA's early implementation is covered well in McJimsey, *Harry Hopkins, Ally of the Poor and Defender of Democracy*, 78–55 and MacMahon et al., *The Administration of Federal Work Relief*, 66–78, 89–120. This account also relies heavily on the *New York Times* and the *Survey* for 1935. See in particular *Survey* 71, no. 10 (October 1935): 310 and no. 12 (December 1935): 375.

14. *Survey* 71, no. 11 (November 1935): 342–343; *New York Times*, April 28, 1935, IV, 3; June 26, 1935, 4; August 16, 1935 16; November 4, 1935, 20.

15. *New York Times*, September 14, 1935, 2; December 24, 1935, 1, 4; Howard, *The WPA and Federal Relief Policy*, 565–566.

16. In December 1936, the *Survey* reported that in a national sample of 10,800 general relief cases, 46 percent had at least one employable member who would have been on the WPA but for quota limitations. Another 22 percent were receiving relief to supplement WPA wages. Only 20 percent were listed as "chronic unemployables." Gertrude Springer, "Off Again—RELIEF—On Again," *Survey* 72, no. 12 (December 1936): 357. See also McMahon et al., *The Administration of Federal Work Relief*, 181, for a 1939 WPA estimate that there were 869,380 workers "certified and waiting for assignment" to the WPA.

17. Stephen T. Early to FDR, November 7, 1935, FDR Papers—Official File 444, FERA, August–December 1935; *Survey* 72, no. 1 (January 1936): 3–7; *New York Times*, January 12, 1936, 2; February 15, 1936, 17; February 16, 1936; Jacob Fisher, *The Response of Social Work to the Depression* (Boston: Schenkman, 1980), 143–146. Howard, *The WPA and Federal Relief Policy*, 70–96 reviews the studies of general relief after 1935.

18. McMahon et al., *The Administration of Federal Work Relief*, 174.

19. Badger, *The New Deal*, 211–213. For the classic study of the conservative counterrevolution in Congress see James T. Patterson, *Congressional Conservatism and the New Deal* (Lexington: University of Kentucky Press, 1967).

20. John Morton Blum, *From the Morgenthau Diaries: The Years of Crisis, 1928–1938* (Boston: Houghton Mifflin, 1959), 279–281. Recent studies have stressed Roosevelt's fiscal conservatism during this period, prior to the triumph of Keynesian theory in New Deal circles in response to the recession of 1938. See Alan Brinkley, *The End of Reform* (New York: Alfred Knopf, 1995); Dean May, *From New Deal to New Economics* (New York: Garland, 1981), 85–86; Mark Leff, "Taxing the Forgotten Man: The Politics of Social Security Finance in the New Deal," *Journal of American History* 10 (September 1983): 376–379; Badger, *The New Deal*, 111–112.

21. *New York Times*, February 2, 1936, IV, 3; February 7, 1936, 4; February 16, 1936, IV, 10; March 7, 1936, 4; March 17, 1936, 20; April 24, 1936, IV, 3; June 7, 1936, 6; Blum, *From the Morgenthau Diaries*, 260.

22. Aubrey Williams, "Address . . . at the National Conference on Social Work," May 26, 1936, Aubrey Williams Papers, FDR Library, Box 42, File no. 3; *New York Times*, February 16, 1936, 35; May 27, 1936, 1; Fisher, *The Response of Social Work to the Great Depression*, 150.

23. *New York Times*, March 22, 1936, IV, 3. Krock, who supported reduced emergency expenditures, was hardly an unbiased observer. (According to Jordan Schwarz, he "heeded the advice" of financier Bernard Baruch on economic matters.) These views may well have been ideology disguised as political analysis. Yet his frequent *New York Times* pieces on fiscal politics provide strong evidence of the kinds of political and ideological pressures tending to reduce WPA outlays in 1936 and 1937. Jordan A. Schwarz, *The New Dealers* (New York: Random House, 1994), 99.

24. McJimsey, *Harry Hopkins*, 88–89; Blum, *From the Morgenthau Diaries*, 246, 267–268, 279.

25. *New York Times*, March 6, 1936, 2; March 13, 1936, 4. Federal officials appear to have developed an informal understanding with the organizations of the unemployed, particularly the Workers Alliance, that the announcement of program cuts would generate protests at the grassroots. See also Frances Fox Piven and Richard A. Cloward, *Poor People's Movements* (New York: Random House, 1977), 85–90, for a critical analysis of the tactics of the Workers Alliance during this period.

26. *New York Times*, December 3, 1936, 6; December 4, 1936, 1; December 6, 1936, IV, 3; *Survey* 73, no. 1 (January 1937): 16; Blum, *From the Morgenthau Diaries*, 276; Blumberg, *The New Deal and the Unemployed*, 88–89, 94, 101–104.

27. As Alan Brinkley has pointed out, "many members of the administration who did not believe deficits were administratively dangerous considered them a political rebuke. . . . Balancing the budget would mark the triumph of the New Deal." Brinkley, *The End of Reform*, 29.

28. *Survey* 73, no. 5 (May 1937): 150; no. 6 (June 1937): 194; *New York Times*, August 6, 1937, 4; August 14, 1937, 12; September 12, 1937 IV, 7; Patterson, *Congressional Conservatism and the New Deal*, 139–145; Howard, *The WPA and Relief*, 855.

29. Blum, *From the Morgenthau Diaries*, 417–426; May, *From New Deal to New Economics*, chs. 6–7; Brinkley, *The End of Reform*, 83–85, 94–104.

30. *Survey* 74, no. 2 (February 1938): 35; no. 3 (March 1938): 79; no. 7 (July 1938): 329.

31. The total WPA caseload as a percentage of the number of unemployed may have actually declined slightly during the recession because the increase in emergency expenditures did not keep pace with the rise in unemployment.

32. "Public Assistance and Earnings under Federal Work Programs in the United States, 1933–1939," *Social Security Bulletin* 3 (February 1940): 54–55. The total number of cases on state-administered public assistance (categorical and general relief), excluding the WPA, in January of 1938 was estimated to be 3.7 million by the Social Security Board.

33. Brinkley, *The End of Reform*, 104; McMahon et al., *The Administration of Federal Work Relief*, 182.

34. Schwarz, *The New Dealers*; J. Joseph Huthmacher, *Senator Robert F. Wagner and the Rise of Urban Liberalism* (New York: Atheneum, 1968). For a discussion of pre–New Deal public employment that places relatively little emphasis on the political base for such policies see Udo Sautter, *Three Cheers for the Unemployed* (New York: Cambridge University Press, 1991). Schwartz describes the political conflicts over work relief and the distance between public employment and welfare in *The Civil Works Administration*.

35. *New York Times*, April 28, 1935, IV, 3; October 4, 1935, 22; McMahon et al., *The Administration of Federal Work Relief*, 23.

36. Howard, *The WPA and Federal Relief Policy*, 351–371.

37. Russell Kurtz, "No More Federal Relief," *Survey* 71, no. 2 (February 1935): 36; Grace Adams, *Workers on Relief* (New Haven, CT: Yale University Press, 1939), 27–37; McMahon et al., *The Administration of Federal Work Relief*, 174.

38. John D. Millett, *The Works Progress Administration in New York City* (Chicago: Social Science Research Council, 1938), 209; Blumell, *The Development of Public Assistance in the State of Washington*, 259; *New York Times*, December 19, 1935, 3.

39. For the impact of WPA cuts in the summer of 1937 see *Survey* 73, no. 9 (September 1937): 290; Margaret Bristol, "Personal Reactions of Assignees to the WPA in Chicago," 69; Blumberg, *The New Deal and the Unemployed*, 107. In many cases public officials, arguing that "employables" were the responsibility of the federal government, cut local relief caseloads in spite of the reduction in the WPA quota. See Ellery F. Reed, "What Turning Relief Back to the Local Community Meant in Cincinnati," *Social Service Review* 12, no. 1 (March 1938): 8–9.

40. Badger, *The New Deal*, 243–244. Hopkins quote: "Report of July 17 Meeting," Morgenthau Diaries, FDR Library, Book 8.

41. Aubrey Williams, "Address . . . at the American Association of Social Workers," Washington, DC, 1937, Aubrey Williams Papers, Box 43, File no. 3. The early Gallup polls found strong support for reducing emergency expenditures and balancing the federal budget. Yet there was equally strong support for the WPA, as opposed to less costly direct relief. Thus, the administration's limited public employment program appears to conform to "public opinion," at least as measured by these early polls. *The Gallup Poll*, vol. 1 (New York: Random

House, 1972), 1, 12, 45, 55, 61, 80, 84; Blumberg, *The New Deal and the Unemployed*, 87, 288–289.

42. Brock, *Welfare, Democracy and the New Deal*, 41–44.

43. Social workers had consistently expressed doubts that public employment would assist all "employables" on the FERA rolls. See "Informal Report of a Special Committee Advisory to the President's Committee on Economic Security," November 22, 1934, CES Files (National Archives), Box 2, File: Public Employment and Public Assistance; Ewan Clague, "No More Federal Relief," *Survey* 71, no. 2 (February 1935): 35–37.

44. *Survey* 72, no. 7 (July 1936): 210; Millett, *The Works Progress Administration in New York City*, 210; Brock, *Welfare, Democracy and the New Deal*, 321; David M. Schneider and Albert Deutch, *The History of Public Welfare in New York State* (Chicago: University of Chicago Press, 1941), 263–264.

45. Brock, *Welfare, Democracy and the New Deal*, 285–286, 303–305; *Survey* 72, no. 8 (August 1936): 240; Arthur D. Miles, "Relief in Illinois without Federal Aid," *Social Service Review* (1940): 283–300.

46. Blumell, *The Development of Public Assistance in the State of Washington*, 305–309; Reed, "What Turning Relief Back to the Local Community Meant in Cincinnati."

47. Ewan Clague, "1932—When Relief Stops—1937," *Survey* 71, no. 11 (November 1935): 328–329.

48. Dorothy Kahn, "What Is Worth Saving in 'This Business of Relief'?," *Survey* 73, no. 2 (February 1937): 38.

49. "Cruelties of the Illinois Three-Year Settlement Provisions," *Social Service Review* 14 (June 1940): 347; Wilfred S. Reynolds,"Public Welfare Administration A Patchwork in Illinois," *Social Service Review* 11 (March 1937): 5–6; Miles, "Relief in Illinois without Federal Aid," 300.

50. Arthur Dunham, "Public Welfare and the Referendum in Michigan," *Social Service Review* 12 (September 1938: 438–439; *Survey* 74, no. 10 (October 1938): 320; 75, no. 3 (March 1939): 184; Patterson, *The New Deal and the States*, 146–150; William Haber, "Social Work and Politics," *Survey* 74, no. 5 (May 1938): 139; Margaret Orelup, "Private Values, Public Policy, and Poverty in America, 1890–1940" (Ph.D. diss., University of Massachusetts, Amherst, 1995), ch. 4.

51. Haber, "Social Work and Politics," 140.

52. Gertrude Springer, "This Business of Relief," *Survey* 74, no. 2 (February 1938): 26; 74, no. 12 (December 1938): 383. These estimates are supported by a number of state studies. Blumell's study of relief in Washington concluded that by March of 1938, "more people were receiving some form of public assistance, including those on the federal work programs, than at any time during the entire depression." Blumell, *The Development of Public Assistance in the State of Washington*, 411; Reynolds, "Public Welfare Administration A Patchwork in Illinois," 2.

53. "Public Assistance and Earnings under Federal Work Programs in the United States, 1933–1939," *Social Security Bulletin* 3 (February 1940): 49–51; Brown, *Public Relief*, 472–473.

54. Gertrude Springer, "Relief in November 1938," *Survey* 74, no. 11 (November 1938): 340; no. 4 (April 1938): 114; Charles Ernst, "Clients Aren't What They Used to Be," *Survey* 74, no. 5 (May 1938): 142–144. Piven and Cloward have argued that there was a significant decline in relief protests after 1935 as a result

of the return of relief to the states and the turn away from disruptive tactics by the increasingly centralized organizations of the unemployed. See *Poor People's Movements*, 84–90.

55. MacNeil, *Seven Years of Unemployment Relief in New Jersey*, 214; Blumell, *The Development of Public Assistance in the State of Washington*, 419–427.

56. See Edwin Amenta and Yvonne Zylan, "It Happened Here: Political Opportunity Theory, the New Institutionalism, and the Townsend Movement," *American Sociological Review* 56, no. 2 (April 1991): 254–256.

57. Joanna Colcord, "The West Is Still Different," *Survey* 73, no. 8 (August 1937): 244; *Survey* 74, no. 4 (April 1938): 115; APWA Round Table, "The Administration of Public Assistance," December 11, 1937, 8–11; Ernst, "Clients Aren't What They Used to Be," 143.

58. Blumell, *The Development of Public Assistance in the State of Washington*, 334; Martha Derthick, *The Influence of Federal Grants* (Cambridge, MA: Harvard University Press, 1970), 54–55.

59. "Public Assistance and Earnings under Federal Work Programs in the United States," 54–55.

60. Ibid.: the Division of Public Assistance of the SSB estimated that the ADC caseload rose from a monthly average of approximately 110,000 families in 1935 to an average of 300,000 thousand in 1939. See also Dorothy R. Bucklin, "Public Aid for the Care of Dependent Children in Their Own Homes, 1932–1938," *Social Security Bulletin* 2 (April 1939): 24–35.

61. Brown, *Public Relief*, 370–371; Howard, "Sowing the Seeds of 'Welfare,' " 214. I believe that Howard's interpretation of the APWA guidelines, adopted by approximately half the states by 1939, is mistaken. The guidelines attempted to transform the clause from one emphasizing moral judgment to one that stressed "meeting the standards of care and health, fixed by the laws of this State and the rules and regulations of the State department thereunder." The latter was an expansive definition of eligibility that focused on improving relief standards. See Winifred Bell, *Aid to Dependent Children* (New York: Columbia University Press, 1965), 30–33.

62. Blumell, *The Development of Public Assistance in the State of Washington*, 339–341, 375–380; Derthick, *The Influence of Federal Grants*, 62; Stafford, *Government and the Needy*, 117, 202–205; *Survey* 75, no. 6 (June 1939): 184.

63. Blanche Coll, *Safety Net: Welfare and Social Security, 1929–1979* (New Brunswick, NJ: Rutgers University Press, 1995), 82–83. On efforts to transfer relief cases to the federally funded Aid to Dependent Children program see letters and memos in Aubrey Williams' papers, FDR Library, Box 27, File no. 2.

64. These reform coalitions closely resemble the groupings described by Ellis Hawley and Stephen Skowronek. The following pages on the modernization of public welfare draw on the ideas of "organizational synthesis" of historians and social scientists writing from the perspective of "American political development." See Stephen Skowronek, *Building the New American State* (New York: Cambridge University Press, 1982), 165–176, 286; Ellis Hawley, *The Great War and the Search for a Modern Order* (New York: St. Martin's Press, 1992), 123–127 and Hawley, "Social Policy in Twentieth Century America," in Donald Critchlow and Ellis Hawley, eds., *Federal Social Policy: The Historic Dimension* (College Park: Pennsylvania State University Press, 1988), 128–129. Hawley has also stressed the

"anti-bureaucratic tradition" and the failure of the New Deal to construct an administrative state of the European type. See Hawley, "The New Deal State and the Anti-Bureaucratic Tradition," in Robert Eden, ed., *The New Deal and Its Legacy: Critique and Reappraisal* (Westport, CT: Greenwood Press, 1989).

65. Brown, *Public Relief*, 307–308, 408; Gordon, *Pitied but Not Entitled*, 277–279.

66. Brian Balogh, "Securing Support: The Emergence of the Social Security Board as a Political Actor," in Donald Critchlow and Ellis Hawley, eds., *Federal Social Policy: The Historic Dimension* (University Park: Pennsylvania State University Press, 1988), 61–63; "The Social Security Board and the Effective Administration of Public Assistance," *Social Service Review* 12 (December 1938): 690–691; Albert Aronson, "Merit-System Standards in Social Security Administration," *Social Security Bulletin* 2 (February 1939): 15–16 and Aronson, "Six Months of State Merit-System Progress," *Social Security Bulletin* 3 (July 1940): 25–27.

67. "Annual Meeting of the Professional Schools," *Social Service Review* 12 (March 1938): 139. Brown, *Public Relief*, 422–423, argues that a decline in federal influence immediately after the dismantling of the FERA was reversed in the late 1930s.

68. Cates, *Insuring Inequality*, ch. 5.

69. *Survey* 75 (July 1939): 219; APWA, *Conference Report Series*, "The Administration of Public Assistance," December 11, 1937, 8–10; Ethel J. Hart, "Legal Responsibility of Relatives for the Care of the Aged: Administrative Policies of State Assistance Agencies," *Social Service Review* 15 (June 1941): 299–300; Marietta Stevenson and Alice McDonald, "Recent State Welfare Legislation," *Social Service Review* 15 (September 1941): 416–417.

70. Balogh, "Securing Support," 63. In reviewing the Board's publications in the late 1930s and early 1940s, I found little of the hostility to public assistance that Cates attributes to the SSB. In 1941, for example, the *Social Security Bulletin* reported favorably on increased state OAA payments in response to more liberal federal reimbursement policies. Later in the year, the *Bulletin* reported approvingly of the "many liberalizations in eligibility requirements." See "The Effect of Increased Federal Participation in Payments for Old Age Assistance in 1940," *Social Security Bulletin* 4 (June 1941): 15–17; "Legislative Changes in Public Assistance—1941," *Social Security Bulletin* 4 (November 1941): 12–19.

71. Howard, "Sowing the Seeds of 'Welfare,' " 214.

72. Marietta Stevenson, "Public Welfare Reorganization," *Social Service Review* 11 (September 1937): 349; Fred Kohler, "Be It Enacted . . . ," *Survey* 73, no. 8 (August 1937): 246–248; Martha Chickering, "States Look at Public Welfare," *Survey* 73, no. 5 (May 1937): 135–137.

73. *Survey* 173, no. 5 (May 1935): 135; 75, no. 1 (January 1939): 21; Stevenson, *Public Welfare Administration*, ch. 2.

74. Brown, *Public Relief*, 383, 387.

75. Stevenson, *Public Welfare Administration*, 351; George B. Tindall, *The Emergence of the New South, 1915–1945* (Baton Rouge: Louisiana State University Press, 1967), 488–492.

76. Brown, *Public Relief*, 320–321; Kohler, "Be It Enacted . . . ," 246; William Haber, "The Public Welfare Problem in Massachusetts," *Social Service Review* 12 (June 1938): 179–204; William Haber and Herman M. Somers, "The Administration of Public Assistance in Massachusetts," *Social Service Review* 12 (September

1938): 409–410, 415–416; Dunham, "Public Welfare and the Referendum in Michigan," 438; Haber, "Social Work and Politics," 139.

77. David Adie, "Our Social Geography," *Survey* 76, no. 9 (September 1940): 259–260.

78. *The Gallup Poll* (1938), 98.

79. *Survey*, 76, no. 6 (June 1940): 206, 74, no. 6 (June 1938): 208; Helen Cody Baker, "What Is Starvation?," *Survey* 76, no. 1 (January 1940): 10; Corrington Gill, "Local Work for Relief," *Survey* 76, no. 5 (May 1940): 157. At a session of the New England Historical Association, Margaret Orelup of the University of Massachusetts at Amherst presented an excellent survey of public attitudes toward relief in the late 1930s. Margaret Orelup, "What Is Poverty? Depression-Era Debates over Relief Standards, Chiseling and Entitlement," paper presented at the New England Historical Association, October 26, 1995.

80. Blumell, *The Development of Public Assistance in the State of Washington*, 236.

81. Ibid., 295, 375–378.

82. Leiby, *Charities and Correction in New Jersey*, 204, 276; MacNeil, *Seven Years of Unemployment Relief in New Jersey*, 54.

83. MacNeil, *Seven Years of Unemployment Relief in New Jersey*, 61.

84. Leiby, *Charities and Correction in New Jersey*, 271–284; Stafford, *Government and the Needy*, 111–112, 188–199.

85. Stafford, *Government and the Needy*, 273.

86. Blumell, *The Development of Public Assistance in the State of Washington*, 411–416; Stafford, *Government and the Needy*, 132, 134, 140; MacNeil, *Seven Years of Unemployment Relief in New Jersey*, 243 and MacNeil, "1936—Relief In New Jersey-1937," *Survey* 73, no. 4 (April 1937): 99–100. This analysis includes employment and expenditures for the federal work program. For example, in New Jersey, expenditures for all forms of relief, including the WPA, averaged $26 million in 1932, rose to $90 million under the FERA (1935) and reached a peak of nearly $147 million during the recession of 1938. If we omit the WPA and focus only on "direct relief," categorical and general, then post-1935 policies appear more like a return to pre-FERA levels. In 1932 total expenditures for public assistance in New Jersey averaged $30,000. Virtually all of these funds were state and local. Total state/local spending remained at approximately this level during the FERA period. It fell slightly, to approximately $29,000, in 1936 and 1937 and then rose to over $37,000 during the recession of 1938.

87. Blumell, *The Development of Public Assistance in the State of Washington*, 356–357, 414–415; Ernst, "Clients Aren't What They Used to Be," 144; Stafford, *Government and the Needy*, 128. Between 1935 and 1939 the caseloads of the categorical programs in New Jersey rose from 42,000 to approximately 60,000. Meanwhile, the state general relief program remained at approximately 200,000 recipients. Expenditures for categorical relief doubled during this period, to over $14 million, while general relief spending averaged around $20 million.

88. Haber, "Social Work and Politics," 140–141.

89. Blumell, *Public Assistance in the State of Washington*, 310–311.

Conclusion

This study has focused on a crucial episode in the history of the American welfare state, the expansion and federalization of relief from 1930 through 1935. I have argued that the traditional framework that interprets these developments primarily in terms of the depression and the New Deal ignores crucial features of welfare policy during this era. It ignores the significant expansion of relief-giving prior to the depression and the impact of efforts to modernize and professionalize welfare services during the 1920s. The conventional wisdom conveys the impression that most local relief efforts were characterized by a traditional voluntarism during the Hoover regime, when, in fact, there was a significant expansion of public welfare spending culminating in the first federal welfare program, the Emergency Relief and Construction Act of 1935. Not only did the ERCA finance most relief nationwide during the winter of 1933–1934, but Hoover's Reconstruction Finance Corporation was forced to play a much more active administrative role than has generally been assumed.

There was no great expansion of federal relief spending during the first months of the New Deal. While the Federal Emergency Relief Administration embraced a more aggressive regulatory role than that of its predecessor, its primary goal was to reduce the national relief caseload and federal spending role (while raising relief standards). Indeed, the New Deal was almost as hostile to the "dole" as was the Hoover administration. Yet, as numerous historians have stressed, this hostility led to unprecedented experimentation with forms of public employment, beginning with the CWA and culminating in the Works Progress Administration. Still, the work relief policy of 1935 was not an inevitable consequence of the values of New Deal officials. Rather, it was produced by the unexpected expansion of federal relief in 1934, the political controversies that the federal grant program engendered and the impact of these developments on debates within the administration over fiscal policy. The WPA was an unprecedented experiment in public employment, but it was underfunded, causing large numbers of workers to apply for the state-level dole. This helped institutionalize public welfare. While the Social Security Act, through its categorical provisions, also played an important role in this process, its impact tends to be exaggerated by historians of American social policy. The purpose of the 1935 program was to eliminate federal relief, not institutionalize it.

More broadly, I view welfare as we have come to know it as an unintended and unwanted consequence of the modernization of welfare services coupled with the failure to adequately finance alternatives (social insurance and public employment). Efforts to modernize poor law relief and private charity centered on the professionalization of social work, the adoption of business forms of organization by public and private agencies and the centralization of both the provision of services and fundraising. They also involved reforms designed to reduce dependence on public "doles," such as mass voluntarist fund drives and various work relief experiments. New, centralized welfare organizations were created in large urban areas that were thrown into crisis at the very outset of the depression. The reform movements of the 1920s also shaped efforts to find alternatives to the emerging dole, as seen in Hoover's unprecedented national Liberty Loan campaign in the fall of 1931 and in the dramatic CWA experiment two years later.[1] The public welfare movement created the vehicles for the institutionalization of welfare in the late 1930s—state welfare departments. Perhaps most importantly, by portraying unemployment and relief as a public responsibility, institutional modernization appears to have encouraged mass applications for the "dole."

To support the last point would require a developed social history of relief during the 1930s. While such a history would certainly portray the devastating impact of unemployment on families, it would also show that the decision to apply for relief was a complex one involving interactions between the family economy, economic conditions and public policies. Large numbers of recipients were able to avoid going "on the dole" by relying on their savings, borrowing, living with family and friends, reorganizing household economies, taking odd jobs and bartering. The seemingly endless depression increasingly exhausted these sources of support, forcing many recipients onto the relief rolls. But the decision to apply for relief might also have been influenced by a mass private relief drive, a work program billed as an alternative to relief, the opening of a new public agency in a neighborhood or even a referral by a friendly social worker, teacher or local politician. In effect, the aggregate national relief caseload was the product of thousands of individual decisions by workers and their families who not only exhausted their own resources but increasingly came to reject the stigma of the "dole."

But this was not a heroic struggle for relief. While there was a significant increase in mass protest during the depression that played an important role in shaping relief policy, much of it was directed against the emerging "dole" and in favor of public employment. Indeed, one of the most striking features of the relief system of the 1930s was how broadly unpopular the policy was and how closely the complaints about it resembled contemporary criticisms of "welfare." The early Gallup polls suggest that the public believed that relief costs were too high and that recipients were "getting too much."[2] Political attacks on relief were a persistent feature of life in the 1930s, particularly strident during the election of 1934. Social workers constantly complained that programs were poorly administered and inadequate. Both liberals and conservatives believed that doles undermined the work ethic and created dependence. These very different, even contradictory criticisms of relief created a dismally negative aura that enveloped the emerging public welfare system.

These conclusions have influenced my thinking on recent academic research on the origins of the American welfare state and on the broader public debate over welfare reform. On the academic side, I view my findings as consistent with the work of organizational historians who have stressed centralization, professionalization and technology as the driving forces in twentieth-century history (the so-called organizational synthesis popularized by Louis Galambos, Robert Weibe and Brian Balogh).[3] They are also consistent with much of the "new institutionalism" in the social sciences, which has emphasized the efforts of reformers to reconstruct the nineteenth-century "state of courts and parties," to use Steven Skowronek's formulation.[4] Like the institutionalists, I believe that the organization of the state and the nature of the party system, rather than ideology or class conflict, tend to explain the unique character of the American welfare state. However, it would seem that the public relief system that emerged was not the goal of the reformers, bureaucrats and interest groups that tend to dominate most institutional history. The crisis that produced the first federal welfare state occurred, in a sense, at the intersection of state and society.

The study of the unemployment relief system of the early depression has caused me to question some of the conclusions of recent research that attempts to explain the low status of "welfare" in American social policy. This work generally begins by noting the sharp distinction between social insurance and public assistance, a distinction embedded in the Social Security Act of 1935. Social insurance programs like the federal pension program for the elderly have, until recently, been politically popular (almost unassailable) and relatively well funded; public assistance, particularly the welfare entitlement for single-parent families, has been poorly funded and politically unpopular and has shown a great deal of variation from state to state.[5]

Why should this be so? Some critics have stressed the ideology of early twentieth-century reformers who held paternalistic views about the poor or believed in sharp distinctions between "welfare," targeted to the poor, and social insurance, a "universalist" program linked to employment. Feminist historians have emphasized that these policy differences were magnified by gender distinctions, with social insurance serving male workers and welfare designed to restrict women's role in the labor force. There has also been much criticism of the implementation of public assistance programs, particularly the Mothers' Pension programs, which served as the foundations for modern "welfare." With the decline of the "maternalist" movement that lobbied for mothers' aid, political support weakened, and these state programs came to look more like traditional relief. By the time the mother's aid was incorporated in the Social Security Act (as Aid to Dependent Children), its status had already been lowered relative to social insurance.[6] This problem was exacerbated by the policies of the Social Security Board, which denigrated public assistance in order to promote the federal insurance program for the elderly ("insuring inequality," according to Jerry Cates' influential study).[7] In the late 1940s the racial composition of ADC appeared to change with large numbers of African Americans applying for relief. This made the policy vulnerable to racist attacks ("Nobody minded welfare until blacks applied for it," is a popular formulation of the impact of this trend).[8] Finally, women's status in the labor force changed radically in the postwar years. As more and more women worked to help support their families (and this came to be seen as the norm), a program designed to encourage single, female parents not to seek employment seemed, at best, archaic.

All these developments no doubt influenced the fate of the welfare entitlement targeted to single-parent families. But do they explain why "welfare" is so unpopular and vulnerable to political attack? In my view they do not, because they presume (1) that the low status of relief can be explained by the historical trajectory of the entitlement for single-parent families and (2) that a different history might have produced a different policy that would have been more acceptable. Consider these assumptions in the context of the unemployment relief system of the early 1930s. Here was a welfare program whose caseload consisted primarily of white male heads of intact families during the most severe economic crisis in American history. Yet the policy was still attacked for creating dependence, bankrupting the government and failing to provide work.[9]

The sad reality is that relief programs have always been unpopular, and this stems from the fact that they are modernized versions of traditional poor law relief. Social insurance was designed, in part, to do away with this policy legacy. Relief and social insurance are, in fact, quite different. This is not a mythology constructed by reformers, politicians or welfare administrators. I also argue that there never was a golden age of mothers' aid or public welfare. The apparent consensus in support of mothers aid evaporated almost as soon as the programs were implemented and caseloads began to expand—that is, as soon at it was obvious that they were relief programs.[10] "Welfare" had positive connotations in its early years because it was seen as quite different from traditional relief. The low status of relief cannot be blamed on the framers of the Social Security Act or the Social Security Board, whose policies significantly liberalized mothers' aid. Race and gender have certainly influenced the politics of relief, but my research leads me to believe that a means-tested welfare policy with a different caseload composition would not have been significantly more popular.

At this point a caveat is necessary. I am not arguing that "public opinion," in the form of attitudes toward the poor or myths about welfare, is the primary source of the unpopularity of relief. It may be true that Americans have a tendency to blame the poor for their own misfortune and hold distorted views of the cost and caseload composition of relief programs. But Americans have also been prone to idealistic appeals to end poverty, as seen in the rhetoric of the Community Chests, the work experiments of the New Deal and the "War on Poverty."[11] Even the Welfare Reform Act of 1996 was justified in terms of ending poverty by encouraging employment. If Americans dislike welfare because they embrace the "work ethic," why have we not implemented more generous public employment and social insurance policies to replace relief?

My argument is that the political vulnerability of relief is not primarily a product of public attitudes but a result of the fact that the program, an unwanted stepchild of other reforms, has never had a strong political base of support. Indeed almost everyone, for his or her own reasons, has had something bad to say about it.[12] Even academics and welfare rights advocates who have been the program's most ardent defenders have spent much time complaining that welfare imposes "social control" on the poor, enforces labor market norms and "regulate[s] the lives of women." These criticisms, however justified, have certainly done little to build political support for the entitlement.

My research on the history of unemployment relief in the 1930s has also influenced my views of the 1996 welfare reform bill. Perhaps the central argument of conservative supporters of that law is that AFDC, as a social policy, has "failed." The assumption seems to be that at some point in the past there was an effective system of local private charity that was replaced by a federal welfare "entitlement," designed by liberals to end poverty. Oddly enough, liberals and welfare advocates who opposed the 1996 reforms base their argument on a similar set of assumptions. They tend to argue that the Great Depression revealed the inadequacies of private charity, they laud the New Deal for establishing a public welfare safety net and they denounce President Clinton, who signed the Republican bill, for deviating from the principles of liberalism. This study has argued that there never was a golden age of private charity prior to the 1930s and, more importantly, that the modern "dole" was never central to the liberal reform agenda. In fact, liberals like the New Deal's Harry Hopkins have often shown extreme hostility to the federal relief program. Whatever one might say about Clinton's decision to sign the Republican welfare bill, his promise to "end welfare as we know it" places him squarely within the liberal reform tradition. On the other hand, the Republicans' militant opposition to universal health coverage and expanded federal employment policies (note their bitter attack on Clinton's modest "economic stimulus" program in early 1993) is part of a long political tradition of successful opposition to social insurance and public employment, creating a vacuum that has made "welfare" necessary.

Finally, if the conclusions of this study are valid, then we should also be quite skeptical of claims that the 1996 law has ended welfare. Press accounts have emphasized important changes in federal welfare law (time limits, the end of the entitlement, mandatory work requirements) and the decline in the national caseload as if there had never been dramatic shifts in welfare policy in the past. But the 1930s saw a good deal of legislative activity designed to reduce the "dole" and cuts in the national relief caseload nearly as dramatic as that produced by the bill Clinton signed. (Between March and September of 1933, for example, the caseload declined by over 30 percent.) But in the absence of well-funded alternatives, relief eventually expanded to fill in the gaps of U.S. social policy. This could well happen again.

A central theme of this study is that the efforts to reform relief have produced unexpected policy outcomes. The Community Chest campaigns of the 1930s and early 1930s appear to have encouraged applications for relief. Similarly, big increases in federal relief spending resulted from the CWA, an experiment designed to eliminate the direct dole. The 1935 reforms implemented under the New Deal eventually produced a state-administered welfare entitlement.

The recent welfare reforms may well produce similar results. For example, press accounts and the back-patting rhetoric of reformers ignore a rather glaring irony produced by the "Personal Responsibility Act"—

federal welfare spending is considerably *higher* today than if the 1996 reforms had not passed. This is because Republicans sought to end the entitlement by "level-funding" the new welfare program at 1994 levels (approximately $16 billion annually).[13] This meant that a national caseload increase would not, by law, trigger an increase in federal expenditures. (An entitlement program is one whose funding must automatically increase if more eligible recipients apply for aid.) But since 1996 the relief caseload has *declined* significantly, a trend that would ordinarily have produced a comparable reduction in federal expenditures. Yet federal welfare spending remains at previous levels. According to one estimate, the federal payments to states were $6 billion higher in 1998 than they would have been under the old welfare regime, and per family subsidies are approximately 64 percent above previous levels.[14] This is one of the reasons that states have been able to expand day care, health care and employment programs for former recipients. Yet when the next recession strikes, and caseloads rise, pressure will mount for an increase in federal aid to the states. This may well ratchet up federal welfare expenditures from a level higher than would have been the case in the absence of the 1996 reforms.

There are other reasons that the history of relief should encourage us to withhold judgment on the long-term impact of the 1996 reforms. The new law has been portrayed as giving welfare back to the states because the state officials purportedly know best how to handle "their own poor." But the history of unemployment relief provides little evidence that state policies are, in fact, produced by careful analysis of the unique characteristics of the local poor. When state fiscal conditions deteriorate, there has been a persistent appeal to the much-despised federal "bureaucrats" for money. Furthermore, despite claims that the 1996 law is a devolution of welfare to the states, it is also a massive, unfunded, federal mandate. This is because the law requires all states to have at least half of its welfare caseload in work and job-training programs by fiscal year 2002.[15] If there is one lesson to be learned from the efforts to reform relief in the 1930s, it is that work programs are a good deal more expensive than direct relief. The federal work requirement has, so far, not proved to be a burden because the level-funding of federal aid has meant that most states have more money to spend on work programs. But this could well change when the 50 percent mandate kicks in, particularly if this occurs in the context of a recession.

We should even be skeptical of claims that the federal "entitlement" has ended. While this is technically true, since under the new law a caseload increase will not automatically trigger an increase in federal spending, the new state programs do not yet show the central characteristic of a non-entitlement program—waiting lists for benefits. (Press reports often erroneously suggest that the time limits and work require-

ments under the new law constitute an end to the entitlement.) It is hard
to imagine that states will simply start denying some poor women aid
if a new recession causes caseload increases. The creation of the welfare
"entitlement" was a slow process that involved small changes in federal
welfare law, court decisions and habits of administration. It will be difficult to change the character of the program by legislative fiat.

So, "welfare as we know it" may not have ended but simply entered
a new phase, much as it did in the late 1930s. To avoid ending this study
on such a dismal conclusion—and adding to the overwhelming negativ-
ism that has enveloped welfare policy—let me suggest a more optimistic
scenario that may well emerge. One of the lessons of history, after all, is
that each time period is unique, that history does not necessarily repeat
itself and that the future is highly unpredictable (certainly the study of
relief policy during the Great Depression supports this last point). Perhaps we live in a time when the political culture is at last willing to
finance alternatives to relief. This may seem like a fantastic dream, given
the need to balance the federal budget and, above all, the political ascendancy of the Republican Party. But there are reasons to be optimistic.
The states are presently spending more on employment, job training, and
day care programs than ever before. Many are experimenting with so-
called earnings disregards, policies that allow recipients to keep more
money than they earn on the labor market. The earned income tax credit,
a significant subsidy for low-wage workers, has expanded and now costs
the federal government more than the old AFDC program at its most
generous. If liberals would renew the struggle for universal health coverage, fight for adequate funding of the federal employment mandate
and pressure for an expansion of food stamp and day care subsidies, we
might have a welfare policy that would be more closely linked to employment and thus appear as something radically different from "welfare."

Another reason to be optimistic is that the critics of "welfare" claim
to have radically transformed the system into one that focuses on employment. However one may evaluate this claim, it does, to some degree,
transform the nature of the welfare debate. The would-be reformers have
been compelled to show that their reforms "work" and have thus come
to support increased spending for job training, day care and the extension of Medicaid to working families. Liberals should build on this trend,
rather than simply pointing to the inadequacies of the new reforms. Furthermore, since the new welfare system is—according to the public rhetoric—now the creation of Republicans and centrist Democrats, it can no
longer be attacked politically as the product of a failed liberal policy
legacy. This, perhaps more than any feature of the 1996 reforms, could
transform the nature of the welfare debate.

Transforming the 1996 law into real welfare reform, however, will require some big changes in the excessively ideological stance with which activists on the Right and the Left approach welfare.[16] The conservatives will have to curb the apparently irresistible tendency to use the welfare issue as a club to beat liberals over their heads. The view that welfare is a liberal program that has caused poverty, an analysis that few serious scholars of the welfare state support, must be abandoned. Conservatives might even admit that their opposition to universal health care and public employment has contributed to welfare dependence. Liberals and welfare rights activists will also have to do some serious soul-searching. They will have to abandon the currently popular view on the Left that all welfare reforms must be opposed because they derive from myths about welfare recipients or efforts to drive women into the labor market. More importantly, they will also have to resist the appeal of a welfare rights strategy that creates the appearance of bringing back the old system—burrowing into the implementation process to try to carve out exemptions for various classes of recipients, liberalizing work requirements to make them useless and using court challenges to reverse losses in the political arena. This will be an extremely difficult tendency to resist since the advocacy approach to welfare that has dominated since the 1970s is enormously comfortable with these tactics. Finally, the Left will need to stop complaining and present a positive agenda for reform that is politically realistic. This will require less emphasis on attacking the myths that justify welfare reform and more on promoting those aspects of the reform program that help low-wage workers—day care subsidies, job-training programs and, above all, universal health coverage.[17]

The 1996 reforms do not change welfare as radically as both supporters and critics of the new law seem to believe. But they do create a window of opportunity to expand programs for the working poor, reduce the role of means-tested relief and perhaps transform the nature of the debate over the American "dole."

NOTES

1. The national relief drive sponsored by the President's Committee on Unemployment Relief was clearly modeled on the Liberty Loan drives of World War I and the Commmunity Chest campaigns they spawned in the 1920s. For an analysis of the CWA that stresses its origins in the efficiency movement of the World War I era see Bonnie Fox Schwarz, *The Civil Works Administration* (Princeton, NJ: Princeton University Press, 1984), 11–14.

2. *The Gallup Poll*, Vol. I (New York: Random House, 1972), 98.

3. See especially Ellis Hawley, *The Great War and the Search for a Modern Order*, 2nd ed. (New York: St. Martin's Press, 1992); Louis Galambos, "Technology, Political Economy and Professionalization: Central Themes of the Organizational Synthesis," *Business History Review* 57 (Winter 1983): 471–493; Brian Balogh, "Re-

organizing the Organizational Synthesis," *Studies in American Political Development* 5 (1991): 119–172.

4. Theda Skocpol, *Protecting Soldiers and Mothers* (Cambridge, MA: Harvard University Press, 1992), and Skocpol, *Social Policy in the United States* (Princeton, NJ: Princeton University Press, 1995), ch. 1; Stephen Skowronek, *Building the New Administrative State: The Expansion of National Administrative Capacities, 1877–1920* (Cambridge: Cambridge University Press, 1982); Margaret Weir, *Politics and Jobs: The Boundaries of Employment Policy in the United States* (Princeton, NJ: Princeton University Press, 1992); James G. March and Johan P. Olsen, "The New Institutionalism: Organizational Factors in Political Life," *American Political Science Review* 78 (1984).

5. Barbara J. Nelson, "The Origins of the Two-Channel Welfare State: Workmen's Compensation and Mothers' Aid," in Linda Gordon, ed., *Women, the State and Welfare* (Madison: University of Wisconsin Press, 1990), 123–151; Linda Gordon, "Social Insurance and Public Assistance: The Influence of Gender in Welfare Thought in the United States, 1890–1935," *The American Historical Review* (February 1992): 19–21 and Gordon, *Pitied but Not Entitled* (New York: Free Press, 1994), 5–6.

6. Gordon, *Pitied but Not Entitled*, chs. 6, 9; Skocpol, *Social Policy in the United States*, ch. 6 and Skocpol, *Protecting Soldiers and Mothers*, 535–536; Cristopher Howard, "Sowing the Seeds of 'Welfare': The Transformation of Mothers' Pensions, 1900–1940," *Journal of Policy History* 4, no. 2 (1992): 188–227.

7. Jerry Cates, *Insuring Inequality* (Ann Arbor: University of Michigan Press, 1983), especially ch. 6.

8. Margaret Orelup, "Private Values, Public Policy, and Poverty in America 1840–1940" (Ph.D. diss., University of Massachusetts, Amherst, 1995), ch. 4.

9. Jill Quadagno, *The Color of Welfare* (New York: Oxford University Press, 1994), 117; Martin Gilens, *Why Americans Hate Welfare: Race, Media, and the Politics of Antipoverty Policy* (Chicago: University of Illinois Press, 1999); William Julius Wilson, *When Work Disappears: The World of the New Urban Poor* (New Yok: Alfred Knopf, 1996), 162, 166.

10. Joanne Goodwin, *Gender and the Politics of Welfare Reform* (Chicago: University of Chicago Press, 1997), 185, 188–190.

11. Gilens, *Why Americans Hate Welfare*, 27–30; Hugh Heclo, "The Political Foundations of Antipoverty Policy," in Sheldon Danziger and Daniel H. Weinberg, eds., *Fighting Poverty: What Works and What Doesn't* (Cambridge, MA: Harvard University Press, 1986), 332.

12. Michael Katz, *Improving Poor People* (Princeton, NJ: Princeton University Press, 1995), 20–21; National Research Council, *A Common Destiny: Blacks and American Society* (Washington, DC: National Academy Press, 1989), 254–255, Quadagno *The Color of Welfare*, 117.

13. U.S. Department of Health and Human Services, "Comparison of PRIOR LAW and the PERSONAL RESPONSIBILITY AND WORK OPPORTUNITY RECONCILIATION ACT OF 1996" (P.L. 104–193), September 28, 1999, http://aspe.os.dhhs.gov/hsp/isp/reform.htm.

14. Jason, DeParle, "Leftover Money for Welfare Baffles, or Inspires, States," *New York Times*, August 29, 1999, 1, 30–31.

15. U.S. Department of Health and Human Services, "Comparison of PRIOR LAW," 1.

16. Stephen Teles, *Whose Welfare? AFDC and Elite Politics* (Lawrence: University of Kansas Press, 1996), 76–78.

17. Jason DeParle, "The Silence of the Liberals," *The Washington Monthly* 31 (April 1999): 17; Center on Budget and Policy Priorities, *Reinvesting Welfare Savings: Aiding Needy Families and Strengthening State Welfare Reforms* (Washington, DC, March 1998); Sandra Venner and J. Larry Brown, *State Investments in Income and Asset Development for Poor Families*, Center on Hunger and Poverty, Tufts University, January 1999.

Appendix

Relief Estimates and the Children's Bureau Series

Efforts to collect data on relief spending began in the late 1920s and were, in part, a response to the unanticipated growth of public and private relief during the decade.[1] The Children's Bureau series derived from two sources: a Russell Sage Foundation study of urban relief begun in 1926 and a project for the "registration of social statistics" initiated by a joint committee of the Association of Community Chests and Councils and the University of Chicago School of Social Service administration. These efforts were taken over by the Children's Bureau, which was receiving frequent requests from relief officials in the Hoover administration for data on the volume of relief spending, in early 1931. The Bureau began publishing a monthly bulletin summarizing the data, which was occasionally used in the debate over the adequacy of relief and the need for a federal program. The Children's Bureau series was, to some degree, superseded by the data collected by the agencies administering the early federal relief programs. However, the Bureau continued to update the urban series until 1936, when it was transferred to the Bureau of Public Assistance of the Social Security Board.

The 1936 study by Helen Winslow used to create Tables 1, 3 and 4 is a compilation of the data from 1929 through 1935. Winslow published estimates of spending for the 120 urban areas and caseloads and relief standards for smaller samples. I have omitted her estimates for 1929 in order to be consistent with the estimates of unemployment based on the April 1930 census.

RELIEF SPENDING

The spending estimates presented in Table 1 were based on Winslow's Table A in Appendix B (pp. 69–71). I simply aggregated her monthly estimates for public and private direct and work relief into quarterly totals. My totals are lower than Winslow's because I have omitted spending for mothers' aid, Old Age Assistance and Aid to the Blind. These programs were not primarily assisting the unemployed and were not receiving federal subsidies prior to the Social Security Act. Second, I have also reduced her expenditure estimates for 1934 and 1935 by 4 percent to adjust for a change in the sample size. In 1934 the Children's Bureau began using data received from the Federal Emergency Relief Administration. The size of the "urban areas" reporting to the FERA was, in some cases, larger than in the original relief series. Using Winslow's table on the geographical divisions reporting to the Bureau, I have estimated a population increase of 4 percent in 1934 and adjusted her data downward accordingly.[2]

CASELOADS AND BENEFIT LEVELS

Winslow published annual, rather than monthly, estimates of caseloads and benefits in the form of average monthly number of cases and average monthly relief per case. The sample of agencies reporting caseloads and benefits was smaller than the spending sample. Finally, Winslow made annual caseload and benefit estimates for different categories of agencies but did not attempt to make aggregate estimates for the entire sample (see Table 8, "Trends in Urban Relief," 29–30).

To create caseload and benefit estimates consistent with the spending estimates in Table 1, I have:

1. Produced aggregate annual estimates of average monthly relief standards for agencies dispensing direct and work relief (as in Table 1, "special allowances" like mothers' aid are excluded). These have been weighted using the caseloads of different types of agencies.

2. Assuming that averge monthly standards in the larger spending sample (Table 1) were the same as the caseload/benefit sample, I divided annual average monthly spending (estimated from Table 1) by the estimate of relief standards. This produced the caseload estimate shown in Table 3.

As was noted in the text, these are extremely rough estimates, and I would not put much stock in the small changes in relief standards from 1930 to 1933. But the data does suggest that relief standards changed little during the Hoover years, that they were approximately one-half of those provided by the Mothers' Pension programs and the more generous private agencies and that the New Deal was able to raise benefit levels by approximately 50 percent.

UNEMPLOYMENT AND PERCENT UNEMPLOYED ON RELIEF

I have created estimates of average monthly unemployment in the urban areas using data from the census of unemployment conducted in conjunction with the 1930 census. Using the census as a benchmark, I have projected forward using monthly data on the labor force and employment collected by the National Industrial Conference Board[3]:

1. From the census, I derived estimates of the labor force and unemployment in the 120 urban areas for April 1930. Employment estimates were derived by subtracting the latter from the former.

2. Using monthly estimates of changes in the labor force and employment for urban occupations published by the National Industrial Conference Board, I estimated monthly trends for these categories in the Children's Bureau's urban sample. The number of unemployed was then estimated by subtracting employment from labor force estimates from the former. Annual monthly averages consistent with the caseload data were then calculated.

This procedure, of course, assumes that the 1930 census represented an accurate count of the number of unemployed in April of 1930. The census was widely criticized for undercounting the number of jobless, primarily because workers who claimed to be only temporarily or seasonally unemployed were often counted as employed by the census takers. It is therefore quite possible that the number of unemployed in April and throughout the series was higher than the estimate used here. Estimating the size of the "labor force" also requires making many difficult assumptions (How many of those working in 1930 became "discouraged" and stopped actively looking for work? How many family members, particularly women, not employed in 1930 joined the labor force?). Finally, there has been considerable debate about how to count the employees of the New Deal's public employment programs. Obviously, for the purposes of this exercise, those on work relief must be counted as unemployed.

While use of the 1930 census may well undercount the number of unemployed, producing a higher percentage on relief, the assumption that there was one unemployed worker per case has the opposite impact. A variety of studies suggested that the average relief "case" contained more than one worker defined as unemployed. Again, one encounters difficult questions about the nature of the labor force and its relationship to the family economy of the 1930s. The issue is further complicated by

Table 6
Unemployment Rates: Estimates for 120 Urban Areas and Other National Estimates

Year	120 Urban Areas	Lebergott	NICB
1930	9.8%	8.9%	7.8%
1931	19.7%	16.3%	16.3%
1932	29.8%	24.1%	24.9%
1933	30.4%	25.2%	25.1%
1934	24.3%	22.0%	24.9%
1935	22.8%	20.3%	16.3%

the fact that the relief caseload increasingly absorbed people defined as "unemployable" in the mid-1930s. These included those who perhaps should have qualified for the "categorical" programs (mothers' aid, Old Age Assistance, etc.). In 1934 New Deal officials appear to have believed that approximately 20 percent of the caseload consisted of "unemployables," and the estimates of some social workers were even higher.

Table 6 compares unemployment rates derived from my estimates for the 120 urban areas with those of Lebergott (the most widely cited estimates) and the the NICB.[4] The other estimates appear to be lower, in part, because they include agricultural employment, which declined at a much slower rate between 1930 and 1933.

NOTES

1. Emma A. Winslow, *Trends in Different Types of Public and Private Relief in Urban Areas, 1929–1935* (Children' Bureau Publication No. 237) (Washington, DC: Government Printing Office, 1937), 2–3; Katherine Lenroot, "Government Provision for Social Work Statistics on a National Scale," *Proceedings of the National Conference on Social Work* (Chicago: University of Chicago Press, 1931), 415–418; Ralph Hurlin to Emma Winslow (December 10, 1936), Children's Bureau Files, Box 821, File 12–8–1.

2. For the "urban areas" and their population see Winslow, *Trends in Different Types of Public Private Relief Urban Areas*, 1929–1935, 65–68.

3. National Industrial Conference Board, *Conference Board Economic Record* (March 20, 1940), 81–82. The procedure used here is similar to that used by the Conference Board in its annual unemployment estimates. See 89–92.

4. Ibid., 84. Lebergott's estimates as cited *in Historical Statistics of the United States*, Series D 1–10, 126. There were attempts to revise Lebergott's data in the 1970s to take into account the "discouraged worker" effect on the labor force and the impact of the New Deal's employment programs. The latter effort, in particular, created considerable controversy among scholars of American eco-

nomic history. For a review of these revisions that tends to support Lebergott's estimates, see Gene Smiley, "Recent Unemployment Estimates for the 1920s and 1930s," *Journal of Economic History* 43 (June 1983): 487–493. For a review of various estimates made during the 1930s see Paul Samuelson and Russell Nixon, "Estimates of Unemployment in the United States," *Review of Economic Statistics* 22 (August 1940): 107–110.

Bibliography

ARCHIVAL COLLECTIONS

Boston College, Social Work Library
  Proceedings of the National Conference on Charities and Correction, Social
    Work, 1910–1942
Georgetown University, Lauinger Library, Special Collections
  Senator Robert F. Wagner Papers
National Archives, Washington, DC
  Children's Bureau (RG 102)
  Federal Emergency Relief Administration/WPA (RG 69)
  President's Emergency Committee for Employment (RG 73)
  Reconstruction Finance Corporation, Relief Division (RG 234)
  Social Security Administration (RG 47)
Franklin D. Roosevelt Library, Hyde Park, NY
  Harry L. Hopkins Papers
  Harry L. Hopkins, Personal File
  Henry Morgenthau, Jr. Papers
  Frances Perkins Papers
  Franklin Delano Roosevelt Papers
  Robert E. Sherwood Papers
  Aubrey Williams Papers
University of Washington Collections
  Charles F. Ernst Papers
  Pacific Northwest Collection

GOVERNMENT DOCUMENTS

Bogue, Mary F. *The Administration of Mothers' Aid in Ten Localities*. U.S. Depart-
    ment of Labor, Children's Bureau, Publication no. 184. Washington, DC:
    Government Printing Office, 1928.

Boston Overseers of the Poor/Public Welfare. *Annual Reports*, 1890–1940.

Carothers, Doris. *Chronology of the Federal Emergency Relief Administration*. WPA Research Monograph no. 6. Washington, DC: Government Printing Office, 1937.

Geddes, Anne E. *Trends in Relief Expenditures, 1910–1935*. WPA Research Monograph no. 10. Washington, DC: Government Printing Office, 1937.

Federal Works Agency. *Final Statistical Report of the Federal Emergency Relief Administration*. Washington, DC: Government Printing Office, 1942.

Palmer, Gladys L. and Wood, Katherine D. *Urban Workers on Relief*. WPA Research Monograph no. 4. Washington, DC: Government Printing Office, 1936.

U.S. Congress, House, Committee on Banking and Currency. *Unemployment Relief*. Hearings on HR4606. 73rd Cong., 1st Sess., April 11–18, 1933.

U.S. Congress, Senate, Committee on Banking and Currency. *Unemployment Relief*. Hearings on Secs. 4632, 4727, 4755, and 4822. 72nd Cong., 1st sess., June 2–13, 1932.

U.S. Congress, Senate, Committee on Commerce. *Unemployment in the United States*. Hearings on Secs. on 3059, 3060, and 3061. 71st Cong., 2nd sess., March 18–April 1, 1930.

U.S. Congress, Senate, Committee on Manufactures. *Federal Aid for Unemployment Relief*. Hearings . . . on Sec. 5125. 72nd Cong., 2nd sess., January 3–17, 1933.

U.S. Congress, Senate, Committee on Manufactures. *Unemployment Relief*. Hearings . . . on Secs. 174 and 162. 72nd Cong., 1st sess., December 1931–January 1932.

U.S. Department of Commerce. *Statistical Abstract of the United States*. Washington, DC: Government Printing Office, 1936.

U.S. Department of Health and Human Services. "Comparison of PRIOR LAW and the PERSONAL RESPONSIBILITY AND WORK OPPORTUNITY RECONCILIATION ACT OF 1996" (P.L. 104–193), September 28, 1999. http://aspe.os.dhhs.gov/hsp/isp/reform.htm.

Winslow, Emma. *Trends in Different Types of Public and Private Relief in Urban Areas, 1929–1935*. Children's Bureau Publication 237. Washington, DC: Government Printing Office, 1937.

PERIODICALS

Boston Globe
Family
The Nation
The New Republic
New York Times
Social Service Review
Survey Midmonthly/Survey Graphic
Washington Post

MONOGRAPHS AND ARTICLES

Abramovitz, Mimi. *Regulating the Lives of Women*, 3rd ed. Boston: South End Press, 1992.

Achenbaum, W. Andrew. *Shades of Gray*. Boston: Little, Brown, 1983.

Adams, Grace. *Workers on Relief*. New Haven, CT: Yale University Press, 1939.

Amenta, Edwin. *Bold Relief: Institutional Politics and the Origins of American Social Policy*. Princeton, NJ: Princeton University Press, 1998.

Amenta, Edwin and Parikh, Sunita. "Capitalists Did Not Want the Social Security Act: A Critique of the 'Capitalist Dominance' Thesis." *American Sociological Review* 56 (1991): 124–129.

Amenta, Edwin and Zylan, Yvonne. "It Happened Here: Political Opportunity Theory, the New Institutionalism, and the Townsend Movement." *American Sociological Review* 56 (1991): 250–265.

Badger, Anthony. *The New Deal*. New York: Hill and Wang, 1989.

Bakke, E. Wright. *The Unemployed Worker: A Study of the Task of Making a Living without a Job*. New Haven, CT: Yale University Press, 1940.

Balogh, Brian. "Reorganizing the Organizational Synthesis." *Studies in American Political Development* 5 (1991): 119–172.

Balogh, Brian. "Securing Support: The Emergence of the Social Security Board as a Political Actor." In Donald Critchlow and Ellis Hawley, eds., *Federal Social Policy: The Historic Dimension*. University Park: Pennsylvania State University Press, 1988, 55–78.

Barry, John M. *Rising Tide: The Great Mississippi Flood of 1927 and How It Changed America*. New York: Simon and Schuster, 1997.

Beito, David. *Taxpayers in Revolt*. Chapel Hill: University of North Carolina Press, 1989.

Bell, Winifred. *Aid to Dependent Children*. New York: Columbia University Press, 1965.

Berkowitz, Edward G. and McQuaid, Kim. *Creating the Welfare State: The Political Economy of Twentieth Century Reform*. New York: Praeger, 1980.

Bernstein, Irving. *The Lean Years*. Boston: Houghton Mifflin, 1960.

Best, Gary Dean. *The Politics of American Individualism: Herbert Hoover in Transition, 1918–1921*. Westport, CT: Greenwood Press, 1975.

Best, Gary Dean. *Pride, Prejudice and Politics: Roosevelt versus Recovery, 1933–1938*. New York: Praeger, 1991.

Beveridge, Albert. "Unemployment Insurance in the War and After." In Thomas Hill et al., eds., *War and Insurance*. London: Humphrey Milford, 1927, 229–230.

Biles, Roger. *A New Deal for the American People*. De Kalb: Northern Illinois Press, 1991.

Blum, John Morton. *From the Morgenthau Diaries: The Years of Crisis, 1928–1938*. Boston: Houghton Mifflin, 1959.

Blumberg, Barbara. *The New Deal and the Unemployed: The View from New York City*. Lewisburg, PA: Bucknell University Press, 1977.

Blumell, Bruce. *The Development of Public Assistance in the State of Washington during the Great Depression*. New York: Garland, 1984.

Brandenburg, Clorinne M. *Chicago Relief and Service Statistics*. Chicago: University of Chicago Press, 1932.

Brandt, Lilian. *An Impressionistic View of the Winter of 1930–31 in New York City*. New York: Welfare Council of New York City, 1932.

Bremer, William W. "Along the American Way: The New Deal's Work Relief

Programs for the Unemployed." *The Journal of American History* 62 (December 1975): 636–652.

Bremer, William W. *Depression Winters: Social Workers and the New Deal*. Philadelphia: Temple University Press, 1984.

Bremner, Robert H. "The New Deal and Social Welfare." In Harvard Sitkoff, ed., *Fifty Years Later: The New Deal Evaluated*. Philadelphia: Temple University Press, 1985, 69–92.

Brinkley, Alan. *The End of Reform*. New York: Alfred Knopf, 1995.

Brinkley, Alan. "Writing the History of Contemporary America: Dilemmas and Challenges" *Daedalus* 113, no. 3 (Summer 1984): 121–141.

Brock, William R. *Welfare, Democracy and the New Deal*. Cambridge: Cambridge University Press, 1988.

Brown, Josephine. *Public Relief, 1929–1939*. New York: Henry Holt and Co., 1940.

Burner, David. *Herbert Hoover: A Public Life*. New York: Atheneum, 1984.

Burns, Arthur. "The Federal Emergency Relief Administration." In Clarence E. Ridley and Orin F. Noltin, eds., *The Municipal Yearbook, 1937*. Chicago: International City Managers Association, 1937, 382–418.

Burns, Arthur and Williams, Edward A. *Federal Work, Security and Relief Programs*. New York: Da Capo Press, 1971.

Calkins, Clinch. *Some Folks Won't Work*. New York: Harcourt Brace and Co., 1930.

Castles, Francis C. "The Impact of Parties on Public Expenditures." In F. Castles, ed., *The Impact of Parties: Politics and Policies in Democratic Capitalist States*. Beverly Hills, CA: Sage Publications, 1982, 22–34.

Cates, Jerry. *Insuring Inequality: Administrative Leadership in Social Security, 1935–1954*. Ann Arbor: University of Michigan Press, 1983.

Center on Budget and Policy Priorities. *Reinvesting Welfare Savings: Aiding Needy Families and Strengthening State Welfare Reforms*. Washington, DC, March 1998.

Chambers, Clarke. *Seedtime of Reform: American Social Service and Social Action, 1918–1933*. Minneapolis: University of Minnesota Press, 1963.

Chambers, Clarke. "Toward a Redefinition of Welfare History." *Journal of American History* 73 (September 1986): 407–433.

Charles, Searle F. *Minister of Relief: Harry Hopkins and the Depression*. Syracuse, NY: Syracuse University Press, 1963.

Cohen, Lizbeth. *Making a New Deal*. Cambridge: Cambridge University Press, 1990.

Colcord, Joanna. *Cash Relief*. New York: Russell Sage Foundation, 1936.

Colcord, Joanna, Koplovitz, William and Kurtz, Russell. *Emergency Work Relief*. New York: Russell Sage Foundation, 1932.

Coll, Blanche. *Safety Net: Welfare and Social Security, 1929–1979*. New Brunswick, NJ: Rutgers University Press, 1995.

Cowley, Robert. "The Drought and the Dole." *American Heritage* 23, no. 2 (February 1972): 16–19.

Cronin, James. *The Politics of State Expansion*. London: Routledge and Kegan Paul, 1991.

Crouse, Joan M. *The Homeless Transient in the Great Depression: New York State, 1929–1941*. Albany: State University of New York Press, 1986.

Davis, Kenneth. *Franklin D. Roosevelt: The New Deal Years, 1933–1937*. New York: Random House, 1986.

DeParle, Jason. "The Silence of the Liberals." *The Washington Monthly* 31 (April 1999): 12–17.

Derthick, Martha. *The Influence of Federal Grants*. Cambridge, MA: Harvard University Press, 1970.

Dubofsky, Melvyn, ed. *The New Deal: Conflicting Interpretations and Shifting Perspectives*. New York: Garland, 1992.

Feder, Leah H. *Unemployment Relief in Periods of Depression*. New York: Russell Sage Foundation, 1936.

Fine, Sidney. *Frank Murphy: The Detroit Years*. Ann Arbor: University of Michigan Press, 1975.

Flora, Peter and Alber, Jens. "Modernization, Democratization and the Development of Welfare States in Western Europe." In Peter Flora and Arnold J. Heidenheimer, eds., *The Development of Welfare States in Europe and America*. New Brunswick, NJ: Transaction Press, 1981, 37–80.

Fraser, Nancy. "Struggle over Needs: Outline of a Socialist-Feminist Theory of Late-Capitalist Political Culture." In Linda Gordon, ed., *Women, the State and Welfare*. Madison: University of Wisconsin Press, 1990, 199–225.

Friedel, Frank. "Hoover and FDR: Reminiscent Reflections." In Lee Nash, ed., *Understanding Herbert Hoover: Ten Perspectives*. Stanford, CA: Hoover Institution Press, 1987, 125–140.

Galambos, Louis. "Technology, Political Economy and Professionalization: Central Themes of the Organizational Synthesis." *Business History Review* 57 (Winter 1983): 471–493.

Galbraith, John Kenneth. "Blame History Not the Liberals" *New York Times*, September 19, 1995, A21.

Galbraith, John Kenneth. *The New Industrial State*, 2nd ed. Boston: Houghton Mifflin, 1971.

The Gallup Poll, Vol. I. New York: Random House, 1972.

Garraty, John A. *Unemployment in History*. New York: Harper and Row, 1978.

Gibson, Mary Barret. *Unemployment Insurance in Great Britain*. New York: Industrial Relations Counselors, 1931.

Gilens, Martin. *Why Americans Hate Welfare: Race, Media, and the Politics of Antipoverty Policy*. Chicago: University of Chicago Press, 1999.

Gill, Corrington. "The Civil Works Administration." In Clarence E. Ridley and Orin F. Noltin, eds., *The Municipal Yearbook, 1937*. Chicago: International City Managers Association, 1937, 419–432.

Glick, Frank Z. *The Illinois Emergency Relief Commission*. Chicago: University of Chicago Press, 1940.

Goodwin, Joanne. *Gender and the Politics of Welfare Reform*. Chicago: University of Chicago Press, 1997.

Gordon, Linda. "The New Feminist Scholarship on the Welfare State." In Linda Gordon, ed., *Women, the State and Welfare*. Madison: University of Wisconsin, 1990, 9–35.

Gordon, Linda. *Pitied but Not Entitled: Single Mothers and the History of Welfare*. New York: Free Press, 1994.

Gordon, Linda. "Social Insurance and Public Assistance: The Influence of Gender in Welfare Thought in the United States, 1890–1935." *The American Historical Review* (February 1992): 19–54.

Greenbaum, Fred. *Fighting Progressive: A Biography of Edward P. Costigan.* Washington, DC: Public Affairs Press, 1971.

Grim, Carolyn. "The Unemployment Conference of 1921: An Experiment in National Cooperative Planning." *Mid-America* 55 (April 1973): 83–107.

Grønbjerg, Kirsten A. *Mass Society and the Extension of Welfare.* Chicago: University of Chicago Press, 1977.

Grønbjerg, Kirsten, Street, David and Suttles, Gerald D. *Poverty and Social Change.* Chicago: University of Chicago Press, 1978.

Hage, Jerald, Hanneman, Robert and Gargan, Edward T. *State Responsiveness and State Activism.* London: Hyman, 1989.

Hall, Helen. *Case Studies in Unemployment.* Philadelphia: University of Pennsylvania Press, 1931.

Hamilton, David E. *From New Day to New Deal.* Chapel Hill: University of North Carolina Press, 1991.

Hamilton, David E. "Herbert Hoover and the Great Drought of 1930." *Journal of American History* 68, no. 4 (March 1982): 850–875.

Hawley, Ellis. *The Great War and the Search for a Modern Order,* 2nd ed. New York: St. Martin's Press, 1992.

Hawley, Ellis. "Neo-Institutional History and the Understanding of Herbert Hoover." In Lee Nash, ed., *Understanding Herbert Hoover: Ten Perspectives.* Stanford, CA: Stanford University Press, 1987, 66–84.

Hawley, Ellis. "The New Deal State and the Anti-Bureaucratic Tradition." In Robert Eden, ed., *The New Deal and Its Legacy: Critique and Reappraisal.* Westport, CT: Greenwood Press, 1989, 77–92.

Hawley, Ellis. "Social Policy and the Liberal State in Twentieth Century America." In Donald Critchlow and Ellis Hawley, eds., *Federal Social Policy: The Historic Dimension.* University Park: Pennsylvania State University Press, 1988, 117–139.

Heclo, Hugh. "The Political Foundations of Antipoverty Policy." In Sheldon Danziger and Daniel H. Weinberg, eds., *Fighting Poverty: What Works and What Doesn't.* Cambridge, MA: Harvard University Press, 1986, 312–340.

Henretta, James, et al. *America's History,* 3rd ed., vol. 2. New York: Worth Publishers, 1997.

Higgs, Robert. *Crisis and Leviathan.* New York: Oxford University Press, 1987.

Hillman, Arthur. *The Unemployed Citizens League of Seattle.* University of Washington Publications in the Social Sciences, vol. 5, no. 5. Seattle: University of Washington Press, 1934.

Hines, John Earl. "The Rank and File Movement in Social Work." *Labor History* 6, no. 1 (Winter 1975): 78–98.

Hopkins, Harry. *Spending to Save: The Complete Story of Relief.* New York: W.W. Norton, 1936.

Hopkins, June. *Harry Hopkins: Sudden Hero, Brash Reformer.* New York: St. Martin's Press, 1999.

Howard, Christopher. "Sowing the Seeds of 'Welfare': The Transformation of Mothers' Pensions, 1900–1940." *Journal of Policy History* 4, no. 2 (1992): 188–227.

Howard, Donald S. *The WPA and Federal Relief Policy.* New York: Russell Sage Foundation, 1943.

Huntington, Emily P. *Unemployment Relief and the Unemployed in the San Francisco Bay Area*. Berkeley: University of California Press, 1939.

Huthmacher, J. Joseph. *Senator Robert F. Wagner and the Rise of Urban Liberalism*. New York: Atheneum, 1968.

Huthmacher, J. Joseph and Susman, Warren, eds. *Herbert Hoover and the Crisis of American Capitalism*. Cambridge, MA: Schenkman, 1973.

Ickes, Harold. *The Secret Diary of Harold Ickes, the First Thousand Days*. New York: Simon and Schuster, 1953.

Jenkins, J. Craig and Brents, Barbara A. "Social Protest, Hegemonic Competition and Social Reform: A Political Struggle Interpretation of the Origins of the American Welfare State." *American Sociological Review* 54 (1989): 891–909.

Karl, Barry. *The Uneasy State: The United States from 1915 to 1945*. Chicago: University of Chicago Press, 1983.

Katz, Michael. *Improving Poor People*. Princeton, NJ: Princeton University Press, 1995.

Katz, Michael. *In the Shadow of the Poorhouse*. New York: Basic Books, 1986.

Kelso, Robert. "Recent Advances in the Administration of Poor Relief." *The Journal of Social Forces* 1, no. 2 (January 1923): 90–92.

Kelso, Robert. *The Science of Public Welfare*. New York: Henry Holt and Co., 1928.

Korpi, Walter. *The Democratic Class Struggle*. London: Routledge and Kegan Paul, 1983.

LaMonte, Edward Shannon. *Politics and Welfare in Birmingham, 1900–1975*. Tuscaloosa: University of Alabama Press, 1995.

Lane, Marie D. and Steegmuller, Francis. *America on Relief*. New York: Harcourt, Brace and Co., 1938.

Lebergott, Stanley. *Manpower in Economic Growth*. New York: McGraw-Hill, 1964.

Leff, Mark. "Taxing the Forgotten Man: The Politics of Social Security Finance in the New Deal." *Journal of American History* 10 (September 1983): 359–381.

Leiby, James. *Charity and Correction in New Jersey: A History of State Welfare Institutions*. New Brunswick, NJ: Rutgers University Press, 1967.

Leiby, James. *A History of Social Welfare and Social Work in the United States*. New York: Columbia University Press, 1978.

Levine, Daniel S. *Poverty and Society: The Growth of the American Welfare State in International Comparison*. New Brunswick, NJ: Rutgers University Press, 1988.

Lloyd, Craig. *Aggressive Introvert: A Study of Hoover and Public Relations Management*. Columbus: Ohio State University Press, 1972.

Lorence, James J. *Organizing the Unemployed: Community and Union Activists in the Industrial Heartland*. Albany: State University of New York Press, 1996.

Louchheim, Kate, ed. *The Making of the New Deal: The Insiders Speak*. Cambridge, MA: Harvard University Press, 1983.

Lowitt, Richard and Beardsley, Maurice, eds. *One Third of a Nation: Lorena Hickock Reports on the Great Depression*. Urbana: University of Illinois Press, 1981.

Lubove, Roy. *The Professional Altruist: The Emergence of Social Work as a Career*. New York: Atheneum, 1983.

Lubove, Roy. *The Struggle for Social Security*. Cambridge, MA: Harvard University Press, 1968.

Lynn, Laurence E., Jr. and Whitman, David deF. *The President as Policymaker:*

Jimmy Carter and Welfare Reform. Philadelphia: Temple University Press, 1981.

MacMahon, Arthur W., Millett, John D. and Ogden, Gladys. *The Administration of Federal Work Relief*. Chicago: Social Science Research Council, 1941.

MacNeil, Douglas H. *Seven Years of Unemployment Relief in New Jersey*. Washington, DC: Social Science Research Council, 1938.

March, James G. and Olsen, Johan P. "The New Institutionalism: Organizational Factors in Political Life." *American Political Science Review* 78, no. 3 (September 1984): 734–749.

Marcus, Grace L. *Some Aspects of Relief in Family Casework*. New York: Charity Organization Society, 1929.

Martin, George S. *Madam Secretary: Frances Perkins*. Boston: Houghton Mifflin, 1976.

May, Dean. *From New Deal to New Economics*. New York: Garland, 1981.

May, Elaine Tyler. *Homeward Bound*. New York: Basic Books, 1988.

McElvaine, Robert S. *The Great Depression*, 2nd ed. New York: Times Books, 1993.

McJimsey, George. *Harry Hopkins, Ally of the Poor and Defender of Democracy*. Cambridge, MA: Harvard University Press, 1987.

Milkman, Ruth. "Women's Work and the Economic Crisis: Some Lessons from the Great Depression." In Nancy F. Cott and Elizabeth Pleck, eds., *A Heritage of Her Own*. New York: Simon and Schuster, 1979, 507–541.

Millett, John D. *The Works Progress Administration in New York City*. Chicago: Social Science Research Council, 1938.

Mitchell, Virgil L. *The Civil Works Administration in Louisiana: A Study in New Deal Relief, 1933–1934*. Lafayette: University of Southwest Louisiana Press, 1976.

Mohl, Raymond. "Mainstream Social Welfare History and Its Problems." *Reviews in American History* 7 (December 1979): 469–476.

Mullins, William H. *The Depression and the Urban West Coast, 1929–1933*. Bloomington: Indiana University Press, 1991.

Muncy, Robyn. *Creating a Female Dominion in American Reform, 1890–1935*. New York: Oxford University Press, 1991.

Myers, William Starr, ed. *The State Papers and Other Writings of Herbert Hoover*. Garden City, NY: Doubleday, Doran and Co., 1934.

Myles, John. *Old Age in the Welfare State*. Boston: Little, Brown, 1984.

National Research Council. *A Common Destiny: Blacks and American Society*. Washington, DC: National Academy Press, 1989.

Nelson, Barbara J. "The Origins of the Two-Channel Welfare State: Workmen's Compensation and Mothers' Aid." In Linda Gordon, ed., *Women, the State and Welfare*. Madison: University of Wisconsin Press, 1990, 123–151.

Nelson, Daniel. *Unemployment Insurance: The American Experience, 1915–1935*. Madison: University of Wisconsin Press, 1969.

O'Connor, James. *The Fiscal Crisis of the State*. New York: St. Martin's Press, 1973.

Olsen, James Stuart. *Herbert Hoover and the Reconstruction Finance Corporation 1931–1933*. Ames: Iowa State University Press, 1977.

Parry, Tom Jones. "The Republic of the Penniless." *Atlantic Monthly* 150, no. 4 (October 1932): 449–457.

Patterson, James T. *America's Struggle against Poverty*, 3rd ed. Cambridge, MA: Harvard University Press, 1994.

Patterson, James T. *Congressional Conservatism and the New Deal*. Lexington: University of Kentucky Press, 1967.

Patterson, James T. *The New Deal and the States: Federalism in Transition*. Westport, CT: Greenwood Press, 1981.

Piven, Frances Fox and Cloward, Richard A. "Explaining the Politics of the Welfare State or Marching Back toward Pluralism?" In R. Friedland and A.F. Robertson, eds., *Beyond the Marketplace: Rethinking Economy and Society*. New York: Aldine de Gruyter, 1990, 245–269.

Piven, Frances Fox and Cloward, Richard A. *Poor People's Movements*. New York: Random House, 1977.

Piven, Frances Fox and Cloward, Richard A. *Regulating the Poor*. New York: Random House, 1971.

Poppendieck Janet. *Breadlines Knee Deep in Wheat: Food Assistance and the Great Depression*. New Brunswick, NJ: Rutgers University Press, 1986.

Quadagno, Jill. *The Color of Welfare*. New York: Oxford University Press, 1994.

Quadagno, Jill. "Theories of the Welfare State." *Annual Reviews in Sociology* 13 (1987): 109–128.

Quadagno, Jill. *The Transformation of Old Age Security: Class and Politics in the American Welfare Scene*. Chicago: University of Chicago Press, 1988.

Quadagno, Jill S. "Welfare Capitalism and the Social Security Act of 1935." *American Sociological Review* 49 (October 1984): 632–647.

Rimlinger, Gaston. *Welfare Policy and Industrialization in Europe, America and Russia*. New York: Wiley, 1971.

Rodgers, Daniel. *Atlantic Crossings: Social Politics in a Progressive Age*. Cambridge, MA: Belknap Press of Harvard University Press, 1998.

Romasco, Albert U. "Hoover–Roosevelt and the Great Depression: A Historiographic Inquiry into a Perennial Comparison." In John Braeman, Robert H. Bremner and David Brody, eds. *The New Deal: The National Level*. Columbus: Ohio State University Press, 1973, 3–26.

Romasco, Albert U. *The Poverty of Abundance*. New York: Oxford University Press, 1965.

Rosenman, Samuel L., ed. *The Public Papers and Addresses of Franklin D. Roosevelt*. New York: Random House, 1938.

Rosenzweig, Roy. "Radicals and the Jobless: The Musteites and the Unemployed Leagues, 1932–1936." *Labor History*, 6, no. 1 (Winter 1975): 52–77.

Salmond, John. *Southern Rebel: The Life and Times of Aubrey Williams*. Chapel Hill: University of North Carolina Press, 1983.

Samuelson, Paul. "Estimates of Unemployment in the United States." *Review of Economic Statistics* (1940).

Sautter, Udo. *Three Cheers for the Unemployed*. Cambridge: Cambridge University Press, 1991.

Scharf, Lois. *To Work and to Wed: Female Employment, Feminism and the Great Depression*. Westport, CT: Greenwood Press, 1980.

Schlesinger, Arthur, Jr. "Hoover Makes a Comeback." *The New York Review of Books* (May 8, 1979): 10–16.

Schneider, David M. and Deutch, Albert. *The History of Public Welfare in New York State*. Chicago: University of Chicago Press, 1941.

Schwartz, Bonnie Fox. *The Civil Works Administration: The Business of Emergency Employment in the New Deal*. Princeton, NJ: Princeton University Press, 1984.

Schwartz, Bonnie Fox. "Social Workers and New Deal Politicians in Conflict: California's Branion-Williams Case, 1933–1934." *Pacific Historical Review*, 43, no. 1 (February 1973): 53–73.

Schwartz, Bonnie Fox. "Unemployment Relief in Philadelphia, 1930–1932: A Study of the Depression's Impact on Voluntarism." In Bernard Sternsher, ed., *Hitting Home: The Great Depression in Town and Country*. Chicago: Quadrangle Books, 1970, 60–84.

Schwarz, Jordan A. *The Interregnum of Despair*. Urbana: University of Illinois Press, 1970.

Schwarz, Jordan A. *The New Dealers*. New York: Random House, 1994.

Sealander, Judit. *Private Wealth and Public Life: Foundation Philanthropy and the Reshaping of American Social Policy from the Progressive Era to the New Deal*. Baltimore: Johns Hopkins University Press, 1997.

Seligman, Lester G. and Cornwell, Elmer E., eds. *New Deal Mosaic*. Eugene: University of Oregon Press, 1965.

Shalev, Michael. "The Social Democratic Model and Beyond." *Comparative Social Research* 6 (1983): 315–351.

Sherwood, Robert. *Roosevelt and Hopkins*. New York: Bantam Books, 1950.

Skidelsky, Robert. *John Maynard Keynes: A Biography*, vol. 2. New York: Viking Penguin, 1994.

Skocpol, Theda. *Protecting Soldiers and Mothers*. Cambridge, MA: Harvard University Press, 1992.

Skocpol, Theda. *Social Policy in the United States*. Princeton, NJ: Princeton University Press, 1995.

Skocpol, Theda and Amenta, Edwin. "Did Capitalists Shape Social Security?" *American Sociological Review* 50 (August 1985): 572–575.

Skowronek, Stephen. *Building the New Administrative State: The Expansion of National Administrative Capacities, 1877–1920*. Cambridge: Cambridge University Press, 1982.

Stafford, Paul Tutt. *Government and the Needy: A Study of Public Assistance in New Jersey*. Princeton, NJ: Princeton University Press, 1941.

Stephens, John D. *The Transition from Capitalism to Socialism*. London: Macmillan, 1979.

Stevenson, Marietta. *Public Welfare Administration*. New York: Macmillan, 1938.

Teles, Stephen. *Whose Welfare? AFDC and Elite Politics*. Lawrence: University of Kansas Press, 1996.

Thane, Pat. *The Foundations of the Welfare State*, 2nd ed. London: Longman, 1996.

Tindall, George B. *The Emergence of the New South, 1915–1945*. Baton Rouge: Louisiana State University Press, 1967.

Trattner, Walter I. *From Poor Law to Welfare State*, 6th ed. New York: Free Press, 1979.

Trolander, Judith. *Settlement Houses and the Great Depression*. Detroit: Wayne State University Press, 1975.

Trout, Charles H. *Boston, the Great Depression, and the New Deal*. New York: Oxford University Press, 1977.

Trout, Charles H. "Welfare in the New Deal Era." *Current History* 65 (July–December 1973): 11–14.

Venner, Sandra and Brown, Larry. *State Investments in Income and Asset Development for Poor Families.* Medford, MA: Center on Hunger and Poverty, Tufts University, January 1999.

Walker, Forrest. *The Civil Works Administration: An Experiment in Federal Work Relief, 1933–1934.* New York: Garland Publishing Company, 1979.

Warren, Harris Gaylord. *Herbert Hoover and the Great Depression.* New York: Oxford University Press, 1959.

Watson, Donald S. "The Reconstruction Finance Corporation," *The Municipal Yearbook* (1937): 375–381.

Weed, Clyde P. *The Nemesis of Reform: The Republican Party during the New Deal.* New York: Columbia University Press, 1994.

Weinstein, James. *The Corporate Ideal in the Liberal State.* Boston: Beacon Press, 1968.

Weir, Margaret. *Politics and Jobs: The Boundaries of Employment Policy in the United States.* Princeton, NJ: Princeton University Press, 1992.

Weir, Margaret and Skocpol, Theda. "State Structures and the Possibilities for Keynesian Responses to the Great Depression in Sweden, Britain and the United States." In Peter B. Evans, Dietrich Rueschmeyer and Theda Skocpol, eds., *Bringing the State Back In.* Cambridge: Cambridge University Press, 1985, 107–163.

Whiteside, Noel. *Bad Times: Unemployment in British Social and Political History.* London: Faber and Faber, 1991.

Whiteside, Noel. "Welfare Legislation and the Unions during the First World War." *Historical Journal* 23, no. 4 (1980): 857–874.

Wilensky, Harold. *The Welfare State and Equality.* Berkeley: University of California Press, 1975.

Wilensky, Harold and Lebeaux, Charles. *Industrial Society and Social Welfare.* New York: Free Press, 1965.

Williams, Edward A. *Federal Aid for Relief.* New York: Columbia University Press, 1939.

Wilson, Joan Hoff. *Herbert Hoover: Forgotten Progressive.* Boston: Little, Brown, 1975.

Wilson, William Julius. *When Work Disappears: The World of the New Urban Poor.* New York: Alfred Knopf, 1996.

DISSERTATIONS

Bauman, John F. "The City, the Depression and Relief: The Philadelphia Experience, 1929–1939." Ph.D. diss., Rutgers University, 1969.

Elder, Jeanette. "A Study of One Hundred Applicants for Relief in the Fourth Winter of Unemployment." Masters thesis, University of Chicago, 1933.

Hannah, James H. "Urban Reaction to the Great Depression, 1929–1933." Ph.D. diss., University of California, 1963.

Hogan, John Arthur. "The Decline of Self-Help and the Growth of Radicalism among Seattle's Organized Unemployed." Master's thesis, University of Washington, 1934.

Kahn, Eleanor. "Organizations of the Unemployed as a Factor in the American Labor Movement." Master's thesis, University of Wisconsin, 1934.

Kerr, Clark. "Productive Enterprises of the Unemployed, 1931–1938." Ph.D. diss., University of California, 1939.

Leader, Leonard. "Los Angeles and the Great Depression." Ph.D. diss., UCLA, 1972.

Maurer, David. "Public Relief Programs and Politics in Ohio." Ph.D. diss., Ohio State University, 1962.

Orelup, Margaret. "Private Values, Public Policy, and Poverty in America, 1890–1940." Ph.D. diss., University of Massachusetts, Amherst, 1995.

Wallis, John Joseph. "Work Relief and Unemployment in the 1930s." Ph.D. diss., University of Washington, 1981.

Index

About the Author

JEFF SINGLETON has taught American history at a number of universities and community colleges. He also has done research for and been active in community organizations, advocacy groups, and human service organizations. Presently he is teaching at Boston College.